Hogwarts and All

PETER LANG
New York • Washington, D.C./Baltimore • Bern
Frankfurt • Berlin • Brussels • Vienna • Oxford

Gregory G. Pepetone

Hogwarts and All

Gothic Perspectives on Children's Literature

PETER LANG
New York • Washington, D.C./Baltimore • Bern
Frankfurt • Berlin • Brussels • Vienna • Oxford

Library of Congress Cataloging-in-Publication Data

Pepetone, Gregory G.
Hogwarts and all: gothic perspectives on children's literature /
Gregory G. Pepetone.
p. cm.
Includes bibliographical references and index.
1. Children's literature—History and criticism. 2. Gothic revival (Literature)
I. Title.
PN1009.A1P444   809'.89282—dc23   2011051550
ISBN 978-1-4331-0060-4 (paperback)
ISBN: 978-1-4539-0577-7 (e-book)

Bibliographic information published by **Die Deutsche Nationalbibliothek**.
Die Deutsche Nationalbibliothek lists this publication in the "Deutsche
Nationalbibliografie"; detailed bibliographic data is available
on the Internet at http://dnb.d-nb.de/.

© 2012 Peter Lang Publishing, Inc., New York
29 Broadway, 18th floor, New York, NY 10006
www.peterlang.com

Printed in the United States of America

Table of Contents

Foreword

Turning north onto Amsterdam Avenue from 110th Street in Manhattan's Upper West Side, you look up and see the massive and seemingly ancient façade of the Cathedral Church of St. John the Divine. Stepping inside you might be tempted to think you have stepped back in time by several hundred years, but the structure actually is barely a century old, a revival of the style of Gothic architecture so readily identified with the Middle Ages. As you glance around the interior, taking in the vaulted ceiling, the stone walls, the stained glass, you are struck by the fact that "gothic" does not equate simply with "dark" or "foreboding"—far from it. Rather, you are surprised to find that as you move deeper into the mystery and awe-full-ness which envelop you in that Gothic space, you actually find your soul illumined, your mind enlightened. You depart somehow more fully attuned to larger realities, more…whole.

In this marvelous collection of essays, university professor and concert pianist Greg Pepetone offers s similar experience of the Gothic, not in architecture but rather in the apparently incongruous realm of children's literature. As in his earlier book, *Gothic Perspectives on the American Experience*, Dr. Pepetone conveys his impressive knowledge of the subject through reflections that are at once both accessible and engaging. His fascination with the Gothic is contagious, as each turn of a page phrase invites the reader to re-enter a world to which we were somehow more open in our youthful years before adult pragmatism made us, like Hamlet's dear friend Horatio, forget that there are indeed more things in heaven and earth than are dreamt of in our philosophies.

So, find a comfortable chair near the warm fireplace and follow your able guide into Hogwarts and all those other special places of mystery and awe, where the darkness serves simply to illumine and enlighten and entrance anew.

> —Dr. C. K. Robertson is an Episcopal priest and author of many books and articles, including A Dangerous Dozen.

Preface: Kinder-Goth and Pottermania

The Romantic Cult of Childhood

The second half of the twentieth century witnessed a proliferation of literature aimed at a younger audience. Much of it has to do with supernatural Gothic subject matter including ghosts, witches, wizards, monsters, vampires, angels, demons, and other mythological or legendary entities. Commercially, the most successful of these books (perhaps the most successful series of books since the Bible) are a recent product of this specialized industry. I refer, of course, to J. K. Rowling's phenomenally successful *Harry Potter* series. Rowling's compelling saga did not, however, arise in a vacuum. Indeed, the way for "Pottermania" was paved two centuries earlier by Romantic educators, poets, novelists, painters, and musicians who conceived of childhood as what the English poet Wordsworth famously called the "seedtime of the soul." What they had in mind was not the result of statistical studies in child psychology, but a widely shared perception of childhood as a code for certain values—such as openness, vulnerability, imagination, and candor—that define our common humanity throughout our adult lives. They intuited that these values were threatened by industrial, scientific, economic, and political changes then sweeping the European continent.

"Old age does not make childish..." writes Goethe in *Faust*, "it merely finds us children yet" (Goethe 5). More than hundred years after the completion of *Faust*, Madeleine L'Engle made the same point when she stated, "I need not belabor the point that to retain our childlike openness does not mean to be childish. Only the most mature of us are able to be childlike" (L'Engle, *Walking On Water*, 74). This core insight, recently somewhat cheapened by pop-psychology as a celebration of the "Child Within," is crucial to understanding the appeal that Rowling and other children's literature holds for many adult readers. I myself first encountered the literature discussed in this volume as an adult, though my wife (an elementary and middle school teacher) and I were later privileged to read much of it aloud to our two young daughters. I have fond memories of both experiences. Indeed, it is on the intersection of adult and childhood perception, sometimes referred to as "the child mind" on which this volume will focus. Why has the magical mixture of fantasy, sci-fi, mystery, and supernatural gothic horror found in the writings of Susan Cooper, Antonia Barber, Madeleine L'Engle, Ray Bradbury, and J. K. Rowling and others, i.e., the cult of childhood in literature, so captivated the imaginations of millions of adults, as well as children worldwide? That is a question I intend to address as this discussion unfolds.

The Gothic Imagination and Childhood

A second, closely related, question has to do with how this unique body of literature under consideration fits into the larger scheme of what might be termed "the gothic imagination." For the past few years, I have taught an undergraduate level course that seeks to explain and contextualize the modern appeal of all things gothic from superheroes, angels, and aliens, i.e., beings that postulate a hidden or "implicate" order of reality, to conspiracy theories premised on a *hidden history* lurking beneath the surface of transformative world events. My object is to understand, not debunk, such notions. "There are more things in heaven and earth, Horatio, than are dreamt of in your philosophy," is a Shakespearean insight to which I personally subscribe and one that might be taken as the motto of the gothic imagination.

It should go without saying that good gothic story-telling, though sensational by its very nature, is not reducible to an immature taste for the sensational. On the contrary, the history of gothic arts suggests that an appetite for the mysterious and the bizarre signals a healthy mind, not a morbid one. A belief that such arts provide a useful mechanism for coping psychologically with life's traumas is an underlying premise of this book (though admittedly one for which I do not pretend to offer statistical validation). One of the more valuable lessons of the gothic imagination is that the modern manqué for such statistical validation is unwise as well as unnecessary. As a literary genre the gothic arose during the second half of the eighteenth century, a revolutionary era that provided horrors a-plenty while at the same time discouraging the consolations of religious faith. It flourished and matured during a century of convulsive political and social upheaval that included two political revolutions (the American and the French) as well as Industrial Revolution that transformed both the pace and content of modern life. More recently, Gothic cinema has picked up where nineteenth- century Gothic literature, music, and painting left off, providing, a much needed psychological outlet for the traumas of war and psychic displacement induced by our own age of rationalized irrationality, dystopia, and unremitting warfare.

Political Gothic

Two World Wars, a Cold War, and now a "War on Terror" have undoubtedly shaken our adult sense of security and ordered well-being. Something, it seems, is indeed rotten in the state of America (as well as the rest of Western civilization) though die-hard "conservatives" refuse to admit it. These traumatic events, difficult enough for adults to process, must have utterly transformed the inner life of children and perhaps even signaled an end to the romantic cult of childhood. While it is true that the young have always been early casualties of political conflict, disease, and natural disaster, the modern era has added significantly, if not to the quotidian catalogue of childhood terrors, at least to the level of childish awareness that modern communication technologies have rendered inescapable. Serial crime, genocide, "collateral damage," dysfunctional families, the largely unchallenged intellectual and aesthetic primitivism of most pop culture icons, highly publicized instances of sexual predation (committed by clerics and high-ranking politicians), dysfunctional families, rumors of alien abduction, random shootings, the reemergence of torture as a supposedly legitimate tool of warfare, the systematic despoliation of the environment, and the threat of terrorist attacks from abroad or within (some allegedly sponsored by our own government) are among the newer entries associated with the unique stress of growing up in the post-WWII era.

To this list, gleaned from the daily headlines and news broadcasts, many would add a deepening erosion of trust in social, political, and religious institutions among adults. Such erosion—though submerged beneath layers of denial, hypocrisy, pseudo-patriotism and mock piety— is bound to have a profound impact on the impressionable minds of youth. To quote from an essay by the late biologist Lewis Thomas, "If I were sixteen or seventeen years old and had to listen to that or read things like that [referring to adult rationalizations for atomic brinksmanship during the Cold War], I would want to give up listening and reading. I would begin thinking up new kinds of sounds, different from any music heard before, and I would be twisting and turning to rid myself of human language" (Thomas 168). Social conservatives are fond of blaming the breakdown of respect for authority on the permissiveness of an excessively permissive culture, when we need look no further for a plausible explanation than to the stark irrationalities and, in some cases, criminal conduct practiced on high. Why should the young respect authority (or the old, for that matter)?

Thomas's poignant *cri de coeur* recalls us to our theme, namely the role of the gothic imagination in the lives of today's younger generation. Much has been made of the way in which J. K. Rowling's novels have triggered a renewed appetite for reading among her younger fans (deservedly so in my view); but, as I have already suggested, Harry and friends did not simply "disapparate" unto the literary scene out of nowhere. John Granger (author of *Harry Potter's Bookshelf*) has documented many of her literary sources. Though most of the books discussed in this volume are not mentioned, I would be surprised if J. K. Rowling's vision was not directly or indirectly influenced by at least some of them. Whether it was or not, Dickens, L'Engle, Cooper, Bradbury and the others are, as I hope to demonstrate, kindred spirits. Moreover, I expect that to a lesser (though still considerable) extent, a nascent interest in books and the pleasures of reading have been nurtured over many decades by each of these authors.

A word of caution before embarking on the substance of this discussion: This is clearly not a book about all gothic literature for children and young adults. Nor is it necessarily a book about only the best such literature— though judging from their longevity as well as the awards conferred on many of them, each of the titles I deal with has been widely recognized as a classic in its genre. Essentially, this is a book about narratives that I personally honor for their artistry, imagination, and entertainment value. That they happen to have been marketed for an age group to which lurid sex, foul language, gratuitous violence, pretentious verbiage, and a cynical world view is unsuited only enhances their worth, in my view. Conversely, neither their popularity nor their Gothic genre necessarily disqualifies them as serious art. In the words of Madeleine L'Engle, "The artist...must retain the vision which includes angels and dragons, and unicorns, and all the lovely creatures which our world would put in a box marked *Children Only*" (L'Engle, *Walking on Water* 21). This book is therefore not an objective academic survey but a personal and unabashedly subjective expression of homage and gratitude for countless hours of innocent and thought-provoking pleasure.

It only remains to explain my idiosyncratic use of certain terms and concepts. To immodestly quote from an earlier book, "The Gothic imagination gives expression and meaning to life's darkly mysterious, painful, frightening, and *seemingly* irrational experiences by embracing them as a potential source of insight and transcendence" (Pepetone 22). This definition of what one of my colleagues has dubbed "the *broad* Gothic imagination" encompasses all historical periods from antiquity to the present and applies equally to all art mediums, e.g., literature, painting, architecture, music, and film. It includes various subgenres of the gothic as well such as science fiction, fantasy, adult fairytale, burlesque parody, and the literature of detection.

As suggested above, within these subgenres I find it helpful to draw a further distinction into categories based on theme and content. *Supernatural gothic*, probably the most familiar of these categories, deals with occult (i.e., literally "hidden") realities and alien, i.e., non-human, intelligences. In one way or another, it postulates the existence of a multi-verse beyond the normal reach of our five human senses and deals with the tension between reality and appearance to which such a cosmology necessarily gives rise. *Psychological gothic* deals with the hidden life belonging to what psychologists refers to as the subconscious or collective unconscious, i.e., the shadow side of the human psyche, as well as the interior and relational tensions to which it gives rise. Finally, *political gothic* explores the tensions between consensus history, i.e., academically accepted, officially endorsed notions of how human events unfold, and hidden history, i.e., narratives that subvert such notions. It is the province of conspiracy theories and explorations of the abuse of power.

Despite the historical origins of what might be called the nineteenth-century "cult of childhood," gothic arts aimed at the young are profoundly unromantic, if by the term "romantic" one means to imply that which is irresponsible escapist in nature. Far from seeing childhood as a privileged subculture isolated from the cares of adulthood, those of a gothic mind-set who write pointedly for the young confront head-on the issue of when-bad-things-happen-to-good (children or adults). The short list of childhood terrors offered above is the stuff of what I sometimes refer to as Kinder-Goth (to coin a phrase) as well as adolescent gothic literature. Many of those who object to the genre on principle do so, I suspect, out of a laudable desire to shield children from an awareness of those terrors. Though compassionate, this motive, in my view, is unrealistic. Thanks to the "information age" in which we live, the young are inevitably aware of disturbing images and behaviors. That is why the insular lifestyle endorsed by those who see the products of the gothic imagination as inimical to "family values" is unsustainable. Its advocates are protecting a chimera that, in my experience, young people themselves overwhelmingly reject. Moreover, adults who advocate such a narrow pedagogy are, I suspect, in denial about the often harsh realities that shape all our lives, irrespective of our age group. As J. K. Rowling might say, "Ignorance may be bliss but it makes a terrible Patronus charm." Indeed, the value of the gothic imagination to readers of all ages resides precisely in its usefulness as a vicarious means of coping with life's true Dementors, i.e., its forces of negation and destruction.

The Gothic Imagination and Socialization

Far more so than their parents, the young instinctively prefer unpleasant truths to comforting lies—though like the rest of us they may conceal their concerns behind an unconvincing façade of cynical indifference. The issue that we face as parents and mentors is therefore not how best to filter out and block an awareness of the discordant aspects of life from the young, but rather how to mediate them in ways that are age–appropriate. Rather than turning them into impregnable fortresses from which to wage "culture wars," perhaps we should transform our homes and classrooms into intellectual and spiritual sanctuaries within which our children might hope to acquire a better understanding of how to withstand and oppose the ruthlessness, ugliness, and deepening nihilism of modern life. In the absence of such havens, kids have little choice but to seek refuge in the welcoming insubstantialities of celebrity culture (and eventually to embrace extremist religious and political ideologies that reduce life's complexities to a collection of simplistic bumper-sticker slogans).

Burned in New Mexico

Speaking of such ideologies, just yesterday, I came across a magazine listing of books banned by American schools and libraries. Topping this right-wing "enemies list" is the *Harry Potter* series, which has (according to a September 2010 issue of *AARP Bulletin*) been subject to a book burning in the state of New Mexico and legally challenged in nineteen others. What a sad commentary on the spiritual health and intellectual vitality of a modern democracy! Writing of Albus Dumbledore, Betsy Towner explains the animosity the Hogwarts headmaster has aroused in some quarters by noting that he embodies "the allegedly demonic attributes of the series—witchcraft, sorcery, and *rebellion against authority* [emphasis added]" (Towner 39)

Either my own grasp of modern history is fuzzy of the infamous Tea Party crowd (some of which sees our current president as a latter day Hitler) is lacing its liquid refreshment with more than cream and sugar. I was under the impression that book burning was a discredited tactic once especially favored by fascists. Then again, the only way to make sense of the farrago of today's so-called "conservatism" is to recognize it as a psychological projection far more applicable to itself than to its allegedly demonic and "un-American" opponents. Allow me to repeat that assertion: *The only way to make sense of the farrago of today's so-called "conservatism" is to recognize it as a psychological projection.* The conflation of the demonic with the subversive lies at the core of conservative *angst* about not only about *Harry Potter* in relation to purportedly Christian/family values, but about such values in relation to our constitutional democracy. As I hope to demonstrate, the cult of childhood arose historically from Christian parables that, in fact, represent some of the most liberal, potentially subversive sayings attributed to Jesus. Conservative fulminations against Rowling are therefore unwarranted from both a theological and a political perspective. The authentically sacramental worldview found in the *Gospels* (and mirrored in many of the classics of gothic literature for children) is fundamentally antagonistic to the very political and cultural status quo that social conservatism and libertarianism strive to conserve. The illegitimacy of the term "conservative" arises from the fact that the political and economic status quo is always changing, always in flux—as are the flagrantly inconsistent rationalizations used by right-wing conservatives and libertarians to defend it).

"Ultimately, gothic literature," writes John Granger in *Harry Potter's Bookshelf*, "is about having the moral courage to see the world as it is and to make a choice to seek a way out. That choice is by definition and tradition a moral one—to flee death and pursue life, to seek light rather than darkness. We see the horror in the world—and in monsters without conscience—and draw away from it" (Granger 104). This same author devotes an entire chapter to the gothic aspects of Rowling's imaginative thought-world, which he identifies with the following motifs: Hogwart's castle i.e., its Gothic architectural features, the books supernatural atmosphere, the presence of the horrific, subterranean passages, fragmentation and reunion (synonymous with dismember/re-member, another gothic pairing referred to later in this volume), prophesy and the notion of an ancestral curse, tainted blood and bonds formed by blood, graveyards and corpses, decay and aristocratic privilege, the importance of the forest and other wilderness settings, sacrificial bravery, memories and dreams, a magic or prophetic book, *Doppelgängers* (doubles and evil twins), scars or telltale marks, mysterious strangers, confused origins, mist and fog, the distant past , and death itself (Granger 91-98). As we shall see, all of these motifs figure prominently in other childhood classics as well.

As for the alleged "demonic" attributes of the gothic imagination, the hostility toward *Harry Potter* exhibited by some Evangelical Christians is more revealing of their own skewed vision than of Rowling's worldview (as projections necessarily are), premised as it is on a thorough misunderstanding how to read books, including their favorite book. Incapable of bringing a nuanced perception to their reading of the Bible, such Evangelicals are at a loss as to how to construe the example and teaching of Jesus, or how those teachings relate to founding principles on which modern democracy was premised (including a respect for liberal education and the separation of church and state). In his revisionist history of the events of 9/11, theologian David Ray Griffin offers a fresh and highly pertinent understanding of the demonic, shared by some of our most astute purveyors of the gothic imagination in children's literature. It exposes modern Evangelical theology for what it is—a "demonic" perversion of fundamental Christian and democratic precepts...in a word, heresy.

The unequivocally pacifist, communitarian gospel of Christ, Griffin argues (as do all exponents of an enlightened spirituality), is the very antithesis of the aggressive individualism and triumphalism preached by today's political and religious Right. Today's pseudo-conservative, pseudo-democratic Evangelical mind-set, argues Griffin, is a by- product of an objective, i.e. trans-personal, force powerful enough to enthrall whole societies, thanks largely to the nature and reach of modern communication technologies. The objective force he has in mind—represented by the gothic imagination (and its near relative the religious imagination) as "the demonic"—is the power of the mass media to shape and limit our ability to question basic assumptions about human destiny in relation to the divine will. At heart, however, technology is not at the culprit. The ideological distortions of modern conservatism are, at their root, attributable to the innate human faculty to construct secondary realities from words and non-verbal symbols such as visual images. Carefully controlled and reinforced constructs of this sort give rise to elaborate belief systems, impregnable symbolic structures difficult to perceive, much less oppose. According to Griffin, Evangelicals who believe in evil as an objective force are therefore correct in believing that they have adopted an authentically biblical stance, albeit one they themselves completely misunderstand. Evil and sin are—right enough—external to individual human will and therefore not susceptible to eradication by individual acts of will. However, that does not mean that they are a direct result of supernatural intervention. Rather, according to the Bible, evil represents a collective assault on human sensibilities that emanates from the nature of imagination itself, creating an environment akin to an all-encompassing cultural climate of thought and feeling. Whereas Evangelicals interpret sin as a perversion of individual will-power and redemption as a baptism of that individual power, the New Testament presents it as a complacent yielding to one's social environment. In light of this biblical—specifically Christian— understanding, the traditional icon of the fish as an identifying symbol seems particularly appropriate. What water is to fish, evil is to humanity (i.e., a sustaining cultural environment—unavoidable, omnipresent, and therefore virtually invisible).

In confronting the military might of Rome and the religious might of Judaism, Jesus (asserts Griffin) was up against precisely such objective evil—as we all are when challenging political and religious establishments (see *Christian Faith and the Truth Behind 9/11* 121-148). It follows that to oppose imperial and nationalistic hysteria, systematic war propaganda, and the violence to which they lead, is to confront evil as Christ did. Conversely, to participate in and promote the social rituals that support demonic belief systems (i.e., those that justify war, economic exploitation and other forms of physical or psychological coercion) is to sin against both the Prince of Peace and the Spirit of 1776 (promulgated by those who sought to create a free and open society from which "the demonic"—in Griffin's sense—would be debarred, or at least restrained). It is perhaps fitting that modern proponents of the cult of childhood have used gothic story-telling as their weapon of choice in fighting such evil within our own culture, much as Christ sought to disperse the fog of tribal pride by telling stories—including parables about the closeness of children to the Kingdom of God.

My hope is that *Hogwarts and All* will help parents and educators become better, more beneficial custodians of youth through identifying and sharing stories suited to inculcating a mature and humane outlook on life (whether sacred or secular). If you are largely unfamiliar with Gothic literature for children other than the Harry Potter books (or perhaps the *Chronicles of Narnia* by C. S. Lewis) you will hopefully be pleased to make the acquaintance of other well-crafted and engaging narratives written from a variety of religious, political, and philosophical perspectives. If some or all of the books I am about to discuss are already known to you, perhaps this attempt to analyze and contextualize them differently will amplify and deepen your own pleasure (and by extension, that of your offspring and/or students). Where we disagree…well, that too can be instructive.

1 Märchen, Adult Fairytales, and Cyclic Journeys: *A Christmas Carol* in Context

The artistic cult of childhood is closely linked with a German literary genre known as *Märchen*, or adult fairy tale. At the close of the eighteenth and early part of the nineteenth century, German authors such as Eichendorff, E.T.A. Hoffmann, Novalis, and Goethe all contributed to a literature of adult fantasy in the manner of a children's tale that is often rife with Gothic images, themes, and settings. This new literary genre was modeled on the less sophisticated folk tales (*Volksmärchen or Hausmärchen*) of anthologists such as the Brothers Grimm and Hans Christian Andersen. Though aimed at children, *Hausmärchen* were in fact symptomatic of romanticism's obsession with the primitive and the nationalistic, obviously adult preoccupations that would hold little attraction for the young. Their adult counterpart, on the other hand, satisfied a growing demand for a literature that would celebrate and nurture those childlike qualities that romantics regarded as threatened by a new scientific ethos bent on reducing the spiritual dimension of life to the status of a fairy tale kept alive by superstition and mindless sentiment.

A mechanistic worldview derived from the science of Sir Isaac Newton (who was himself personally committed to an occult and mystical view of life) left no room for human free will, nor did it recognize the existence of "trans-rational" modes of perception such as divine revelation, intuition, clairvoyance, artistic afflatus, and insight derived from dreams. The gothic imagination, predicated as it is on a "childlike" belief in an open universe fraught with infinite possibilities, offered a bulwark against Mathew Arnold's receding sea of faith. In effect, the gothic paradigm embraced by European romanticism constituted an intellectual counter-culture to that of scientific materialism. E.T.A. Hoffmann's *The Golden Pot* is (like the German romantic culture that spawned it) is no longer familiar to the average reader. Its dualistic world of serpentine intelligences, alchemy, and mythic vibrancy lurking just beyond the sensory reach of a quotidian world of bureaucratic rules, rigid class distinctions, and a Philistine preoccupation with material comfort. Hoffmann's German romantic vision nevertheless does live on through still popular world classics influenced by *Hausmärchen* and *Kunstmärchen* (artistic narratives in the manner of a fairy tale but pitched to a more mature readership) such as *A Christmas Carol* by Charles

Dickens—a work that has seeped into the bloodstream of a popular culture largely unaware of its literary antecedents.

According to literary critic M. H. Abrams, German romantic *Märchen* provide a clear template for what I have referred to elsewhere as the archetypal journey of the gothic hero. "They embody, "writes Abrams, "an implicit theodicy [a justification of the ways of God to humanity], for the journey [of the protagonist] is a spiritual way through evil and suffering which is justified as necessary means to the achievement of a greater good; and usually, although with greater or less explicitness, this process is conceived as a fall from unity [wholeness] to division [dismemberment] and into a conflict of contraries which in turn compel the movement back toward a higher integration [synthesis]" (Abrams 193) Scrooge, like the unredeemed solicitor Mr. Blunden in Antonia Barber's *The Amazing Mr. Blunden* or the irredeemable Lord Voldemort in J. K. Rowling's *Harry Potter* saga, is a typical gothic anti-hero. Such individuals are proud, obsessive, unconventional, alienated, insensitive, and selfish.

Moreover, Scrooge's journey toward spiritual regeneration is not linear—progressing through an orderly sequence to ever higher levels of insight, one logical step at a time—rather it is cyclic and episodic—progressing through a somewhat random series of seemingly unrelated vignettes to an organic transformation in which Dickens's misanthropic miser must circle back to the future. Scrooge, like Mr. Blunden, must return to his past, not to undo what was done, but to regain those forgotten childlike qualities that he has incrementally relinquished. Furthermore, his spiritual condition at the conclusion of his journey, i.e., his transcendence of his gothic dilemma, though it may resemble the innocent pleasures of his early youth, is in fact characterized by a deeper, more authentic joy precisely because it represents a new synergy of the past, the present, and the future subsequent to a long and precipitous fall from grace, a fall that is marked by many numbing years of renunciation, neglect, and alienation. In other words, a visual representation of Scrooge's *Bildungsreisse* (the German term for a journey of personal enlightenment) would appear not as a steadily ascending line, but rather as an ascending spiral of concentric circles, each tier of which covers essentially the same or very similar ground, though on a higher level of awareness. In such a representation, it is the perception of the viewer rather than the view itself that changes. This cyclic model of Scrooge's educative process recalls the trials of Meg Murphy who, in L'Engle's time trilogy (discussed in a later chapter), must expose herself repeatedly to an excruciating assault that carries with it the threat of being "un-named" or "X-ed" by forces of negation known as Echthroi. Like the farandole Sporos in *A Wind in the Door* (another of L'Engles religiously oriented science fiction fantasies for the young), Mr. Scrooge experiences a transformation that might best be described as a deepening rather than a logical progression.

The Naming of Ebenezer Scrooge

Apart from the fact that it represents a still vital link with a largely forgotten cultural heritage, there are several reasons for including a discussion of what is clearly a piece of adult fantasy in an anthology of essays about gothic literature for children and adolescents? First, the specter of Dickens's "ghostly little book" hovers in the background of much of the children's literature we are about to consider, especially that which is explicitly Christian in its orientation. Second, the *Carol* is, in terms of its literary quality, a premier example of Gothic literature for the "childlike." Third, although Dickens's Christmas novella is perhaps no longer read by adults or children as widely as it once was, various films (now available in a home video format), CDs, literary, and television adaptations of *A Christmas Carol* (including adolescent narratives based on the original and even comic book, cartoon, and graphic novel versions pitched to a "post-literate" audience), continue to proliferate. The outcome of this Dickensian cottage industry is that Victorian England's most familiar skin flint has become an iconic, instantly recognizable figure in popular culture. Fourth, it would be difficult to find a more compelling example of the synthesis of the three principle genres of the Gothic imagination (supernatural, psychological, and political) or the defining themes of the gothic imagination such as redemptive memory, duality, and the transformative journey of the gothic hero.

Perhaps most of those who read this book can be expected to have seen one or more of the many film adaptations of *A Christmas Carol*. Many will have watched their favorite version more than once. Fewer, possibly, will have read Dickens's Christmas novella, and fewer still will have undertaken a lengthy independent study of the complete Dickens oeuvre with its attendant biographical and critical studies. It is only after doing so, however, that one can hope to experience the *Carol* in its widest cultural context—a context that embraces gothic literature, Victorian cultural and political history, and Christian theology. Coming away from such an absorbing project with a new and deepened respect for what may previously have seemed an inconsequential holiday entertainment, those who take this arduous but rewarding journey, will almost certainly come to understand Dickens's almost-too-familiar story as not merely an enduring classic of English literature (as well as an indispensable component of an annual social ritual) but as a Rosetta Stone that holds the key to an understanding of the ethical, political, and economic dilemmas faced by every thoughtful citizen of Western culture since the dawn of the industrial era.

In retrospect, I can now see that my own early, though uncritical, fascination with the *Carol* derived from an innate sense that there was much more to this unusual ghost story than met the eye. "I wants to make your flesh creep," says the Fat Boy at Dingly Dell in *The Pickwick Papers* and that, according to a great many critics of the sub-genre (ghost story), chiefly accounts for the appeal of the *Carol* in particular and gothic literature in general; but does it? Something about the trinity of Dickens's Christmas specters (past, present, and future) seems to transcend this limited explanation. To fans of the gothic imagination (those old enough to respond at more than a visceral level, at least) it is patently obvious that tales such as *A Christmas Carol* are intended to convey more than cheap thrills; but what exactly does it convey...what enduring insights into the human condition does this Dickensian fantasy in particular and the gothic imagination in general have to offer? By exploring Dickens's timeless tale of a soul dismembered and re-membered, a representative though seldom contextualized example of an English *Kunstmärchen*, this chapter will attempt to answer that question.

Victorian Political Gothic

The literary cult of childhood has a simple premise: Children (and adults who have not altogether relinquished child-like sensibilities) require, an occasional escape—a mental vacation if you will—from the cruelties and irrationalities of life. We need to be inoculated, in a manner of speaking, against the relentless tensions that plague modern industrialized society and the cynicism to which those tensions can give rise. This can be accomplished, in part, by remembering (or vicariously re-living though engagement with the arts) our own childish experience of a time when simple pleasures yielded great and complex joys, a time when the world seemed fresh and welcoming, more a fairy garden than a killing field. Dickens's contemporaries, whose need for such a vaccine was equal to if not greater than our own, looked to their poets and novelists for relief. In providing it, however, nineteenth-century romantics like Wordsworth and Dickens were faced with a choice between providing a transient escape *from* a culture increasingly poisoned by the interrelated creeds of predatory capitalism, scientific materialism, tribal nationalism, and philosophical nihilism and an escape *to* an alternative perspective that would expose the spiritual inadequacies of these soul-destroying creeds? Exponents of the cult of childhood in its earlier phase chose the latter option.

While, as George Orwell notes, none of Dickens's books can be read rightly as political tracts i.e. as doctrinaire propaganda, it is nevertheless true that in the *Carol* its author set out to deal a blow on behalf of the poor against the burgeoning excesses of a capitalist economy that benefited the super rich at the expense of everyone else (Orwell 61). Clearly, Dickens was not Karl Marx; but just as clearly, he saw the *laissez-faire* theories of economic utilitarianism as irreconcilable with a Christian commitment to what a much later orator and political activist, Dr. Martin Luther King, would term "the Beloved Community." England during the "hungry forties" (the *Carol* was first published in 1843) was shot through with an undercurrent of anxiety about the prospect of a revolution comparable to those that had occurred earlier in America and France. Dickens, with his deep seated psychological dread of poverty, was ambiguous with regard to this prospect. He feared the potential consequences to himself and his family of social upheaval as much as he despised the arrogance and insensitivity of the aristocrats and capitalists who rendered such an upheaval distinctly possibility (Houghton 54–58). Arguably, this tension served as both a catalyst to his creative imagination and a contributing factor in his premature death. In any case, the *Carol* makes it abundantly clear that Dickens regarded utilitarian economics and the political agenda that it fostered as ethically abhorrent.

Though decidedly not a political tract, the *Carol* comes close, as does the entire canon of Dickens, to being a liberal defense of Whig history against both the social conservatism of aristocratic Tories and the economic radicalism of the utilitarian economists. The courage and faith required of Dickens in taking this political-gothic stand are difficult to estimate from our own vantage point in time. He was easy prey to the charge of "sentimentality" from adversaries (lampooned in *Hard Times*) who had the statistical "facts and figures" on their side. Thomas Malthus (1756–1834) had shown, with unassailable logic, that England's growing "surplus population" would soon deplete its sustainable food supply. Liberal legislation aimed at relieving the distress of the poor was therefore condemned as shortsighted and sentimental. Economic theorists such as Malthus, James Mill, and Ricardo were proven wrong, however, not because their statistics were wrong but because they had failed to anticipate innovations in transportation technology, such as the steam ship, that would open new markets, thereby alleviating population stress and invalidating their anti-liberal, self-serving political ideology. Deficient in the faith that would have encouraged them to renounce their radical creed in defiance of their statistics, these men chose instead to ignore the human misery that their *laissez-faire* ideology helped to create and deride those who sought to alleviate it. Dickens, who suffered from no such lack of ethical imagination, rebelled in the name of Christian humanitarianism.

Dickens, of course was no more able to see into the future than those whose ideas he would oppose. He simply decided to abide by the biblical injunction to care for the poor and needy despite apparently sound economic reasons for abandoning it. Whether, in the long term, history will vindicate his choice, remains to be seen. That his irrational and sentimental opposition frustrated and angered the Malthusians is understandable given their imaginatively limited frame of reference. In the words of Chesterton, "The faith of Christians angered him [Malthus, who was himself a clergyman] because he was more a pessimist than a healthy man should be. In the same way, the Malthusians by instinct attacked Christianity; not because there is anything especially anti-Malthusian about Christianity, but because there is something a little anti-human about Malthusianism." (Chesterton 96) This seemingly antiquated historical controversy illustrates one of the fundamental insights of the political-gothic imagination, as applicable today as it was then: Inhumane means used to promote some alleged "greater good" inevitably lead to inhumane ends.

Those who indulge their Shadow side in gothic literature, such as Victor Frankenstein, Dr. Henry Jekyll, Ebenezer Scrooge, and Lord Voldemort, invariably rationalize their methods as interim means to a glorious end. Crippled by lack of ethical imagination and blinded by denial, their thoughts and deeds are invariably justified in their own eyes regardless of their consequences or the criticism expressed by others. Their unshakable belief in their own innate rectitude, in other words, provides a Harry Potter-like *Cloak of Invisibility* under which to conceal their cruelty, irrationality, and arrogant disregard for widely accepted norms of human conduct, not just from others, but more importantly from themselves. It is precisely this grotesque disconnect, between idealism and expediency, ends and mean, that defines

Scrooge's Gothic duality. His obsessive need to hoard and possess, rationalized as a devotion to the values of free-market capitalism and commonplace business practice, have turned him into a caricature of humanity devoid of human sympathy, a creature as frightening as any gargoyle or vampire from the darkest recesses of the gothic imagination.

One of the recurrent themes of Gothic literature for the young at heart (as well as the young in years) is that when acted upon, trust, faith in the eternal verities of human conduct and goodwill can often trump logic that is seemingly irrefutable. In a well known Christmas classic novelized by Valentine Davies (*Miracle on 34th Street*), faith is defined as "believing in things when common sensed tells you not to." In upholding his faith in charity, compassion, and liberal public policy over the rationalized cruelties of child labor, class snobbery, and corporate greed Dickens was not only defying the consensus wisdom of the early Victorian era, i.e., upholding a vision of the world as it should be rather than as it appeared to the intellectual vanguard of his age, he was also choosing to heed a childlike sense of wonder and openness to radical possibilities. "There's more of gravy than grave about you, whatever you are," quips Scrooge the scientific materialist (27). "If they [the poor] would rather die they had better do it, and decrease the surplus population," says Scrooge the Malthusian and social Darwinist. "I don't make merry myself and can't afford to make idle people merry," says Scrooge the entrepreneurial self-made man of business (14).

Though we are all encouraged to fear the irrational, justifiably so, many of the worst crimes in history have been committed in the name of logic and reason. Romanticism clearly gave precedence to sound feeling over arid intellectualism. When the Ghost of Christmas Past beckons him to proceed together out the upper story window of his bedroom, Scrooge protests that he is mortal and liable to fall. "Bear but a touch of my hand there, said the Spirit, laying it upon his heart," and you shall be upheld in more than this" (46). The romantic painter Goya warned against the spiritual dangers of intellectual abstraction uninformed by human emotional warmth and sensibility when he warned that "The sleep of reason produces nightmares." Though they sensed that their own nineteenth-century culture, sometimes referred to as the "Age of Ideology," erred on the side of head over heart, practitioners of the gothic imagination knew instinctively that neither "head" (human reason unbalanced by faith and feeling) nor "heart" (faith and human sympathy unbalanced by reason) are a reliable compass with which to navigate the mysteries of this world. Only a synergy of head and heart (i.e., trust in an ultimate outcome informed by sound critical judgment, a feeling heart, and an alert conscience) can hope to prevent the nightmares unleashed by the "sleep of reason."

Consequently, they advocated a transcendent rationality, or "trans-rationality" that—to paraphrase from the screenplay of Jacques Tourneur's Gothic film classic, *The Night of the Demon*—recognizes the value of reason but also the dark shadows that reason can cast, shadows that can blind men to the truth. Dickens clearly felt that the various "isms" of the Victorian era (scientism, capitalism, social Darwinism, and utilitarian radicalism) were blinding men to what Christians call the Social Gospel based on a concern for one's less fortunate neighbors. His answer to the challenge posed by the gun-ho capitalists and social conservatives of his age was to restore the failing ethical vision of his Victorian culture by invoking memory, example, and fear, as embodied by the three spirits of Christmas. In role-modeling the social transformation he hoped to bring about through depicting the politico-ethical transformation of a representative "economic man" in Ebenezer Scrooge—a transformation from *homo de monde* (the narrowly Victorian economic man of the world) into *homo de cour* (an ethically enlightened man of compassion and liberal outlook)—Dickens turned to the adult fairy tale as his genre of choice (Johnson 483–489).

Dismemberment, Remembrance, and Gothic Atonement

In keeping with the Gothic precept that the negative journey of the gothic hero/villain toward *enantiodromia,* i.e., "reversal into the opposite" is a self-inflicted dismembering of past, present, and future (a form of forgetfulness that psychologists term "denial"), Scrooge's way back from denial begins with a survey of past Christmases. "Long past," inquires Scrooge. "No, your past," replies the spirit, described as "a strange figure—like a child; yet not so like a child as like an old man, viewed through some supernatural medium, which gave him the appearance of having receded from the view, and being diminished to a child's proportions" (68). Dickens goes on to describe the enigmatic appearance of this child-like spirit as one adorned with fresh green holy (an emblem of winter or old age) as well as summer flowers (a symbol of youth). Dickens assigns a male pronoun to this somewhat an-drogynous specter (an interesting feature developed more fully in some of the film adaptations) yet its voice and touch are described as being soft and gentle as a woman's. He/she/it emits a jet of bright light from the crown of its head symbolizing the illumination that memory brings. This interpretation is reinforced by Scrooge, who when he spots the extinguisher cap that the spirit holds under its arm, confesses to a desire to see it worn by the spirit. "What," exclaims the ghost, "would you so soon put out, with worldly hands, the light I give? Is it not enough that you are one of those whose passions made this cap, and force me, through whole trains of years to wear it low upon my brow" (69)?

Though Scrooge apologizes on this occasion, later, after memory has reopened the deepest of his suppressed wounds, he reasserts his determined denial by violently forcing the cap upon the spirit. If we look closely at the particular memories invoked by this spirit, we discover that they concern formative influences and decisive turning points along the path traveled by Scrooge's from trauma (e.g., his solitary childhood) to denial and projection (e.g., his refusal to acknowledge to his former fiancée that he has changed and his mental habit of blaming the "harshness of the world" rather than accepting responsibility for his own harsh decisions) and finally to that reversal by which he is transformed into a monster of greed and selfishness, the very embodiment of the forces that shaped and stunted his own spiritual development in youth. At each of these milestones, Scrooge is bidden to reclaim himself by remembering the joys, sorrows, and misspent opportunities of a past hidden behind a dense wall of denial: "You recollect the way," inquires the spirit with regard to the path leading to an old school house. When Scrooge, overcome with emotion, exclaims that he could walk it blindfold, the spirit comments, "Strange to have forgotten it for so many years" (70)!

This theme, prominent in the *Carol*, is central to another of Dickens's Christmas *Kunstmärchen*, *The Haunted Man and the Ghost's Bargain*. The man in question, is the book's central character, Professor Redlaw—a solitary, Byronic figure who, as the title suggests, is haunted by his past. The ghost, incidentally, is that of a childish *Doppelgänger*, a disturbing image of the savage, ignorant ragamuffin that Redlaw might have become (he is also a literary stand-in for the author had he not been rescued from the blacking factory). In an episode reminiscent of Dorian Gray in Oscar Wilde's classic Gothic masterpiece, Redlaw thoughtlessly wishes that he could be relieved of the burden of memory; but when his ill-considered wish is granted, he finds that this supposed blessing is in fact a curse (one he inadvertently passes on to the detriment of every one with whom he comes into contact). As one literary and film critic Fred Guida remarks, "It's closing line—'Lord keep my Memory Green'—is not only a fitting coda for his [Dickens's] work in the Christmas book genre, but, in a sense, perhaps even a summation of all that he hoped to accomplish (at least personally) through his work" (Guida 151). When one considers the lengthy list of hard-hearted plutocrats, such as Gradgrind and Mr. Dombey, who strut through the pages of his novels—men who have forgotten what it is to be human by forgetting what it is to be a child, Guida's generalization seems warranted.

In both the *Carol* and *The Haunted Man*, the principle characters, Scrooge and Redlaw, are personalities divided against themselves, like Robert Louis Stevenson's Dr. Jekyll and Mr. Hyde. Fragmented, dismembered, lacking in that wholeness, which according to cult-of- childhood author Madeleine L'Engle, is also a mark of holiness, these men are held hostage by a sinister alter ego, a beast within. The Jungian term for this archetypal psychic component, inherent in each of us, is the "Shadow." According to the gothic imagination, it is this latent monster with whom we must achieve a reconciliation (or synergy), if we are to function in a creative and benevolent fashion. Prior to the depth psychology of Jung, gothic artists such as Dickens gave expression to this same principle, often through the use of the *Doppelgänger* motif. Like Mr. Blunden in Antonia Barber or Harry Potter in Rowling's *The Prisoner of Azkaban*, both Scrooge and Redlaw are confronted by their "doubles" (apparitions of their present or former selves)—confrontations that force a radical reassessment of their current identities and values.

Scrooge, confronted by a memory of himself as an abandoned child (and later as a young adult) aided and abetted by his loving sister Fan, is compelled by conscience to reassess his relationship with his nephew Fred, Fan's orphaned child to whom he should have become a surrogate parent following his mother's untimely death in childbirth. His remembrance of himself as a grateful apprentice to Mr. Fezziwig (one of Dickens's last literary portrayals of benevolent capitalism) forces Scrooge to reevaluate his obligations as an employer to Bob Cratchit. Scrooge as a once ardent suitor turned into a cold and lonely misanthrope, induces Scrooge to reconsider not only his own solitary and emotionally barren lifestyle, but his earlier sour verdict on the marriage of his nephew. During Fred's most recent Christmas-Eve confrontation with his uncle, he makes it quite clear that his recent marriage was "the making of him," despite its failure to bring him any financial advantage (L'Engle, as we shall see, might have called it the "naming" of him). Scrooge, of course, insists it was the ruin of him.

Unlike Mr. Blunden in Antonia Barber's cult-of-childhood Christian parable (discussed presently), Ebenezer Scrooge is not offered an opportunity to undo his "life's opportunities misused" up to the time of his meeting with the spirits. He is, however, granted time in which to make amends subsequent to their visitations: "Men's courses will foreshadow certain ends, to which, if persevered in, they must lead...But if the courses be departed from, the ends will change. Say it is thus with what you show me," pleads Scrooge with the Ghost of Christmas Yet to Come. (124) Unlike his former business partner Jacob Marley, Scrooge (through Marley's timely intercession) is indeed granted an opportunity to depart from the ways he has chosen. The various narratives discussed so far affirm the existence of an open-ended, morally conditioned, i.e. undetermined, universe in which individuals are left to work out their own salvation, as the Danish Christian philosopher Kierkegaard suggests "with fear and trembling." This insistence on the possibility and importance of free will, i.e., the ability to make choices that alter outcomes in ways that are meaningful, is one of the hallmarks of the cult of childhood.

Dickens's Romantic Christianity and the Gothic Imagination

Numerous biographers and critics have noted that Dickens did not affiliate himself with any particular Christian denomination, nor did he attend church regularly. Moreover, his portrayal of "religious" people (from the unctuously pious Mr. Pecksniff in *Martin Chuzzlewit* and the lay preacher Mr. Chadband in *Bleak House* to the opium-addicted choirmaster of Cloisterham Cathedral (John Jasper in *The Mystery of Edwin Drood*) is far from flattering. In his children's version of the Christian Gospels (*The Life of Our Lord*), Dickens removes most references to the supernatural, presenting Jesus as something of a public spirited, liberal-minded Victorian gentleman. Indeed, the consensus among literary critics seems to be that Dickens himself was a "Culture Christian," whose religious commitment amounted to little more than "a jackdaw fondness for cathedrals."

Admittedly, Dickens is emphatically un-doctrinaire, but then, one might argue, Christ was also. As with his political stance, which is also ideologically fluid and difficult to categorize using current ideological markers, it is a mistake to underestimate either the depth of Dickens's faith or the extent to which it informed his writings. Those who question the authenticity of his Christianity must offer a plausible explanation for his many scriptural references such as his epithet of David Copperfield's loyal nurse Peggotty ("thou good and faithful servant,") or his poignant portrayal of Steven Blackpool whose dying vision invokes the Star of Bethlehem, or his favorable portrait of Esther Summerson's authentic Christian charity in comparison with the tractarian "telescopic philanthropy" of Mrs. Pardiggle.

Given his own explicit professions of religious commitment, his contempt for those who abused or misrepresented it, and the sheer number of scriptural references found in his writings, the only alternative that suggests itself is a purely cynical and mercenary desire to manipulate his audience—an explanation that seems decidedly implausible, notwithstanding the iconoclasm of authors such as Dan Simmons (author of *Drood*), whose fictionalized realization of the unsolved mystery posed by Dickens's uncompleted last novel is only the most recent entry in a lengthy catalogue of Gothic entertainments and scholarly psycho-dramas devoted to the "dark side" of Mr. Dickens. That he had a dark side is undeniable, even *de rigueur* according to the Gothic imagination. That the Shadow-side of Dickens led him to profess an essentially spurious Christianity is not.

One could easily multiply examples of Christian citations and allusions found in Dickens's work. Each of these, in isolation from all the rest, can perhaps be dismissed as shallow appeals to conventional Victorian sentiment. Their cumulative effect, however, leaves a different impression. Indeed, the vast majority of Dickens's readers, now as during his lifetime, instinctively associate Dickens's art with his faith. A close reading of *A Christmas Carol* can only strengthen that association. Apart from its obvious connection with a festival whose historical origins are certainly sacred, if not initially Christian, Dickens himself, pointedly references the nativity as a source of inspiration. Indeed, the gothic imagination and the religious imagination are closely allied in many respects. One of the Church's earliest creedal statements, for example, the *Athanasian Creed*, includes the so-called "Harrowing of Hell" wherein the crucified Christ, prior to ascension, pays a visit to Lucifer's nether realm in order to liberate spirits sentenced to perdition merely because they lived prior to the incarnation. Indeed, the Christ of Christian orthodoxy, though not proud is a typical gothic hero in other respects, i.e., isolated, intelligent, sensitive, wise beyond his years, old before his time, unconventional, and conversant with alternate realities. He is, moreover, a demigod endowed with preternatural powers (e.g., precognition, time travel, spontaneous healing, resurrection, and *ex nihilo* materialization, to name only a few). He is also a melancholy "Man of

Sorrows" who carries the heavy emotional burden implicit in his clairvoyant anticipation of a humiliating and painful death.

When Scrooge tactlessly reminds Marley's Ghost that since he travels "on the wings of the wind" he might have covered a quantity of ground in the seven years since his death, his distraught former partner explodes: Oh! Captive bound and double ironed," exclaims the specter, "not to know that any Christian spirit working kindly in its little sphere, whatever it may be, will find its mortal life too short for its vast means of usefulness. Not to know that no space of regret can make amends for one's life's opportunities misused! Yet such was I! Oh! Such was I!...Why did I walk through crowds-beings with my eyes turned down, and never raise them to that blessed Star which led the Wise Man to a poor abode? Were there no poor homes to which it light would have conducted me" (62)? In view of passages such as this, one must strain more mightily than the fabled camel seeking passage through the eye of a needle not to see a genuine connection between Christianity and the philosophy of Dickens. The fact of the matter is that the spiritual worldview, with its acceptance of a transcendent reality inhabited by otherworldly agencies is, as mentioned above, inherently as well as historically linked to, if not inseparable from, the gothic imagination.

From its opening presentation of Victorian London as fog-enshrouded dystopian Inferno (bitter cold, like the frozen ninth circle in Dante) a strong association in the *Carol* between the terrible fate of Marley's ghost and familiar representations of Christian damnation: "There was something very awful, too, in the specter's being provided with an infernal atmosphere of its own," writes Dickens. "Scrooge could not feel it himself, but this was clearly the case; for though the Ghost sat perfectly motionless, its hair, and skirts, and tassels, were still agitated as by the hot vapor from an oven"(60). The essence of the anguish experienced by Marley as well as the spirits who accompany him is that they have forfeited their power to interfere for good in human affairs. It is when Scrooge attempts to console Marley by extolling his former business acumen that the ghost vents his pent up remorse, proclaiming that his true business was the common welfare and that the dealings of his trade were but "a drop of water" in the comprehensive ocean of his business (61). It is important to remember that in Dickens—as in Dante, L'Engle, Barber, and Cooper, Rowling and other contributors to the cult of childhood—damnation is not an extrinsic punishment but a subjective choice.

G. K. Chesterton, an early twentieth-century convert to Catholicism who revered Dickens, nevertheless once accused him of displaying a typically Victorian religious provincialism for having created the three Spirits of Christmas, thereby ignoring the saints and martyrs of Christian tradition (presumably a trinity of L'Engle's cherubim in *The Wind in the Door* would have been more to his liking). This argument, of course, misses the point of Dickens's brand of romantic Christianity. The *Carol* is no more an Evangelical tract than it is as a political pamphlet. Dickens's religion as well as his politics was grounded, as mentioned above, in what Christian theologians refer to as "the social Gospel." It was rooted in a genuine conviction that the example and teachings of Jesus are authoritative, but that the linked concepts of sin and redemption have a socio-economic as well as a personal bearing. Based on his reading of the Gospels, he concluded that the essence of Christian faith was "love your neighbor as yourself" and "render unto Caesar, i.e., the secular authority, those things that belong to Caesars (and those things only). In short, he saw the teaching and example of Jesus as an injunction to care for the needy and resist any secular authority whose call to violence and acquisitiveness contradict the requirements of compassion.

In a hypocritical culture (not unlike our own) in which self-congratulatory pietism was often confused with genuine piety, Dickens was no doubt eager to distance himself from the Evangelical fervor of men like Mr. Chadband (*Bleak House*) and Rev. Brocklehurst in C. Brontë's *Jane Eyre*. Intelligent Christians have always understood that humanity's relationship with the Mysterious Other should be spoken of, if at all, with reticence, thoughtful restraint, and circumspection. One has only to compare the delicate sympathy exhibited by Esther Sommerson with the heavy-handed charity of Mrs. Pardiggle (both professing Christian's from the pages of *Bleak House*) to appreciate the distinction. As the Spirit of Christmas Present affirms, "There are some upon this earth of yours who lay claim to know us, and who do their deeds of passion, pride, ill-will, hatred, envy, bigotry, and selfishness in our name; who are as strange to us and all our kith and kin, as if they had never lived" (92).

The Ghost of Christmas Present symbolizes the sociable, extroverted aspects of the Christmas festival that Dickens sought to promote. It is in the presence of this robust spirit that we experience the wholesome pleasures of social intercourse and human fellowship at the homes of Scrooge's impoverished clerk, Bob Cratchit, and his high-spirited young nephew, Fred. As Dickens explains, "It is good [for adults] to be children sometimes, and never better than at Christmas, when its mighty Founder was a child himself" (104). Once again, we see, in this passage and throughout *Stave Three*, that Dickens's delight in the more secular aspects of Christmas—drinking, feasting, and the chaste pleasures of the mistletoe, for instance—is rooted in belief that Christians are under no obligation to exceed the sobriety and chastity of Christ. Dickens's answer to the dour religionists of his age (as well as its dour capitalists)—who hadn't time to make merry themselves at Christmas and couldn't afford to make idle people merry—is that Jesus was himself was not adverse to merry-making, as at the Wedding at Cana. Moreover, if the Gnostic Gospels are to be believed, he was not even against bestowing an occasional kiss. To reference a more canonical instance of Christ's conviviality, the Last Supper, during which the sacraments of wine and bread were administered, provides a definitive model of communion and good fellowship that has become the center church ritual. Why then, implies Dickens, should religion be associated only with drab avoidance and an invariably grave demeanor?

He took seriously the Pauline injunction that, though you may possess all knowledge, your faith is in vain if it is devoid of charity, i.e., a sympathetic concern and a spirit of benevolent camaraderie. Paul's dig at those who possess "all knowledge" was probably a dig at both the Greek philosophers of Athens (whose intellectual bent rendered them impervious to his proselytizing) and the burgeoning Gnostic sects of early Christianity (who regarded esoteric knowledge, rather than "unmerited grace," as the key to personal salvation). Nevertheless, as Dickens intuited, it applied equally to those radical economists for whom the politico-economic theories of their own circle carried greater weight than the ethical teachings of the Bible (when read through the lens of the teaching and example of Christ). Dickens's purpose in *Stave Three* of his *Carol* is to bear-witness to (i.e., role-model) this spirit of benevolence wherever it is to be found (and to suggest that it is perhaps to be found more often among the poor than the well-to-do).

Ebenezer Scrooge is encouraged to look for it in the homes and hearts of wayfaring travelers, laborers, and Londoners from all stations in life: in the cheerful dialogue of two mariners stationed in a lonely lighthouse, on the deck of a ship tossed by turbulent seas, and in the hovel of a group of poor miners whose rough voices are joined on Christmas Eve. Though the natural and domestic settings to which Scrooge is conducted in this portion of the

Carol are often sublime, i.e. calculated to arouse a sense dread and awe, Dickens's essential message is, to some extent, at variance with the typical conception of the gothic hero as a loner. In most gothic narratives, the hero carries his or her isolation as a badge of distinction. Having possessed the moral courage to separate from the herd, the gothic hero (like the Gnostic disciple or the Romantic artist) tends to see his or her alienated status as a pre-condition to the attainment of hidden knowledge. Certain prominent nineteenth-century purveyors of the gothic imagination, Dickens and Hawthorne among them, disagreed. These two artists (both of whom contributed to gothic literature as well as to the cult of childhood) viewed the willful isolation of the typical gothic hero as ethically suspect. The reclusiveness of Scrooge and Mr. Redlaw in *The Haunted Man* (like that of Hawthorne's *Young Goodman Brown*) for instance, is seen as a mark of intellectual pride—an emblem of the "original sin" rooted in Satan's cosmic rebellion against the sovereign authority of God, according to Christian mythology. Ultimately, the purpose of the supernatural visitations depicted in Dickens's two Christmas novellas is to persuade its gloomy protagonists to rekindle their communion with the divine by rejoining human society, for it is only in minds and hearts of their fellows that the earthly vestiges of that divinity are to be found.

The Spirit of Christmas Yet to Come: Dickens's Holiday Dementor

Perhaps the most obviously Gothic episode in the *Carol* involves the Spirit of Christmas Yet to Come. A creature echoed in characters from later cult-of-childhood narratives such as Susan Cooper's Dark Riders, Tolkien's sinister Horsemen of the Nâzgul (a.k.a. the Black Riders), and Rowling's Dementors of Azkaban, this final spirit of Christmas is portrayed as a hooded menace. No doubt Dickens, in creating this specter, sought to suggest the impenetrable mystery of what lies ahead, not only in this life but in the next. The unbreakable silence exhibited by this Victorian variant of the Grim Reaper certainly belongs to the connotative complex of death and dying (which includes silence—as in the familiar adage "silent as the grave"). Wishing to impress upon Scrooge the lesson that, "Men's courses will foreshadow certain ends," as Scrooge himself expresses it, the ghost accompanies Scrooge on a guided tour of the ends foreshadowed by his present course. He witnesses his own solitary death, the guilty pleasure it brings to two of his insolvent debtors, the callous indifference of his business associates to his passing, the human misery brought about in part by his own disregard for Ignorance and Poverty (the twin children of humankind shown to Scrooge by the Spirit of Christmas Present), the scavenger-like business transactions carried out by menials (a charwoman, an undertaker, and the pawn shop broker) who seek to profit from his pilfered belongings (a vivid representation of predatory capitalism reduced to its sordid essentials) and finally, he is led to the brink of the abyss, i.e., the spectacle of his own unattended grave site.

Scrooge's terror at the supposition that, like his deceased business partner, he has forever forfeited the power to interfere for good in human affairs (especially his own) serves as the catalyst for his final transformation from miser to philanthropist. Having witnessed the painful trauma of his neglect as a child, his adult denial of any reality beyond that of his "money-changing hole," his projection of his own deep-seated fear of poverty unto a "surplus population" too idle to have merited his own financial success, and the spiritual impoverishment to which that 'success" has brought him, Scrooge, in effect experiences his own "dark night of the soul." Such an "identity crisis," to use the pale parlance of pop psychology, often signals a turning point in the mythic journey of the gothic hero.

To his unspeakable joy and relief, Scrooge awakens in his own bedroom on Christmas morning. What follows is more like the literary equivalent of Handel's *Hallelujah Chorus* than a holiday carol—a sustained peel of jubilation that more than justifies the book's title. Speaking of that musico-literary title, its creator was ironically devoid of musical cultivation. Though his own sister was a pianist who aspired to the concert stage, he typically referred with disdain to the glories of Western musical culture as "scientific music," preferring traditional ballades and (less forgivably) cheap dance hall ditties to the musical equivalents of his own profound and sophisticated prose style. In short, Dickens, whose prose is among the most musical in the English language, had a tin ear for music. This Philistine aspect of his make-up, shared generally speaking by Victorian culture, was not missed by Chesterton, who once characterized Dickens as "a sturdy, sentimental English radical with a large heart and a narrow mind" (Chesterton, *Charles Dickens: Last of the Great Men* 115). It was also Chesterton who elsewhere described the literary geniuses the nineteenth-century generally as "giant dwarfs," his way of saying that they were often unable to achieve in their personal lives the synergy of oppositional forces they endorsed in their art.

The Gothic Transcendence of Ebenezer Scrooge

In *Stave Four*, Dickens envisions a spiritual transformation that, without need of religious rhetoric, offers what is certainly one of the most convincing portrayals of Christian redemption to be found in secular literature. It was for this reason that the great Victorian writer, and Dickens's chief literary rival, William Makepeace Thackeray, characterized the *Carol* as a personal beneficence to each of its readers. To judge by its enduring popularity, it still is. Though for some, the intervening horrors of history may have muffled the celestial music of Dickens's celebrated prose poem, for many his *Carol* still has prophetic power and resonance. Now, as then, there are those who believe, as did Scrooge himself initially, that the conversion experience is more likely result from an undigested meal than a supernatural visitation ("more gravy than grave") and that the depth and intractability of the evil manifested by the Holocaust and Hiroshima have made a mockery of Dickens's cheery Christmas optimism. I suspect that, were he alive today, Dickens would agree. His own sad verdict on Victorianism, even during his lifetime, had moved far beyond the cult-of-childhood philosophy found in the *Carol* by the time he wrote his last novels. Then again, these later novels were not conceived as *Kunstmärchen*.

A Christmas Carol was presented to his "dear readers" as a seasonal ornament. It was intended for those among his fans who, even in the "haggard winter" of their lives, still experienced the season of the nativity as a magical time that, in Dickens's own words, "can win us back to the delusions of our childish days" (*The Pickwick Papers* 374). The open-eyed realism of Dickens, in other words, was not averse to shoring up his own faith and that of his readers in the possibility of a different and better world. At a time of year set aside for the celebration of children and the hope they bring to the world, he created an adult fairytale that facilitated a breakout, a literary escape from the fog-enshrouded netherworld of life inside a the debtor's prison of predatory capitalism (a fitting symbol of a social system designed for the few at the expense of the many) into one that provides for the needs of all. As the character of Puddleglum says to the Witch of the Underworld in the *Chronicles of Narnia*, perhaps his belief in an aboveground realm of sunlight, trees, and fresh air is only a dream, but if so, his dream beats her reality hollow (Lewis, *The Silver Chair* 159).

In *Great Expectations*, Pip is granted no Scrooge-like reprieve from the consequences of his youthful folly. In *Little Dorrit*, absolutely no one's life-sentence behind the prison bars of Victorian England's commercial greed, drab respectability, and class consciousness is commuted. Perhaps, as some modern critics have suggested, this late pessimism signals a deepening of outlook on Dickens's part, i.e., maturation rather than a falling off from a formerly heightened level of inspiration (as earlier critics tended to maintain). Then again, perhaps Dickens, in his Christmas books, simply accommodated his vision to the requirements of the genre in which he was working. Whatever the explanation, *A Christmas Carol* is one of the earliest adult fairy tales to lay bear "modern man in search of a soul," to cite the title of a book by C. G. Jung. The loss of one's soul, cautioned against by Jung as well as cult-of-childhood writers from Dickens to Rowling, is the proverbial fate worse than death. At some point in time (romantics associated this loss with the Enlightenment) Christendom and the Anglo-American liberalism that was both an extension of Christian culture and a reaction against its baser qualities, experienced this dire fate. The key to recovery, according to these writers, lies in an adult appropriation of values and perceptions associated with childhood.

Lacking any social consensus on behalf of a transcendent moral authority, the soul of Western civilization (like that of Lord Voldemort) has been purportedly dismembered and severed from its ultimate source of well-being. Both common decency and traditional religion declare that our collective well-being can only be advanced through personal sacrifice. Within a social system that permits and even encourages the acquisition of unlimited personal wealth, suggests Dickens, we are all liable to become "squeezing, wrenching, grasping, scraping, clutching, covetous" old sinners. Whether presented as a species of individual madness, a symptom of a broadly shared social psychosis, or as a malevolent process set in motion by supernatural agencies, the Negative Journey of the gothic hero, envisioned by Dickens, is arguably one to which our culture, as well as his, seems committed. Its opposite, as envisioned by Madeleine L'Engle, in her children's literature is a process that involves what she terms "naming" a process that affirms, through an act of loving acceptance and faith in a providential pattern, the wholeness and spiritual well-being of the individual in relation to self, society, and the cosmos. To engage in this process of "naming" is to re-member that which has been dis-membered. It signals the restoration of a divinely-sanctioned banquet hall, open to all, that humankind in its "little brief authority" has replaced with a maximum security debtor's prison, in Dickens's imaginative vision.

The way out of this dark fortress (a kind of Azkaban of the spirit) into the sunlight of participation in MLK's "Beloved Community" implies the successful completion of a cyclic journey. That journey extends from the first innocence of childhood and back again to a more mature innocence informed by and grounded in experience (sometimes referred to as a "second childhood." In *A Christmas Carol*, Ebenezer Scrooge (and by extension the Victorian exponents of radical capitalism) experiences just such a journey. In the course of doing so, he and they are recreated or "named," i.e. restored from the living gargoyles they had become under the influence of a narrowly rational, dehumanizing ideology, back into what they once had been as children, namely, human beings stamped with God's image.

In Rowling's cult-of-childhood saga, it is Harry, the Chosen One, who is named. His circular journey takes him from the premature delusions of childish days to a child-like renewal of trust in himself, his friends, his wizarding society, and in the transcendent moral authority endorsed and exemplified by Dumbledore and Hogwarts. As a result, he achieves a wholeness that the fractured and fragmented Lord Voldemort cannot defeat. As John Granger writes, "Harry Potter means 'Heir to the Potter,' which , because 'potter' is a biblical metaphor for God, 'shaper of the human vessel,' used from the Book of Genesis to Revelations, points to his being a Christian everyman and spiritual seeker" (Granger 226). Scrooge, though no spiritual seeker (he's more the one sought—by Marley and the other ghosts) is, like Harry, very much a Christian everyman who fits comfortably into a cyclic narrative tradition traceable to a religious source, as future chapters will show. "Although it is written for adults," say the authors of *The 101 most Famous People Who Never Lived* with regard to Dickens's *A Christmas Carol*, "the story's real target is children" (Lazar, Karlan, Salter 154). Their point, though well-taken, is not quite accurate. This enduring tale is arguably the most successful and enduring *Märchen* of all time. Its appeal is not so much children as to the childlike within each of us.

Ironically, a century and a half after the death of Dickens, we find ourselves grappling with the same injustices and inequalities on a global scale with which Dickens concerned himself on a national level, still imprisoned in a Victorian world on steroids—a corporate global culture divided into disparate groups of haves and have-nots, predators and prey (one can easily infer which groups comprise the statistical minority). A tiny percentage of the world's population (consisting mostly of American plutocrats and their political, military, and intelligence minions) control an inordinate preponderance of its wealth and resources, natural as well as human. Exploitive child labor practices (sweat shops), and a vile trade in prostitutes (in the form "female slaving") are rampant. The forces of corporate greed and organized violence—in the guise of "free market" democracy (an obvious oxymoron) and Christian triumphalism (another surrealistic pairing)—are polluting not only our natural but our intellectual, spiritual, and aesthetic environment. Wall Street hucksters like Bernie Madoff make Ebenezer Scrooge seem a mere hobbyist, while the proverbial wolves-in-sheep's-clothing like Rush Limbaugh, Glen Beck and Pat Robertson fail to meet even minimum standards of ethical decency and intellectual integrity. The result, both here and abroad, has been a massive upward redistribution of wealth at the expense of everyone else—a shift that began the nineteenth century and has gained momentum ever since (much of it within my own lifetime).

This politico-economic change has taken a heavy toll on the spiritual and intellectual tone of our culture. An authentically open and democratic society requires an informed citizenry; a cryptocracy based on inordinate personal wealth backed by governmental secrecy and military might does not. Though he was no more a doctrinaire liberal than he was a doctrinaire Christian, Dickens recoiled at the stench of organized greed backed by jingoism and religious cant. That noxious concoction—like the thick brown fog that envelopes London in the opening pages of the *Carol*—has been brewed on a large scale by the theocratic Right ever since, while its true origins (if not its effects) have been largely ignored on the Left. Dickens knew, as thoughtful Christians of every age and culture have known, that in the hands of the illiterate (or, worse still, the semi-literate) the Bible has been used to sanctify every conceivable perversion of Christ's enlightened ethic from slavery, and war to child abuse, predatory capitalism, and patriarchal oppression. What the intellectual crudity of evangelicalism (then as now) fails to recognize is that in order to read it profitably, one must first know how to read. In a word, divine revelation and blind reliance on the Holy Spirit are not substitutes for a good education, nor is there any warrant for such an absurd conclusion in the New-Testament sayings attributed to Christ. Ultimately, the neo-fundamentalist fog machine of religious and political conservatism has confused and distracted the more generous among us while those operating it have been busy converting Western civilization into "Mac-World"—a mindless, emotionally sterile, immature (childish not child-like), hedonistic, unimaginative, technology-obsessed, violence-prone, homogenized negation of the human spirit. In short, the Victorian debtor's prison that Dickens attempted to demolish with words and upon which he seized as an appropriate symbol of spiritual devastation has been enlarged immeasurably since his demise.

Perhaps, suggests Dickens and other practitioners of the cult of childhood, adults should at long last take seriously the seemingly innocuous injunction to emulate the wisdom of those innocent of power, i.e., those who instinctively seek God's blessing on everyone. Such an inversion of normative values, were it to occur, would go a long way toward realizing the vision of history's great political, religious, and artistic prophets. It would also, of course, lay waste to the current politico-economic system. Indeed, the Utilitarian/capitalist ethic symbolized by Scrooge (and the human misery to which it has given rise) has recently reemerged, bigger and stronger than ever, in the guise of Globalization, i.e., an anarchist form of economic terrorism that—like its political counterpart—is impervious to national and international law. In the meantime, the gothic imagination in children's literature will help to keep the Dickensian vision alive and, in so doing, provide its readers with comfort, innocent entertainment, and the "psychic distance" necessary to cope with the painful realities that surround them.

2 Enantiodromia or Transcendence: The Walker's Dark Journey

Mythic Truth

In *The Dark Is Rising*, volume one of a five book series, Susan Cooper draws upon one of the most enduring of British myths, the legend of King Arthur (as do *Greenwitch*, *The Grey King*, and *Silver on the Tree*). Set in rural England and Wales in the modern era, the cast of Cooper's characters includes Merlin, Guinevere, and Arthur himself. It also features other legendary and quasi-mythical personalities such as the harp-playing Welch bard Taliesan and Owain Glyndwr, the Welch king who sought to unite his people against English domination under Henry Plantagenet. In the first volume of her four-part saga (from whose title the entire sequence takes its name) we are introduced to Will Stanton, on his eleventh birthday, along with his large family of five brothers (Robin, Max, James, Paul and an older, absent Lieutenant in the Royal Navy, Stephen) and three sisters (Barbara, Gwen, and Mary). Will, seventh son of a seventh son, is the youngest member of his family. Mr. Stanton is a jeweler who works in a nearby town of Eton. They live on a rural Buckinghamshire farm not far from the village of Huntercombe bordering the Thames River.

As the story opens, it is Midwinter's Eve and strange events are afoot. The kitchen radio produces only static in Will's presence and the farm animals, dogs and rabbits, cower at his approach. An ominous flock of rooks hover overhead, and as Will and James make their way to the nearby farm of Mr. Dawson to procure hay, they are trailed by a seemingly demented tramp. When they reach their destination, Farmer Dawson, speaking to a farm hand, Old George, is overheard to say, "The Walker is abroad...It will be a bad night...tomorrow will be beyond imagining" (7). He proceeds to offer Will an unusual birthday gift, an ornamental buckle outlining a flat circle quartered by two crossed lines, "You will need it after the snow comes," he tells Will. Later we learn that Will and Mr. Dawson are immortals (a. k. a. "Old Ones") charged with the task of completing the circle of magical signs without which the dark forces of death will prevail against those of light and life.

As Will and James retrace their steps, pushing the hay cart past Rook's Wood on the corner of Church Lane, the tramp, who has apparently been waiting in ambush, is inexplicably attacked and driven off by a flock hovering rooks. Will notices that his newly acquired metal ornament, originally cold to the touch in keeping with the weather, is suddenly warm. Equally strange is the fact that by the time the two brothers return home, the entire incident is wiped from James's memory. Alone in his bedroom later that night, Will is inexplicably seized by a sudden wave of fear. "Something is wrong," he mutters to himself. As the cold wind mounts outside, the catch to the skylight in the roof breaks and snow comes swirling in like a predator, leaving in its wake the wing feather of a rook. As it does so, Will involuntarily shrieks in terror. Paul, a musician and perhaps the most sensitive of Will's many brothers, rushes in to reassure his younger sibling and offers to trade rooms for the night, an offer that Will gratefully accepts.

So begins the bizarre sequence of events that will pit an ostensibly young and ordinary boy against the forces of the Dark, led by a sinister and hooded presence on horseback known as the Black Rider. Devotees of children's fantasy will no doubt recognize in this menacing personage a familiar element borrowed from J. R. R. Tolkien's classic *Lord of the Rings* trilogy. The fantasy worlds of Tolkien and Cooper are strikingly similar in other respects as well: Both depict a decisive series of encounters between good and evil culminating in a pitched battle; in both, wizards and dark lords abound; and in both, good triumphs, but at a steep price, particularly to the humans caught in the crossfire. It is on this last circumstance that I wish to focus because it is in the fate on the human characters that assist either the Light or the Dark that the risks and rewards of Cooper's morally ambiguous otherworld reality fall most heavily. It is with such characters—those with whom mere mortals can most readily identify—that Cooper achieves her finest literary touches and lavishes her most subtle psychological insights.

The Negative and Positive Journey of the Gothic Hero

In *Man's Search for Meaning*, psychologist and concentration camp survivor Vicktor Frankl has written persuasively of our common need to situate our lives within a broader spiritual context as a requirement as fundamental to human survival as food and water. The quest for meaning is one that begins in childhood and mounts in urgency as we approach adolescence and early adulthood. Does our life have ultimate purpose? If so, how are we to discover it? To whom or what can we look for guidance and insight? What if we fail? Is success even possible and what or who defines the rules governing our success or failure? These and a host of other obvious but urgent questions define the heroic journey often referred to as "coming of age" that we must all undertake. It is not just David Copperfield who ponders whether or not he shall become the hero of his own life. Each of us poses that questions to a "darkly painful, mysterious, frightening, and seemingly irrational" world. The questions we ask (or fail to ask) of life can be said to comprise an existential exam administered (according to a strict honor code) at a school we each enter at birth and from which we can rightly be said to have graduated only at the moment of death.

Within this Gothic perspective, students and educators (consigned to the role of bit players in today's social hierarchy) are correctly viewed as principal characters in life's unfolding drama. Accordingly, the extension of human experience provided by an engagement with literature and the fine arts is viewed as an indispensable tool at all times of human development, but particularly during its earlier stages. It follows that the choice we must urge upon the young, as parents and teachers, is not between the "real" world and the bookish world. It is between an examined life and a brutish one—a life devoted to the reasoned pursuit of knowledge and wisdom rather than celebrity, hedonistic pleasure, or material wealth. All truly educated adults recognize that life as experienced unreflectively, i.e., life outside the domain of literature, music, and other expressions of humanity's timeless quest for meaning, lacks any obvious organizing principle or underlying structure. Our initial, uninformed impression is liable to be one of chaos rather than cosmos. The wise and thoughtful among us, however, detect recurrent patterns and colors in life's enormously intricate tapestry. Imaginative literature is one of the means by which the young can discover these hidden threads of meaning.

Nevertheless, it is the essence of the Gothic imagination that informed intellect, though indispensable, is only one tool of perception among many. It suggests that those who pin their hopes on a narrowly defined rationality (whether scientific, religious, or political) will ultimately find themselves ill equipped to face the painful challenges of the human condition. Consequently, Gothic heroes such as Will Stanton or Harry Potter are aided by trans-rational but essentially ordinary faculties such as intuition and emotion as well as by more clairvoyant faculties. I use the somewhat awkward portmanteau term 'trans-rational, rather than the more familiar "irrational" in order to suggest modes of perception that require us to utilize logic, reason, and critical thinking skills without being limited to them. All of us can identify with such characters, whether or not acknowledge the existence of trans-rational powers, because all of us are compelled to face such challenges. The issue then becomes not if but how one is to respond to them. The Gothic imagination poses two fundamental paths, two recurrent patterns of response: The *positive* quest for understanding leads from trauma to introspection and critical self-examination, acceptance (of responsibility for one's own role in bringing about a painful, or undesirable outcome) and finally transcendence, defined as the overcoming of one's Gothic dilemma.

Its *negative* counterpart also starts in the pain, i.e., some personal or collective trauma, but leads through successive stages to a very different outcome. Instead of introspection, those who choose the negative path proceed from trauma to denial (characterized by an inability to confront openly the implications of the circumstances in which they find themselves or to assume responsibility for their own role in bringing them about). This second stage typically leads to projection, i.e., a psychological strategy whereby one literally attributes unacknowledged character flaws and motivations to another individual or group (race, nation, religion, political party etc.) much as a motion picture camera projects a cinematic image upon a blank screen. Frequently, projection terminates in an unintended act of psychic self-mutilation or dismemberment, an act that climaxes ironically in the destruction of that which one most cherishes, in that which one not in the grip of denial and projection would most earnestly seek to protect and nurture. This final stage in the negative journey of the Gothic hero might be dubbed *enantiodromia*, a Greek concept coined by Swiss psychologist C. G. Jung that means literally "the reversal into the opposite" (Jung 238).

Now let us see how these concepts apply to the characters (two in particular) from Susan Cooper's Gothic quartet, *The Dark Is Rising*—both of whom are mortals. Cooper's cosmos, like that of J. K. Rowling, is divided into a consensus reality perceived by ordinary individuals and an alternate reality invisible to most humans most of the time. One of these realities is inhabited by eternal beings (the Old Ones) unbounded by the usual limitations imposed by space and time. In addition to the Old Ones of both the Light and the Dark and their comparatively few human allies and enemies, there is a third category of characters representatives of a yet more primal, reality referred to simply as "the high magic." A comparable cosmology and terminology occurs in the *Narnia Chronicles* of C. S. Lewis in which Aslan, the Christ-like lion who is the legitimate King of Narnia, and the White Witch, who has usurped Aslan's rule, are both subject to a power greater and more binding than their own, also identified with "the high magic."

Although *The Dark is Rising* is told largely from the perspective of Will Stanton and its central plot concerns Old Ones (including a host of legendary figures from British history and mythology such as the medieval sage and magician, Merlin) Cooper's subplot focuses on the tragedy of Hawkin, Merlin's liege man. Hawkins, also referred to as the Walker, is taken out of his own time by the Light, ahead to the nineteenth century, to fulfill a unique mission on its behalf, the retrieval of the *Book of Gramarye*. This magical compendium of all knowledge and wisdom, which must be retrieved by human hands, resides at Greythorne Manor, the aristocratic estate of an exalted creature of the "high magic" referred to simply the Lady or, in her nineteenth-century incarnation, as Miss Mary Greythorne. Will first encounters her at various crisis points in Cooper's narrative. Ultimately his task, and that of his allies, is to secure the "Six Great Signs of the Light" (of which the buckle ornament presented by Farmer Dawson is the first) as well as four powerful objects to assist in the final confrontation between the forces of Light and Darkness (a chalice, a harp, a warestone, and a sword). The first and last of these four additional objects obviously resonate with Arthurian lore. Thus, as in the *Harry Potter* series, which finds its hero in search of seven *Horcruxes* and four *Hallows* (enchanted fragments of Lord Voldemort's corrupt soul and objects of preternatural power associated with the four founders of Hogwarts School of Witchcraft and Wizardry), Susan Cooper's young hero (also a wizard of sorts) is in search of protective talismans against the Dark.

All Times Are As One

Hawkins's first appearance (as the demented tramp lurking in Rook's Alley) suggests someone whose purposes are sinister. At this point in the narrative, has been warned that the Walker (Hawkin' name subsequent to his nineteenth century visit to Greythorne Manor) is abroad. By the time Will notices him in Rook's Alley, Hawkins has long switched his allegiance from the Light to the Dark, for reasons explained later in the story. Meanwhile, the Rider (with the aid of his, by now, reluctant agent) intends to possess the magical talismans. In addition to Will's buckle of iron there are four supernatural *Signs* associated with each of the other four elements—wood, water, fire, and stone. The Walker's unenviable fate is to acquire them from whoever is currently in possession (fearful of both the Light and the Dark) until relieved of his heavy burden by one or the other. *The Dark Is Rising* is therefore largely the tragic story of how Hawkins became known as the Walker through choosing the negative path of the Gothic hero-villain—a path he has travelled for several long centuries prior to the birth of the Sign Seeker, Will Stanton, last of the Old Ones.

As Merlin's liege man, Hawkin's story begins with his relationship with history's most famous magician, a relationship characterized by the established feudal pattern of fealty and fidelity on the one side and *noblesse oblige* on the other. The Walker's first appearance in the story (as Hawkins) occurs on the night that Will first encounters Merlin in the guise of Merriman Lyons, butler to Miss Greythorne in the nineteenth century (as in Will Stanton's twentieth century England he would become simple Farmer Dawson).

On this occasion, Will has travelled back in time to find himself in a Gothic manor in which the oak walls are hung with medieval tapestries and the *Sign* he wears on his belt—which happens to correspond to a Jungian Mandela, a mythic symbol of spiritual completion—is replicated in candlesticks and other household objects scattered throughout the manor: "Here again, as everywhere" notes Will, "was the sign: The cross within the circle, the quartered sphere" (52). When the great doors of the manor house through which Will had entered, identified by Merlin as "our great gateway into Time," suddenly vanish, Merriman comments wryly, "Nothing is what it seems boy. Expect nothing and fear nothing, here or anywhere. There's your first lesson." When the perplexed boy fails to understand, Merriman explains that he has been waiting for him a long time maintaining that they share a common gift and a common mission. "It is a burden," he elaborates with reference to their shared responsibilities, "Make no mistake about that...If you were born with the gift then you must serve it." Like Harry Potter when first informed of his wizarding ancestry by Hagrid, Will protests that "there's nothing special about me." In response Merriman replies, "Minds hold more than they know...particularly yours" (43).

This exchange underscores several concepts central to the psychological Gothic imagination. It reminds us, for instance, that the heroes of Gothic literature for and about children often age prematurely as a result of the heavy burden they choose (and are chosen) to carry. As young men and women who have experienced "a much older person's suffering," to borrow a phrase applied to Albus Dumbledore in *The Deathly Hallows*, they possess insights denied to their peers and companions. As last of the Old Ones, Will Stanton's boyish appearance belies his status as a Gothic hero who is old before his time and wise beyond his years (ostensibly, at least). A corollary of this circumstance is that appearances (consensus understandings of reality) can be, and indeed probably are, deceptive; that we are not to take the stated motivations, of others (or even ourselves) at face value. Merriman's final observation suggests that wisdom; i.e., the cultivation of mind and spirit, is not quite the same thing as "learning" or "knowledge." It was Dr. Samuel Johnson, the famous eighteenth-century philosopher, who said that people need to be reminded more often than they need to be instructed. Applying this maxim to perhaps a larger context than he intended, exponents of Gothic arts such as Susan Cooper constantly stress the connection between wisdom and memory as an active, often a redemptive, faculty.

What such artists seem to have in mind is a combination of the ancient neo-Platonic notion of knowledge as an act of recollecting a prior, transcendental existence and the modern Jungian concept of the "active imagination" whereby—through myths, dreams, and trance states—the underlying group mind that is, according to Jung, the fundamental substratum of the human psyche (he calls it the "collective unconscious") offers insights previously unacknowledged by the percipient's conscious mind. Recent studies of how the brain stores knowledge suggest that nothing to which we are exposed is permanently lost to our unconscious memory. Like a computer with an unlimited storage capacity, the human brain records everything to which it is exposed, though at any given moment most of this information is inaccessible to the conscious mind. Children (or adults, for that matter) who find their powers of immediate recall frustratingly inadequate at times may well take comfort in the notion that "Minds hold more than they know."

Another "lesson" conveyed by stories such as this, in which all historical times and places are available to the characters, is that what recollection is to the individual, history is to the collective experience of humankind. It follows that knowledge of history is, as Cooper expresses it, "a worthy effort to extend one's memory" (Cooper, *The Grey King* 185). One of the more disturbing cultural developments in recent decades, frequently noted and discussed by culture conservatives, is the astonishing absence of historical perspective exhibited by many Americans, young and old alike. To an extent, this is symptomatic of what is now widely referred to as our "post-literate" culture. Whatever its source, its end result is what noted author Gore Vidal has referred to as "the United States of Amnesia." This collective memory loss is reflected in everything from our widespread indifference to the treasures of classical music, to the documented inability of typical high school and college students to place major historical events, such as world wars, in their correct chronological sequence. It manifests itself not simply as a deficient capacity for the retention of names, dates, and facts (though memorization of such raw data is arguably indispensable to an informed historical perspective), but in a fundamental failure to sense the interconnectedness of all times and places, the threads of continuity that connect the past with the present. The inevitable consequence of this failure—a by-product of today's pop-culture focus on the new, the fashionable, and the transient—is an inability to interpret current events within a meaningful historical and ethical context. Though profitable to the corporate interests that sponsor the "now-generation", this focus is impoverishing to the rest of us.

The kaleidoscopic images and sound bites offered by today's twenty-four/seven news cycle is a surrealistic, ever-shifting collage of events, personalities, and "breaking news" items that leaves all of us—the young especially—awash in a turbulent sea of sound and fury signifying nothing. In this dizzying welter, anything that points to even the possibility of an alternative world order is kept well out of sight. Bombarded incessantly by useless and unrelated facts elucidated by shallow commentary, we are indeed reduced as a culture to the condition of a patient suffering from Alzheimer's. Without any solid basis in either personal experience or imagined experience on which to pin their "audacity of hope," a sad state of affairs for which they can hardly be faulted, many of today's young people feign malaise (or else exhibit a misplaced enthusiasm for whatever seems at odds with authority) that is both age inappropriate and, to the extent that it is ungrounded in historical awareness, inauthentic. Understanding too little, they both accept and reject too much. Though the most recent presidential election cycle suggests a ground-swell of longing for something better, without the anchor of an objective vantage point from which to compare what is with what has been or might yet be, the young have little option but to either blandly accept the status quo or blindly attack it. These are, of course, crude, therefore exaggerated, generalizations. As such, they necessarily sound more pessimistic or censorious than circumstances warrant. In my long career as an educator, I have been as often impressed by the openness, curiosity, and basic human decency of my students as by their intellectual deficiencies (which undoubtedly belong to all times, places, and age groups). Two pertinent thoughts occur: First, that the literature we are considering is the product of cultivated minds and imaginations not enthralled by the present. As such, it offers a badly needed antidote to the easy cynicism and cultural short-sightedness fostered by pop culture, and second, Quite possibly, the sensational success of J. K. Rowling's seven-volume compendium of the accumulated wisdom of the cult of childhood can be largely attributed to a hidden, culturally suppressed hunger for a credible alternative to today's intellectually and emotionally sterile status quo, if only one found between the covers of a book.

We will elaborate on this theme when we come to the political Gothic dimension of the *Harry Potter* novels, but to those who understand that historical knowledge is as relevant to a correct understanding of contemporary events as a knowledge of an individual's past experience is to an accurate assessment of their present character and circumstances, the cult of childhood emphases on redemptive memory and denial as a form of dismemberment is a welcome one. As Merriman Lyon (Merlin) explains to Will Stanton, "We of the Circle are planted only loosely in Time...For all times co-exist, and the future can sometimes affect the past, even though the past is a road that leads to the future" (Cooper 54). Many well-known factors contribute to the fixation on the here and now so characteristic of today's youth culture, including television, video games, and computers as well as the fact that in too many public schools "social studies" and the fine arts are taught (if at all) by unqualified classroom teachers rather than bona fide historians and artists. Just as Rowling's books offer a blend of Medieval, Victorian, and contemporary settings, so do the books of Susan Cooper. Perhaps an early involvement with this literature can contribute to the kind historical sense best described by noted historian Johan Huizinga when he writes, "A feeling of immediate contact with the past is a sensation as deep as the purest enjoyment of art...the historic sensation is not the sensation of living the past again but of understanding the world, perhaps as one does when listening to music" (Lukacs 115).

At a later point in the *The Dark Is Rising*, Will Stanton remarks to the local church rector, Mr. Beaumont that, "Everything that matters is outside of time." When an adult suggests that he is referring to infinity, Will responds with wisdom far beyond his years, "Not altogether...I mean the part of all of us, and of all things we think and believe that has nothing to do with yesterday or today or tomorrow because it belongs to a different kind of level. Tomorrow is there too. You can visit either of them. And all Gods are there, and all the things they have ever stood for...and the opposite too" (149). Will's uncanny remarks elicit the following reaction from the rector, "I am not sure whether you should be exorcised or ordained." The difference between the cyclic sense of time espoused by Will and the orthodox concept of eternity parroted from the pulpit by Mr. Beaumont is also the distinction between myth and history. In one sense, mythic and historical consciousness oppose one another in that historical consciousness seeks to understand a particular moment within the broadest relevant context whereas mythic consciousness seeks to understand a temporal moment as the manifestation of an eternally recurring pattern within human affairs. Nevertheless, these two modes of thought can be said to compliment and reinforce one another in that both offer an imaginative escape from the tyranny of the present.

Hawkin's Fatal Choice

When next we encounter the Walker, this servant of the Dark carrying at his waist the Sign of bronze, is ill-advisedly summoned by a careless display of

Will's newly acquired magical powers. "He [Will] knew that he had done something foolish, improper, dangerous perhaps," writes Cooper (61). But on seeing the tramps pitiable condition, Will's alarm turns into compassion for a man stripped of humanity, dismembered by time and painful experience: "I don't trust your kind anymore than I trust the Dark," declares the Walker bitterly" (62). When Will, the Sign Seeker, offers to relieve him of the burden he has been compelled to carry through six centuries of alienation, terror, and abuse from agents of the Dark, the Walker exclaims, his voice "broken and simple as that of a sad child," "It's so heavy...and I've been carrying it so long. I don't even remember why. Always frightened, always having to run away. If only I could get rid of it, If only I cold rest...But I daren't risk giving it to the wrong one. The Old Ones can be cruel, cruel..." (62) Will, pondering this emotional outburst, reaches the sympathetic conclusion that, "He's been frightened for so long...he's forgotten how to stop. How awful to be so absolutely lonely. He doesn't know how to trust me; it's been so long since he trusted anyone, he's forgotten how" (63). Obviously, the Walker's tragic condition is the result of a shattering trauma. Notice too the pointed connection made here between loss of humanity and loss of memory. In effect, the tramp's degradation is a function of his forgetfulness. This Gothic theme is further emphasized by what occurs next.

At this critical juncture, i.e., the second encounter between Will and the Walker, Maggie Barnes appears suddenly. Long perceived by Will as a simple farm girl, she reveals her true nature as a disciple of the Dark. Will wonders if she is being exploited for the occasion or has always been in league with the Rider. "Something flickered in his mind. Some detail of memory flickered, but he could not catch it" (67). As Will struggles to remember this forgotten detail, Merriman materializes to offer the following admonition: "The Walker was waiting for you, stupid boy...I told you that he would find you, and you did not remember. Remember now. In this our magic, every smallest word has a weight and meaning" (69). He goes on to provide a partial explanation for the psychological condition of the Walker: "He has been waiting for you to be born, and to stand alone with him and command the Sign from him, for time past your imagining...Poor soul. He betrayed the Old Ones once, long ago, and this was his doom" (69).

Merriman's cryptic account of the Walker's dilemma serves as a transition from the opening section of the book (subtitled *The Finding*) to the

second (entitled *The Learning*). This second section begins at a modern
Christmas party. A band of Christmas Eve carolers, that includes Will and
members of his family, end up at Greythorne Manor where the traditional
finale of the annual holiday festivities is a rendering of the popular British
carol *Good King Wenceslas*. The concluding verses of their performance
have a pointed bearing on the relationship between Merlin and Hawkins as
well as the sinister events unfolding around them. This music serving—as
music in cult of childhood literature often does—as catalyst for movement
between alternate realities—marks another transition from present to past.
The *Book of Gramarye* is about to be retrieved. In its pages, the hiding places
of the remaining Signs, some in the distant past other in the future (relative to
this nineteenth-century setting) will be revealed to Will who must eventually
possess them. The year is 1875 and Will and Hawkin who is destined to
become the Walker, are introduced in this new temporal setting: "Will...
found himself staring into a thin, lively face, almost triangular, thickly lined
yet not old, with a pair of startlingly bright eyes staring at and somehow into
him. It was a disturbing face, with much behind it" (93). Hawkin then moves
away to engage in an elaborate, but ironic, show of deference to Merriman
(the nineteenth-century incarnation of Merlin)—an act that elicits laughter
from both men.

This episode suggests Merlin's affectionate condescension as well as
Hawkin's ease in the presence of his powerful master. When Will and
Hawkin meet again, Will raises the crucial paradox posed by time travel:
"Here I am brought into the past, a century that's already happened, that's
part of the history books. But what happens if I do something to alter it"
(98)? Hawkin, dressed in an identifying green velvet jacket, explains that,
"Generally you people manage to affect history in ways that no man ever
knows...The Old Ones can travel in time as they choose; you are not bound
by the laws of the Universe as we know them" (98). Merriman, joining them,
elaborates on this theme: "Hawkin is a child of the thirteenth century...I
belong nowhere and everywhere Will. I am the first of the Old Ones [as Will
is the last]" (99). Merriman goes on to explain the nature of his relationship
with Hawkin, "He is my friend who serves me, and I have a deep affection
for him. And hold him in great trust. So great that I have given him a vital
part to play in the quest we will accomplish this century—the quest for your
learning" (99).

It is this act of trust on Merriman's part that precipitates the tragic fate of Hawkin. As the three of them move from the crowded Great Hall to the sequestered library, Merriman informs Will that the knowledge (or "Gramarye") he must acquire this very evening will be imparted by the oldest book in the world, a book that lies hidden in a grandfather clock and that will be destroyed once its pages, written in a secret language, have been perused by Will. "When you have the knowledge, Will Stanton, there will no longer be any need of storing it, for with you the circle is complete" (102). As Merriman reaches into the grandfather clock with one hand, careful to avoid touching its swinging pendulum, he rests his other hand lightly on a terrified Hawkin's shoulder. When, in replacing the Book later on, his hand merely brushes the pendulum by mistake, the result is something like an explosion. Once the book is successfully removed, Hawkins collapses from the obvious strain of its retrieval. Before turning his full attention to the book, Will, observing Hawkin, asks Merriman, "Is Hawkin all right? He looks ill." Looking down sadly at the "small, drooping figure in green," Merriman replies enigmatically, "Too much to ask" (103).

In the course of his "reading," a process comparable to Harry's experience of Tom Riddle's Diary and Dumbledore's "Pensieve," Will learns of the power of the Old Ways, the "patterns of survival against malevolence," and about the origins of the Dark. In Susan Cooper's cosmology, as in the mainstream Judeo-Christian tradition, evil is contingent. It arises whenever someone chooses to be "changed into something more dread and powerful than his fellows...Such creatures were not born to their doom, like the Old Ones," the book explains, "but chose it " (107). Here, Cooper sounds a theme that figures prominently in the cult of childhood, namely, the importance of free choice in shaping our individual and collective destinies as human beings. He learns that the first great uprising of the Dark was thwarted by King Arthur who was "lost in the saving unless one day he might wake and return again." In *Silver on the Tree*, the final books in Cooper's series, he does precisely that. When Will, enlightened but shaken by his experiences, emerges from the library he is greeted by Merriman who comments," As I told you, it is a responsibility, a heaviness. But there it is Will. We are the Old Ones, born into the circle, and there is no help for it." When Will, subsequent to this episode, asks after Hawkin again, Merriman replies with a strange tightness to his voice, "He was not needed *this* time [emphasis added]" (108).

The reason for both Merriman's sadness and Hawkin's terror is explained shortly thereafter: "I have made the greatest mistake an Old One can make," laments Merriman, "To put more trust in a mortal man than he has the strength to take" (111). Merlin/Merriman goes on to explain that it was necessary to involve a human in the retrieval of the *Book of Gramarye*. Had one of the Old Ones been tricked by magic into seizing the book for the Dark, the Light would have had no option but to short circuit the process by destroying Hawkin. A spell of protection woven around the book mandated that Hawkin's presence would be required whenever the book was removed. When Will remarks that Hawkin must be both brave and loving to have run such a risk, Merriman says in a passage reminiscent of Dumbledore's admission of inadequacy to Harry at Kings Cross Station (*The Deathly Hallows*), "I wish that I had made sure he really knew the risk he ran." When Hawkins subsequently realizes that Merlin was prepared to let him die rather than permit the book to fall into the wrong hands, he feels deeply betrayed. He shifts his allegiance to the Dark accordingly, thereby sealing his own fate and placing the entire enterprise of the Light at risk.

The Burden of Moral Ambiguity

The moral ambiguity of this episode adheres in the ethical issues raised not just "when bad things happen to good people," but when they are sanctioned (or even caused by the forces of right and righteousness). This is an issue that goes back at least as far as the biblical *Book of Job*, and it is the central issue of that branch of Christian theology known as apologetics, i.e., justifying the ways of God to humanity. Cooper does not write out of a specifically Christian perspective, but of course the Arthurian lore that serves as a vehicle for her worldview is inseparable from that of Medieval Christendom. Indeed, it is hardly irrelevant that this story unfolds during the Christmas season which, Will says, "has always been a time of magic, to him and all the world" (124). Nevertheless, its magic is always vulnerable to attack, as Will reflects in church on Christmas morning: "Any church of any religion is vulnerable to their attack, for places like this are places where men give thought to matters of the Light and the Dark" (141).

As in Orthodox Christianity, evil, from the time of St. Augustine forward, is typically portrayed as a corruption of the good rather than as a primal force, equal to goodness. The difficulty, of course stems from our human reaction to pain, resentment, and fear. At precisely the moment that Hawkins experiences all three with regard to his precarious allegiance to the Light, he is approached by Maggie Barnes who seduces him to the side of the Dark, "The Dark and the Rider are kinder masters than the Light," she whispers. "So it will go," Merriman tells Will prophetically, "He will have a sweet picture of the Dark to attract him, as men so often do, and beside it he will set all the demands of the Light, which are heavy and always will be. All the while he will be nursing his resentment of the way I might have had him give up his life without reward. You can be sure the Dark makes no sign of demanding any such thing, yet" (114). Merriman concludes with the following remorseful prediction: "And the doom that Hawkin has brought upon himself, by this act…is a dread thing that will make him many times wish that he might die" (115). How often have most of us yearned for the timely intervention of an understanding friend, parent, or teacher at a moment of crisis in our lives? Had Merriman been a better friend to Hawkin, terrible consequences to himself, to the Light along with its human allies, and to Hawkin himself might have been similarly averted.

In terms of the negative /positive journey of the Gothic hero toward either reversal into the opposite or transcendence, Hawkin, in the wake of his painful experience at Greythorne Manor on Christmas Eve 1875, clearly chooses to turn his feet down the dark path of denial, projection, and *enantiodromia*. Accordingly, he blames Merriman, rather than himself, for his subsequent willingness to be deceived by Maggie Barnes, interpreting Merriman's reticence as a betrayal of trust. In reality, of course, it is he, not Merriman, who is ultimately guilty of betraying his own better judgment. Though both decisions are to have unfortunate consequences, Merriman's unwillingness to take Hawkin completely into his confidence, like Dumbledore's secrecy toward Harry, was well-intentioned. As the second assault of the Dark nears its climax (the first was repulsed by Merlin and Arthur centuries earlier), Will's twentieth-century England is threatened by an unprecedented snow storm. Normal lines of human communication are severed as power lines are cut. This is the time of *The Testing* (the title of the book's final section). Will and his flautist brother, Paul guided by a conciliatory rook, discover the unconscious body of the Walker half buried in snow near to the old stone church. Mr. Beaumont, the rector, enjoins them to accommodate the unfortunate tramp at the Stanton home until the storm abates and a doctor can be summoned. Will, realizing the potential danger involved in this plan, objects, but to no avail. The storm, however, does not abate; it worsens. The surly tramp rejects every kindly overture on the part of the Stantons once he regains consciousness. Feigning a total loss of memory, he eventually gives himself away by reacting in terror at the sight of the four Signs (iron, bronze, wood, and stone) that Will, by this time, has added to his belt.

In an attempt to assist in this crisis, Miss Greythorne extends an invitation to the entire village to take refuge at her comparatively warm and well-equipped manor house. Will's father, motivated by what Cooper calls "inverted snobbery," declines this generous offer, though he grudgingly consents to the advisability of relocating the Walker, who is equally unenthusiastic about Miss Greythone's invitation until Will softly warns him in the Old Speech that, "The Dark will come for you." The moving passage in which Cooper relates Hawkin's response to this threat is worth quoting in full:

> There was a pause. Then very slowly the Walker turned his shaggy grey head back again, and Will flinched in horror as he saw the face. For just a moment its history was naked upon it. There were bottomless depths of pain and terror in the eyes, the lines of black experience were carved clear and terrible; this man had known somewhere such a fearful dread and anguish that nothing could really ever touch him again. His eyes were wide for the first time, stretched open, with his knowledge of horror looking out. The Walker said emptily, "The Dark has already come for me. (171)

With this statement the Walker, at that instant at least, acknowledges his own reversal into the opposite. Through his long habit of nurturing resentment against the Light and fear of the Dark he has devolved from the bright-eyed companion of Merlin into his own worst enemy; a miserable and crafty vagrant devoid of friends, family, and hope. Destined to wander alone for more than half a millennium, he has brought himself to the point of assisting in the destruction of all that he had once most valued and sought to protect.

The Gothic lesson here is obvious: As we sow, so shall we reap. In betraying our ideals we merely betray ourselves. Hell, to practitioners of the Gothic imagination from Dante to Susan Cooper, is not a so much a matter of punishment as it is a state of mind, a self-absorbed forgetting of all that truly matters to our deepest selves. As Madeleine L'Engle (whose work we will consider presently) reminds us, "wholeness" and "holiness" are closely related concepts.

Dismembered By the Dark/Remembered By the Light

I spoke earlier of memory as the redemptive faculty. The Gothic imagination stresses the connection not only between "whole" and "holy" but also that of another closely related pairing, remembering/dismembering. Rowling's Lord Voldemort loses his soul by fragmenting it into seven Horcruxes. In doing so, he literally fails to see the "whole" picture, i.e., not only in terms of the consequences of his actions toward others but also in terms of the limitations his Death-Eater sensibility imposes upon himself. It is precisely those limitations that render him vulnerable to Harry. The classic monsters of Gothic fiction from Frankenstein's creature onwards (and He-Who-Must-Not Be-Named certainly qualifies) are often icons of dismemberment as well as forgetfulness. This nexus of associative concepts is eloquently illustrated by Susan Cooper at a crucial moment in which the Walker, finding himself included in an extended family of villagers who have sought refuge at the manor, seems suddenly to recall his former self: "From the corner of his eye he [Will] saw, with a shock, the figure of the Walker...For an instant Will saw his face, and was astonished. All guile and terror were gone from that lined triangle; there was only sadness on it, and hopeless longing...It was the face of a man shown something immensely precious that he had lost" (181). A short while later, transported once more out of time, the Walker is confronted by Merriman, temporary butler to Miss Greythorne. "Hawkin," says Merriman, "there is still time to come home...every man has a last choice after the first, a chance of forgiveness" (185). Unable to seize his final chance at redemption, the Walker "mad with bitterness" shrieks his answer in a last display of projection: "You risked my life for the Book! You made me carry the Sign! You let the Dark hound me through the centuries, bur never let me die! Now it is your turn!" Cooper punctuates this decisive affirmation of his *enantiodromia* with the following commentary: "The Walker's chance to turn back to the mind and heart of Hawkin had come and been rejected and now it was gone forever" (186, 187).

When Will next encounters him, though still recognizable, Hawkin is fully and unequivocally a creature of the Dark. At this point in the story, the penultimate battle between the Light and the Dark is at hand (the ultimate contest is, of course, deferred to the final volume, *Silver on the Tree*). One of Will's sisters has been kidnapped by the Black Rider and Hawkin seeks to negotiate, offering Will's sister in exchange for the Signs. When Will scornfully declines this bogus offer, Hawkin summons his master who is equally unsuccessful at bargaining with the Last of the Old Ones. Now fully assembled on the final day of Twelfth Night, the forces of the Light, led by the legendary figure of Herne the Hunter and his Hounds of Doom, fly in pursuit of the Dark while the Old Ones seek to complete the Circle of Light. In the ensuing battle, the forces of the Dark are again vanquished for a time, but while surveying the corpse-strewn field of battle, Will and Merriman discover the still living but broken body of Hawkin. "Those who ride with the Lords of the Dark must expect to fall," says the latter, "and men do not fall easily from such heights" (228). Gasping in pain from a broken back, Hawkin pleads with Merriman to be permitted to die: "The last right of a man is to die. You prevented it all this time…And all because I had not the wit of an Old One." Merriman explains one last time that Hawkin's betrayal of the Light was of his own choosing and that once his role as Walker was complete, he could have had "rest forever" rather than choosing to betray the Light a second time. "All your choices have been your own," comments Merriman sadly. As though he has finally understood, Hawkin, turning the bright light in the eyes of his younger self upon Will and Merriman wishes the former well and whispers what proves to be a final and redeeming word…"Master." The Walker is, of course, not the only one burdened by the responsibilities of choosing to serve the right master. Will, whose attentions have been preoccupied with closing the Circle and defeating the Dark, plies Merriman with questions about the fate of his human family. Merriman reminds him that he already knows the answers: "Come, Old One…remember yourself," replies Merriman, "You are no longer a small boy…but sometimes you feel how very much more agreeable it would be if you were." Will agrees conditionally, "Sometimes…but not always" (239).

So ends the first volume of Susan Cooper's *The Dark Is Rising*. In the three succeeding novels, Will quests after the objects of magical power that will permit the ultimate defeat of the forces of Darkness, an outcome in which the legendary King Arthur and his modern-day son, Bran Davies, play a key role. In these books as well, it is mortals like Hawkin, you suffer the cruelest fate, though not always through following the negative path from trauma to *enantiodromia*. Indeed, some (such as John Rowlands) experience a betrayal as deep and devastating as Hawkin, but they are able transcend the Gothic dilemma imposed on them by the Dark. Their triumph, like that of Harry Potter in *The Deathly Hollows*, is a victory of selfless sacrifice and love over the ever-present temptation to self-pity and despair. Nevertheless, as in J. K. Rowling's world, the sacrifices are both real and costly and the virtuous are sometimes hard to distinguish from the villainous. Cooper's Arthurian world—though it relies less on humor and perhaps more on poetic word painting—is as compelling as Rowling's wizarding world. To do full justice to its imaginative detail and narrative sweep would require a volume in its own right. Though we have focused here on essentially a single facet of Cooper's psychologically nuanced vision of the mortal dangers involved in navigating a morally ambiguous universe, the tragic story of the Walker is, in my view, her finest achievement. Seldom (if ever) preachy in tone, Cooper manages (as does Rowling) to create a memorable cast of characters—about whom the reader cares deeply—characters thrust into ethically challenging situations, however fantastic, which all of us can identify. By placing the uncertainties and insecurities of this world in an otherworldly context, Cooper's vision elucidates the nature and consequences of ethically difficult choices we are required to make in this world without being onerously didactic. Though her mythopoeic saga belongs primarily to the supernatural Gothic genre, dealing, as it does with themes such as obsession, denial, projection, and the divided self, it exemplifies the psychological Gothic as well.

A Cinematic Postscript

Having just returned from a matinee showing of *The Seeker*, a film adaptation of Cooper's *The Dark is Rising*, it seems appropriate to offer a few critical observations. My first is this: Don't pre-judge any film by its journalistic reviews. Approach all such "two-stars/three-stars" commentary with a healthy "I'll-judge-for-myself-thank-you-very-much" attitude. Though predictably inferior to the book, in my opinion, *The Seeker* is worthwhile in its own right. British actor Ian McShane is superb as Merriman and the production values are high, with cinematography and special effects ranging from the merely engaging to the spectacular. My principle reservation (a big one as you might infer from having read this chapter) is that the tragedy of the Walker is entirely omitted. This crucial subplot personalizes Cooper's story by anchoring it in the concrete experience of a particular set of characters. Without it, the cosmic struggle between the forces of the Light and the Dark gets lost in its own abstraction. The making of the film was no doubt prompted by the success of the Harry Potter films. Indeed, I first learned of its imminent release at the midnight book-launching party for *Harry Potter and the Deathly Hollows*, at which promotional posters for *The Seeker* were prominently on display. Nevertheless, it would be unfair to fault the former as a clone of the latter. If the question of direct influence is even relevant, it is Rowling who is indebted to Cooper. Though, to the best of my knowledge, there is no mention of Cooper's saga as source material for her *Harry Potter* series in any of Rowling's written or spoken interviews, the affinity between these two modern cult of childhood classics is undeniable, as I hope the preceding discussion has made apparent.

3 How Grim Is the Reaper?

Death and Denial

Where and what is the "Undiscovered Country" of which Prince Hamlet speaks? Of all life's terrors, none is more urgent than that of our inescapable human mortality. The most basic way in which old age finds us children still is in our persistent incredulity at the thought of our own inevitable extinction. To the young, death is a misfortune that befalls others. That life exists at all is astonishing, but that it will one day seek to exist is patently impossible. To the old, it is hardly less so. Throughout our lives, the approaching specter of unavoidable dissolution becomes a nexus for any number of related anxieties, both rational and irrational. Author Leonard B. Meyers speaks of a "connotative complex" of loosely related concepts associated with dying that includes deep, cold, silent, dark, pathos, winter, and decay, all of which are ultimately enfolded in life's final and most unsolvable mystery (Meyers 265).

Elaborating on this theme, Ernest Becker, in his classic study, *The Denial of Death*, discusses death as a complex symbol and—following his mentor, Sigmund Freud—berates expectations of an afterlife. Even so, are such timeless and universal expectations truly reducible to a symptom of denial, or is it the reductionism of the materialist worldview itself to which that proscriptive term applies more appropriately. The gothic imagination, even in literature for the young, does not shirk this issue. Speaking of the terrors of the child's inner world, of which fear of death is surely foremost, Becker writes, "In their tortured interiors radiate complex symbols of many inadmissible realities—terror of the world, the horror of one's own wishes, the fear of vengeance by the parents, the disappearance of things, one's lack of control over anything, really." (Becker 19)

The American writer who has specialized in exploring this "lack of control over anything, really" (death in particular) is Ray Bradbury. Though he is perhaps best known as a purveyor of adult science fiction such as *The Martian Chronicles* and *Fahrenheit 451*, Bradbury's novels and short stories make the gothic theme of death and dying (and related concepts such as the mystery of time, human violence, loss, aging, and other unnamed terrors that lurk in the shadows of human consciousness) the focus of his literary imagination. Many of these works, such as *Dandelion Wine* (as well as its later sequel *Farewell Summer*) and *Something Wicked This Way Comes* are adult meditations on coming-of-age and the ultimate unraveling of life. Others are pitched to a younger readership, including *The Homecoming* (and its extended version *From the Dust Returned*) as well as *The Halloween Tree*. All are preoccupied with human mortality from the dual perspective of youth and old age.

Such tales (particularly such atomic age cinematic thrillers as *It Came from Outer Space* and *The Beast from 20,000 Fathoms*, both scripted by Bradbury) were bound to resonate with a "baby-boomer" generation just beginning to piece together an imperfect picture of the world they inhabited, a world of black-and-white political ideologies and unquestioning loyalties in which government and military officials were the good guys (stalwart, reliable, and reassuringly unimaginative) whereas scientist, artists, ministers, and "egg-heads" generally speaking were a bad risk—emotional, imaginative types untrustworthy in a crisis. Exciting as well as terrifying possibilities lay ahead and, provided the stalwarts continued to hold sway, the monsters from without (never within) would always be thwarted by American military prowess and technological know-how.

Armed with the optimism of early youth, an optimism encouraged by the Cold War culture of the age, "exciting" definitely outweighed "terrifying," initially at least. By the time baby-boomers had reached their teens, however, the scales had decidedly begun to shift for many of us. Then, in 1963, the cinematic monsters forever breached the barrier separating fiction from reality, the proscenium arch from the crowded theater. The periodic earth tremors (I grew up in Las Vegas) associated with above-ground nuclear tests and the radioactive residue of those mushroom clouds wafting across the desert landscape were as nothing compared to the psychological earthquake unleashed upon an unsuspecting generation on a bright November day in Dallas, Texas. Increasingly, from that time forth, the imaginations of those too old to forget and too young to understand began to be haunted by the notion that not all monsters are manageable.

In the film documentary *Universal Horror*, Bradbury states that for him the death of silent film star Lon Chaney was the first public trauma to invade childhood's magic circle of invincibility. Thereafter, childish illusions of personal safety and fundamental human decency were forever shattered. A similar response attended the 1963 execution of President John F. Kennedy. Official denials of conspiracy notwithstanding, the "counter-culture" that emerged from that event knew beyond a reasonable doubt that monsters more sinister than any that the special effects wizardry of Hollywood could conjure—the ogre Death foremost among them—were at large in the land and that no one anywhere was beyond their reach. Bradbury's painful moment of epiphany, i.e., the moment he first realized the certainty of his own eventual demise (captured so memorably through the character of Douglas Spaulding in *Dandelion Wine*) is a recurrent motif in Bradbury's work, sometimes presented in association with characters or situations evocative of "the man of a thousand faces" (as Lon Chaney was popularly known). What the death of Chaney was to the young Ray Bradbury ("If death itself could die, and for me that's what Chaney personified, I wasn't safe."), the death of Kennedy, was to the more prescient members of my own generation, those for whom the fallen leader had personified youthful vitality and intellectual promise. The collective insecurities, anxieties, and suspicions unleashed by that brutal event and its implications are clearly echoed in pages of post-1963 cult of childhood fantasy by Christopher, L'Engle, Rowling, and others. Bradbury's gothic sensibilities, though traceable to different event, are similarly preoccupied with the threat to youthful vitality and intellectual promise posed by death.

Bradbury's Transmogrifying Exposure to Universal Horror

Anyone conversant with Bradbury's writings will immediately recall his many allusions to the silent film classics of gothic horror, such as *The Phantom of the Opera*, a modern re-telling of which forms the plot of Bradbury's own 1990 novel, *A Graveyard of Lunatics*. In *Dandelion Wine*, for instance, Tom, one of its young protagonists from Green Town, Illinois with a penchant for recording his adventures in a notebook declaims, "Four hundred Matinees I seen...eight repeats on *The Phantom of the Opera,* four Milton Sillses, and one Adolph Menjou thing about love where I spent ninety hours in the theater toilet so I could see *The Cat and the Canary* or *The Bat*, where everybody held on to everybody else and screamed for two hours without letting go" (Bradbury 7). The first generation Universal studio talkies such as *Dracula, Frankenstein, The Invisible Man,* and *The Mummy* (*King Kong* was an RKO product) were also films imprinted on Bradbury's youthful imagination. Special effects artist Brian Willis, the Hollywood innovator of the stop-animation technique used in *King Kong* was, of course, a formative influence in the life of Bradbury's longtime friend and colleague

Ray Harryhausen. Bradbury collaborated with Harryhausen on the 1953 Warner Bros. film *The Beast from 20,000 Fathoms*. One of the special features included in the DVD release of that film consists of an interview with these two old friends (Bradbury and Harryhausen). In that special feature, Bradbury explicitly refers to himself and a "man-child," attributing his success to the fact that even in old age he has remained a young boy at heart (*The Beast from 20,000 Fathoms, Harryhausen & Bradbury: An Unfathomable Friendship*). William Wordsworth, the English Romantic poet who fixated on childhood experience, famously proclaimed the child is father to the man. Referring to one of his own literary contributions to the cult of childhood, Bradbury writes, "*Dandelion Wine* is nothing if not the boy-hid-in-the-man" (Bradbury, ix). In a similar vein, he invokes Goethe's "Old age does not make childish, it merely finds us children still" in his humorous assertion that "The first thing you learn in life is you're a fool. The last thing you learn in life is that you're the same fool" (Bradbury, 62).

The Halloween Tree

For all his love of prehistoric monsters and the mysteries of outer space, it was the classics of gothic literature and film to which Bradbury would return repeatedly for the imagery, characters, and settings of his Kinder-Goth meditation on death and childhood entitled *The Halloween Tree*. For Bradbury, the secular celebration of Halloween is obviously a ritual obser-vance as sacramental as the holidays of the church calendar. In this slender volume, imaginatively illustrated by Joseph Mugnaini, he sets out to explain the origins and significance of All Hallows Eve through relating the adven-tures of a group of boyhood friends. On this particular Halloween, the boys experience an adventure that will change, and ultimately shorten, each of their lives. The setting is the same small mid-western town c. 1930 that figures in his other autobiographical writings. It is surrounded by open country and divided by an ominous ravine ("a place where civilization fell away in darkness") that so often seems to haunt Bradbury's memories of his early childhood. The plot concerns the fate of young Joe Pipkin, "the greatest boy who ever lived...an assemblage of speeds, smells, textures; a cross section of all the boys who ever ran, fell, got up, and ran again" (11). Consequently, when Joe fails to appear at the appointed time and place to join his costumed comrades for a traditional evening of tricks or treats, they go to his parent's home to investigate.

In doing so, they learn that their seriously ill friend is unable to summon the energy to join in their holiday revels. Pip, as he is affectionately called, nevertheless promises to join them at a sprawling deserted mansion situated on the far side of the "deliciously frightening ravine." When, upon their arrival, there is no sign of him, his comrades reluctantly decide to inspect the allegedly haunted house more closely. Their ailing friend's nickname inevitably conjures the exploits of another daring youth and another ghostly mansion from Charles Dickens's autobiographical novel *Great Expectations*. In a sense, Bradbury's corpus of work may even be said to have defined the rituals of Halloween in small-town America and fixed them in the popular mind as memorably as Dickens's Christmas novellas capture the essence of that holiday in the Victorian era. That this literary connection is no accident is attested by the fact that Dickens's burlesque gothic masterpiece is explicitly referenced by Bradbury as the boys approach the haunted mansion: "Henry-Hank Smith (for that's who it was), hidden inside his black Witch's costume, cried 'Look!' And all looked at the knocker on the door. Tom's hand trembled out to touch it. 'A Marley knocker...You know, Scrooge and Marley, a *Christmas Carol*!' whispered Tom...Then the front door gave a shake, a twist of its knob, a grimace of its Marley knocker, and flung itself wide" (Bradbury 20).

A spectral voice from the dark shadows within promises only tricks, as the boys pile back out and around the side of the house where they first encounter an enormous tree hung with "a variety of pumpkins of every shape and size and a number of tints and hues of smoky yellow or bright orange," i.e., a Halloween Tree (20). Before they have had time to recover from the impact of this sublime spectacle, they find themselves accosted by a towering figure whose face is a pale skull, reminiscent of the Phantom's ravaged features in Lon Chaney's silent film classic. This skeletal apparition suddenly erupts in laughter, removing his mask, and introducing himself as Carapace Clavicle Moundshroud, master of Halloween tricks (not treats). The possessor of this sonorous sobriquet will serve as their Ghost of Halloween Past, or, to draw from another well-known otherworld journey in literature, their Virgil-like tour guide on a perilous exploration of the historical origins of Halloween. While on this Dickensian/Dante-esque excursion they experience rituals and customs by means of which humankind has sought to commemorate and placate the dread specter of Death, acquiring in the process a new and deeper understanding of the seemingly frivolous rituals observed thoughtlessly by their parents and peers in America during the era of the Great Depression. In doing so, they will perceive these holiday traditions as faint echoes of a rich but somber heritage, for the first time.

"What say lads," intones Moundshoroud, "would you solve two-mysteries-in one? Search and seek for lost Pipkin, and solve Halloween, all in one fell dark blow" (39)? What motivates the boys to accept Mound-shoud's challenge is the appearance of their emaciated friend Pipkin who, before fleeing into the night pursued by some dark thing that "frittered, and danced, and slithered away in the cold night air," promises to join them at the various stages of their otherworld journey. Suspecting that this dark thing is none other than Death itself, the boys, following Moundshroud's example, fashion a makeshift kite from the wind-tattered remnants of old circus posters on the side of a nearby barn—a device that recalls Mr. Dark's Pandemonium Carnival in another of Bradbury's fictional explorations of aging and its inevitable outcome, *Something Wicked This Way Comes.* As the kite begins to rise, the boys (dressed as ghost, skeleton, mummy, witch, ape-man, grim reaper, and gargoyle) hang desperately to it and to one another, ride the stars and "sail off away deep into the Undiscovered Country of Old Death and Strange Years in the Frightful Past" (48).

The Mummy Revisited

Peering down in the moonlight at their first port of call, they recognize a desert vista punctuated by familiar landmarks: the River Nile, The Sphinx, and The Great Pyramids, and the Valley of the Kings where lie buried the mummified remains of Egypt's Pharaohs. Racing into a burial chamber, the boys pass illustrated pillars depicting the golden sun murdered nightly by the onset of the night, and seasonally by the onset of winter, only to be resur-rected with each sunrise and reborn with each recurrence of spring. As he darts from pillar to pillar, Tom (bright and bookish, the Ray Bradbury-like protagonist of *The Halloween Tree*) realizes that these daily/seasonal cycles in nature form the basis of the central religious myth of Egyptian culture, the saga of Osiris, Son of Earth and Sky and King of Death, who is eternally dismembered by Darkness in Autumn and re-membered by his loving sister and consort Isis in the Spring. This mythic ritual explained as "death's festival having to do with the seasons," comprises Moundshroud's "Lesson Number One about Halloween" (53).

In the annual offerings of "warm food steaming on the porches" left by the ancient Egyptians for the benefit of wandering spirits, the boys discover

the origins of our modern day Halloween "treats." A somber funeral proces-
sion for a mummified boy king passes directly before them; only this
particular boy king proves to be a Pip rather than the more celebrated Tut or
Tutankhamen from Egyptian antiquity. Through his funeral wrappings, Pip
mumbles an injunction to meet him at their next destination. How he will
manage to keep this appointment, as he is about to be sealed inside a sar-
cophagus and entombed along with the customary furnishings designed for
use in the Land of the Dead, remains a mystery. As the boys are about to
depart, Moundshroud comments, "The Egyptians, why they built to last. Ten
thousand years they planned for. Tombs, boys tombs! Graves. Mummies.
Bones. Death, Death. Death was at the very heart, gizzard, light, soul, and
body of their life!" Ralph, dressed as a mummy, replies, a light going off
inside his head, "Everyday was Halloween to them" (59)!

Prehistoric and Classical Death

Before undertaking an extended visit to the Middle Ages, the boys are
transported into the even more remote past of pre-historic cavemen, for
whom the discovery of fire—that earthy substitute for the warmth and light
of the sun that Moundshround refers to as "the heart, soul, and flesh of
Halloween"—offers release from the terrors of nightfall and the shortened
winter days. When Tom, noting the absence of any modern ritual comparable
to those practiced by the ancient Egyptians, asks what all of this has to do
with Halloween, Moundshroud replies somewhat testily, "When you and
your friends die every day, there's no time to think of Death, is there? Only
time to run…Halloween, indeed! A million years ago, in a cave in autumn,
with ghosts inside their heads, and the sun lost…Memories, that what ghosts
are, but ape men didn't know that…They could drive away wolves but not
memories, not ghosts. So they held tight to their ribs, prayed for spring,
watched the fire, thanked invisible gods for harvests of fruit and nuts" (62).

Next, the time travelers pay a brief visit to the Greco-Roman world. The
Grecian Festival of the Dead, known as the Feast of Pot, features "tricks
from the dead if you don't feed them," the closure of all holy temples and
shrines on this unhallowed evening, and the painting of black molasses on
front porches to catch the ravenous spirits of those who are abroad and
thereby prevent them from entering until the rising sun forces their departure.
The boys learn that following the Greek lead in this, as in everything, ancient
Roman ritual also required the feeding of the dead. On their fly-by en route

to Europe, the boys catch a fleeting glimpse of "Roman cemeteries where people placed food on graves and hurried off" (67). Mounting the sky again in a whirlwind of autumn leaves, Moundshroud speeds his acolytes to the British Isles where they encounter Samhain, the Druidic God of the Dead, a forty-foot tall harvester of sinful souls. Here, the dread October God not merely dispatches the souls of the unworthy humans, but transforms them into unsavory creatures such as "frogs and toads and multitudes of scaly warts with legs and jellyfish which stank in the light" (72). A madly terrified Pip, in the shape of a small dog, flashes past his friends once again creating a Doppler effect as he enjoins them to, "Meet. Meet. Meet Meee…" (74)

The scene changes to a Druidic ritual of animal sacrifice intended to induce Samhain into releasing the human souls of recently departed loved ones. In history's madcap game of musical chairs, Roman soldiers, under orders from their Emperor, Seutonius, suddenly appear to disperse the pagans and crush their religion. The end of Samhain is symbolized in the fall of a mighty oak, emblem of the Druidic faith: "He was the greatest tree in all existence ever, the tallest oak ever to plummet down and die" (78). Soon, Bradbury's phantasmagorical kaleidoscope of history shifts again. This time it is the Romans themselves who suffer a similar fate at the hands of triumphant Christians. "Aye, boys, see," says Moundshroud, "Gods following gods. The Romans cut the Druids, their oaks, their God of the Dead, bang! Down…Now the Christians run and cut the Romans down" (79).

Witches, Gargoyles, and Hunchbacks

Once more the scene changes, this time the boys, including Pip, find themselves astride broomsticks en route to attend the October Broom Festival, also known as the Annual Migration. History's clock has jumped forward to the Dark Ages, characterized by Moundshroud as "the longest, darkest night ever" (79). The setting is Europe at the height of the cult of witchcraft. "Would you see witches, boys," shouts Moundshroud, "Hags, crones, conjure wives, magicians, black magics, demons, devils? There they be in mobs, in riots, boys. Skin your eyeballs" (84). When Henry-Hank, dressed in a witches costume, inquires as to powers possessed by witches he is told that the etymology of the term "witch" is related to the English "wits": "Wits," said Moundshroud, "Intelligence, that's all it means. Knowledge. So any man or woman, with half a brain and with an inclination towards learning had his wits about him, eh? And so, anyone too smart, who didn't watch out, was called a witch." The rest, Moundshroud assures the boys, was all a tragic misunderstanding that led hysterical mobs in Germany and France "to conspire to burn old women, babes, and virgins in a fire" (86, 87).

Inevitably, given Bradbury's longstanding fascination with Lon Chaney's cinematic portrayals of grotesques such as Quasimodo and the Phantom, Moundshroud's educational outing takes Tom Skelton and the other trick-or-treaters to the steps of Notre Dame Cathedral at the height of the Middle Ages. Gazing up at the imposing twelfth-century façade, Tom recognizes Pipkin, or his spirit at any rate, in a certain bell "hung upside down over Paris, his head for a knocker" (92). Pip cries for help as the bell begins to swing, and the boys mount a flight of stairs that appear magically in keeping with Moundshroud's invitation to join him in the building of this colossal structure. Noticing that the cathedral is devoid of Gargoyles, the boys whistle up a host of creatures out of a Medieval bestiary so that, "All the old gods, all the old dreams, all the old nightmares, all the old ideas with nothing to do, out of work" could be preserved and conscripted into the service of the "true God" and his "only begotten son" here on earth: "And obedient to summons, the mobs, the flocks, the prides, the crush, the collection, the raving flux of monsters, beasts, vices rampant, virtues gone sour, discarded saints, misguided prides, hollow pomps oozed, slid, suckered, pelted, ran bold and right up the sides of Notre Dame. In a floodtide of nightmare, in a tidal wave of outcry and shamble they inundated the cathedral, to crust themselves on every pinion and upthrust stone" (98). With this impressive catalogue (to which he later adds apes, griffins, lions, whales swallowing Jonahs, dragons, the Worm of Conscience, acrobats and tumblers, pigs, and Satanic goats), Bradbury pays verbal homage to the ornate grandeur of gothic architecture.

Stationed inconspicuously among all of these grotesqueries the boys discover "one small round beautiful angel/devil face with a familiar eye, a familiar nose, a friendly and familiar mouth" (102). Pipkin it is, in his fourth and penultimate transformation from mummy to dog to bell-knocker to Gargoyle trapped "inside this rock with all these devils and demons for pals" (105)! No sooner has he uttered an appeal for help than a bolt of lightning strikes the façade of the cathedral, putting an abrupt and seemingly irreversible end to Pip's prospects for survival as well as to the reveler's sojourn in Medieval Paris.

Latin American Rituals

Once again there is a montage-like shift to a locale identified by Mound-shroud as "the last grand travel of this night" (106). A panoramic view of candlelit graveyards throughout the Yucatan Peninsula and all of South America resolves itself into an Argentinean celebration of *El Dia de Muerte*, the *Day of the Dead Ones*. Commemorated with fireworks, sugar candies in the shape of skulls (each one engraved with a familiar name) for sale by vendors, pastries, miniature coffins, and miniature effigies of VIPs and ordinary folk sporting human faces attached to skeletal bodies. This Latin version of Halloween, with its festive *memento moiré*, serves Tom and the others as a final reminder of the scriptural injunction that even in the midst of life we are in death. In a flash of insight, Tom explicitly states the central theme of Bradbury's Halloween homage:

> Up in Illinois, we've forgotten what it's all about. I mean the dead, up in our town, tonight, heck, they're forgotten. Nobody remembers. Nobody cares .Nobody goes to sit and talk to them. Boy, that's lonely. That's really sad. But here, why shucks. It's both happy and sad...I mean it's almost like Thanksgiving huh? And everyone set down to dinner, but only half the people able to eat, but that's no mind, thee there. It's like holding hands at a séance with your friends, but some of the friends are gone (119).

Tom and one of the others notice that two of the children participating bear them an uncanny resemblance, as well they might in keeping with Bradbury's vision of a commonwealth of childhood unlimited by time, place, ethnicity, or culture. They also notice the uncharacteristic absence of their friend, Pip. As they do so, a "man carrying, on his head, lightly, lightly, a small coffin" crosses their field of vision. Suspecting that the figure inside the coffin might be their unhealthy friend, Tom supplicates Moundshoud to take them all home before it is too late to save Pip. "The night's been too long," pleads Tom, "I seen too much" (123). Immediately, Tom's wish is granted as the small group is transported, though not to the comfort and safety of familiar surroundings. Instead they find themselves at the mouth of an immense catacomb on the outskirts of their hometown. Moundshoud orders them to descend, which they do, uneasily and silently, each step carrying them deeper into the unknown and further from the security of their homes to which, by now, they long to return. When their seemingly intermi-nable descent finally ends, they find themselves within a burial chamber lined with the mummified remains of those whose impoverished families had been unable to afford the rental and maintenance of their original burial plot.

The reason for this final descent into an Otherworld realm of the dead is soon made clear. Among the rows of silent mummies, there is one who weeps in a small, terrified voice that Tom recognizes as belonging to Pip. When urged to join them, Pip complains that he is afraid to run the menacing gauntlet that has formed between them, a gauntlet consisting of the "nightmares, the mysteries, the dreadful ones, the dires and the haunts" (129). The others decline to fetch him for that identical reason. Breaking this momentary impasse Moundshround shouts, "Save him with this," holding out a sugar-candied skull from the Day of the Dead inscribed with the name Pipkin. At this critical juncture, Moudshroud makes a startling proposition. Telling them to divide the candied letters of Pips name into eight portions, one for each of them (Is this perchance the origin of Rowling's Horcruxces?), he strikes a bargain: Pip can be ransomed, but only if each one of them agree to sacrifice "one precious year from the far-burned candle-end of your life." "When the time comes," he warns, "you may regret. But, you will be able to say, this year I spent well, I gave for Pip, I made a loan of life for sweet Pipkin, the fairest apple that ever almost fell too early off the harvest tree" (131). They consent with alacrity, first Tom then the rest.

Instantly, uncertain whether or not they have succeeded in rescuing Pip, they find themselves back inside Moundshroud's mansion. The same Dickensian knocker that had heralded their arrival at the beginning of their adventure ushers them out of the house at its conclusion. Literally weeping for joy, Tom looks off into the distance to see his recovered comrade waiting for him. Before bending his feet toward Pip and home, however, he pauses to ask one final question, "Mr. Moundshroud, who are you?" "I think you know boy, I think you know," comes the rejoinder. "Will we meet again," inquires Tom. "Yes, many years from now I'll come for you," says Moundshroud. With an implicit desperation, Will fires off one more parting question: "Will we ever stop being afraid of nights and death?" Moundshroud's reply is as enigmatic as it is comforting. "When you reach the stars, boy, yes, and live there forever, all the fears will go, and Death himself will die," a particularly intriguing remark in light of Bradbury's confession (cited above) that it was the death of Death, i.e., the death of Lon Chaney, that triggered his own Gothic quest to understand life's ultimate mystery (143). But is this prediction a nod at gothic transcendence or an example of Becker's denial of death? Whichever it may be, Bradbury seems to foreshadow not only

Rowling's Isis/Osiris theme (dismember/remember) but also to anticipate her mystical vision of an unspecified afterlife.

So ends Ray Bradbury's historical survey of Halloween as part of humanity's age old struggle to comprehend and, in some measure mitigate, the terrors of life's final destination. Like Susan Cooper, and others who address youthful anxieties about the mysteries of time, aging, and death, Bradbury equates enlightenment with remembrance. To paraphrase Santayana's almost too-famous maxim, those who forget the past are doomed to misconstrue the present. If, as Scripture teaches, the beginning of wisdom is the fear [i.e., awe] of God, it follows that the awakening of our slumbering sense of awe from the denial and projection that the trauma of death can precipitate is the beginning of our release from the self-destructive cycles of behavior that can only end in *enantiodromia*. Paradoxically, the gothic imagination finds an antidote to the corrosive influence of fear in an honest acknowledgement of our irreducible human insecurity and vulnerability. In the body of literature and film that forms the topic of this discussion, childhood (either in the guise of an unchanging archetypal child or in that of the mutable child as gothic hero) is upheld as a symbol and type of the wisdom of insecurity. One of the core themes of the cult of childhood is that we are paradoxically most potent only when we acknowledge and accept the ethical and practical limits of human power.

As in Cooper's *The Dark Is Rising*, we are reminded by Bradbury that the essentials of human nature do not change, that friendship and mutual concern should hold sway over self-preservation, that in the long perspectives of history all times are one and that the transcendence of our gothic dilemma lies in a re-membering of a consciousness that has been dismembered and mutilated by fear. As Moundshroud cries at the climax of this extra-curricular outing:

> Well boys, do you see? It's all one, yes…Always the same but different, eh? every [sic] age, every time. Day was always over. Night was always coming. And aren't you always afraid, Apeman there, or you Mummy, that the sun will never rise again…And they looked up through the levels of the great house and saw every age, every story, and all the men in history staring round about as the sun rose and set. Apemen trembled, Egyptians cried laments. Greeks and Romans paraded their dead. Summer fell dead. Winter put it in the grave. A billion voices wept. The wind of time shook the vast house. The windows rattled and broke, like men's eyes, into crystal tears. Then, with cries of delight, then thousand times a million men welcomed back bright summer suns which rose to burn each window with fire. (136)

According to Bradbury, in other words, we can respond to the challenge of our own mortality as either a devouring monster to be placated at all costs or as a teacher who encourages us to discover within ourselves hidden depths of sympathy, compassion, and courage. The gothic imagination reminds us that there are worse fates in life than dying; that spiritual dismemberment is a fate more terrible than bodily death. The essence of gothic psychology is a belief in human duality, the realization that if we are not busy transforming ourselves into angels we are probably busy transforming ourselves into demons, or to invoke a more secular analogy, if we are not striving to control the Beast Within, it is probably well on its way to gaining control over the Child Within. Tom Skelton and Bradbury's other trick-or-treaters, in subordinating their own (admittedly childish) fears to the demands of loyalty and friendship, pass the test we all must face in life: Do we choose to walk upright as human beings through the Valley of the Shadow or descend to all fours in the vain hope of prolonging a mere animal existence at the expense of our fellows? By sacrificing a remote year of their future lives that Pipkin might live today, the boys demonstrate a wisdom that is peculiar to children who instinctively live in the moment. How often do we adults, who rely on mature calculation and foresight, misjudge the moment, and in so doing, sacrifice future as well as present happiness?

Though Bradbury, like the second and third-century Alexandrian theologians such as Clement and Origin, definitely sees life as a "school for souls," it is characteristic of the best writers of what might be termed Kinder- Goth that they are didactic without seeming moralistic or cloyingly pious. Arguably, children and young adults look to older more experienced grown-ups for guidance as to how best to conduct their lives and process the world around them. They are, however, swift to detect and react against pretension and sham. Bradbury manages to avoid both pitfalls. Mr. Moundshoud, like all good pedagogues, is part preacher, part teacher, and part entertainer. He leads by example, shows more than he tells, dispenses discipline with a tolerant humor, and approaches his students without condescension. So does his creator, whose poetic prose style is probably best appreciated by his adult readership. Nevertheless, a child's aesthetic reach should exceed its grasp and I suspect that Bradbury's signature blend of humor with pathos, child-like immediacy with grown-up nostalgia, homespun Midwestern dialect with rhapsodic gush and verbal pyrotechnics poses an intriguing challenge to the younger members of his readership. Needless to say, Bradbury's youthful audience is not comparable in size to that of J. K. Rowling, but my own hunch is that for all her winning qualities and current popularity, Bradbury's work will enjoy a comparable shelf-life.

4 Fates Worse Than Death: *The Amazing Mr. Blunden* and *A Wind in the Door*

Gothic Christianity and Wordsworth's "Seedtime of the Soul"

Arguably the comparatively recent notion of children as the repository of human values threatened by the "march of progress" is perhaps the most distinctive flower of Christendom. When (in parables such as Mathew 18:3 and 18:6, Mark 10:15, and Luke: 18:17) Jesus makes a child-like disposition and outlook a precondition for entering Heaven and the placing of spiritual impediments in the way of children as a certain path to Hell, he was not only laying the foundation for a developmental concept of spiritual enlightenment, he was also attributing a unique value to emotional susceptibility, vulnerability, and unfettered imagination. These are all qualities associated with childhood that are often stunted in later life (Hoecker 39-49). It is within the context of this distinctively Christian conception of God as a pedagogue and life as a school for souls that the evangelical emphasis on being "born again" needs to be reinterpreted. From the perspective of the cult of childhood, being reborn spiritually has little to do with accepting creedal formulas and Jesus as "Lord and Savior" (which all too often amounts to checking one's brain at the church door) and everything to do with the recognition that in certain respects, children see the world with an unimpaired freshness and sense of wonder—a sense of wonder that poses an implicit challenge to the religious and political assumptions that form the underpinning of civilization itself. Most children, for instance, are by nature pacifists, i.e., they instinctively abhor cruelty and shun those who practice it—until, that is, they are taught the "manly necessity" of aggression and, along with it, the sadistic pleasures of might over right. Most children, including those you grow up to be champions of *laissez-faire* economics, are willing to share with individuals less fortunate than themselves. Not yet responsive to the mesmerizing influence of intellectual abstractions, they neither accept nor ostracize on the basis of political, religious, or racial prejudice. In short, most children are willing to live and let live until their adult role-models teach them to do otherwise. Similar in their needs and vulnerabilities, children are naturally accepting of the Christian injunction to "do unto others." Until conditioned by a civilization oriented competitive, tribalist values into giving their immediate family, their social identity groups, and their nation priority, children quite easily see "others" as themselves.

This childlike predisposition was axiomatic to the tenets of European Romanticism and formed the basis of what is sometimes referred to as the nineteenth-century cult of childhood. Novelists such as Charlotte Brönte in *Jane Eyre* and Charles Dickens in *David Copperfield*, poets such as William Blake in his *Songs of Innocence and Experience* and William Wordsworth in *The Prelude* and *Lines Written A Few Miles Above Tinturn Abbey*, painters such as Otto Phillip Runge in his canvas entitled *Morning*, and composers such as Robert Schumann in *Kinderscenen* (*Scenes From Childhood*, Op. 15) all celebrated childhood as a "seedtime of the soul," a time when innate human attributes essential to a spiritually healthy civilization were ideally cultivated and strengthened. This belated recognition by Western culture of its children as guides and prophets was clearly connected with rise of unbridled capitalism in the nineteenth century—a development that would pave the way for a revival of interest in the gothic imagination in the late twentieth century, particularly as it related to the artistic cult of childhood. In effect, The Romanticism promoted the archetypal Child Within as an alternative to the archetypal Beast Within fostered by predatory capitalism and nationalism.

This post-WWII revival was spearheaded by group of Oxford dons known collectively as the Inklings (C. S. Lewis, J. R. R. Tolkien, Owen Barfield, and Charles Williams). The gothic imagination seems to thrive during periods of social strife; and the turbulent political and social circumstances through which these scholars and fantasists had lived were strikingly parallel to those that pertained during the late eighteenth early nineteenth-century gothic revival in literature. Both were periods of incessant though intermittent warfare and unprecedented political and technological innovation. Its American phase, which, caught on in the 1960s (another era of profound political and social turbulence) was led by writers such as Madeleine L'Engle. Those who would later join the cult of childhood were no doubt influenced by the challenges to a strictly materialistic worldview posed not only by the Inklings but also by other proponents of the supernatural and the paranormal such as Colin Wilson, author of *The Occult* and *Beyond the Occult*, and Louis Pawles and Jacques Bergier who co-authored the widely read (largely unreliable) *Morning of the Magicians*. However, another intellectual tributary that empties into the same estuary as gothic childhood fantasy is science fiction (including UFO lore).

Authors such as Paul Davies (*God & The New Physics*) and Patrick Harpur (*Daimonic Reality:Understanding Otherworld Encounters*) draw upon theories of pan-dimensionality and alien intelligences to portray a multiverse of possibilities that often outstrip the most speculative theology, science fiction, and fantasy. Indeed, in *Walking on Water: Reflections of Faith and Art*, L'Engle, the Newberry prize-winning author of a series of theological science fiction novels for young readers known as the *Time Trilogy* (*A Wrinkle in Time, A Wind in the Door, A Swiftly Tilting Planet*) confesses that her religious imagination is more often inspired by popular science than by her forays into classical or popular theology. One of the implications of the development to which I refer is that the revitalization of the nineteenth-century cult of childhood is perhaps a constituent of a new post-WW II paradigm of reality. This new climate of thought and feeling is one that seems to be groping its way toward a synergy of religion and science that will finally reconcile "the two cultures" posited by C. P. Snow in the earlier part of the twentieth century—unless, of course the culture conservatives (who take issue with science as well as the gothic imagination in children's literature) have their way.

The Amazing Mr. Blunden

First published in Britain under the quotidian title *The Ghosts* in 1969, Antonia Barber's *The Amazing Mr. Blunden*—arguably, an even worse choice—is an exciting Victorian gaslight thriller in the tradition of Charles Dickens and Arthur Conan Doyle. Its seamless blend of supernaturalism with the perennial science-fiction theme of time travel is pressed into the service of a religious parable, a Passion play about redemption, set, appropriately enough, against the backdrop of the Lenten season (Good Friday to Easter Sunday). Nevertheless, the Christian implications of this well-crafted murder mystery are secondary to the requirements of good story-telling (as they are in other, better known examples of children's literature with an explicitly Judeo-Christian slant, such as the *Narnia Chronicles* of C. S. Lewis and the theological science fiction of Madeleine L'Engle).

I first encountered Barber's ghostly tale (which opens in Bob Cratchit's London suburb of Camden Town) not as a child or adolescent but as a young adult living in the London suburb of Hampstead, very near to Camden Town.

As my wife and I, huddled in front of an electric space-heater for a read-aloud—seeking, I suppose, a psychological as much as as physical respite from an incessant, mizzling, rain and the penetrating chill of a poorly insulated English flat in wintertime—we found ourselves transported by Barber to an identical time and setting (minus the space-heater). The first chapter opens with the mysterious figure of an elderly man dressed in antiquated Victorian apparel making his way through the heavy pedestrian traffic of a crowded London street, imperious to the rain by which he is assailed. His destination is the apartment of Mrs. Allen, a young, recently widowed American expatriate and her three small children (Lucy the eldest in her early teens, Jamie, several years younger, and an infant still in the crib). The straightened financial and emotional circumstances of this single-parent family are succinctly captured in Barber's description of Mrs. Allen's cramped basement apartment which belongs to a row of terraced houses, the first of which "lay in a pool of shadow behind a stunted tree" (7).

The mysterious old man introduces himself nervously as a representative of a legal firm with the somewhat redundant cognomen of Blunden, Blunden, and Claverton. Lucy, who is intrigued but suspicious, notes that Mr. Blunden's clothing and manner of speaking are reminiscent of *David Copperfield*. The old man explains to Mrs. Allen that he is there to offer her a responsible position as caretaker to a rural English mansion that, upon the decease of its most recent owner, came under the disposition of his legal firm. As an added inducement, he mentions that the house is equipped with a fine grand piano. This observation prompts Mrs. Allen, a trained classical pianist who has abandoned her musical calling in the wake of her husband's untimely death, to confide in Mr. Blunden concerning her bereavement. Mr. Allen's promising career as a composer/conductor, like the tree outside her apartment, was tragically stunted in an automobile accident, casting the lives of his surviving family into a deep shadow of grief and uncertainty. Mr. Blunden responds sympathetically but predictably that time heals grief. From his enigmatic follow-up to this remark, however, Mrs. Allen senses that there is more to his seemingly glib reaction is than he is telling. "You don't believe me now," the mysterious stranger goes on to say," but you will find that it is true. I am an old man…a very old man…and I have learned wisdom the hard way. It is not grief that scars, but guilt, not the blows we suffer, but the injuries we do to others" (11).

Addressing the children, while Mrs. Allen is out of the room, Mr. Blunden asks, "Do you think you would be afraid if you saw…a ghost" (13)?

Sounding once more a note of remorse, he elaborates on this strange question by pointing out that, "Sometimes, ghosts are people who come back seeking help. They are people who during their lives were not strong enough...or wise enough...or good enough to meet some challenge. They come seeking help because they cannot rest for the knowledge that they did harm and the longing to put it right" (14). Foreshadowing subsequent events, he goes on to suggest that if ghosts were to appear, they would not be of the gibbering, headless variety favored by pulp entertainment but "...much like ordinary people: children of about your own age, perhaps, or even...an old man such as myself" (14).

Memory leavened by introspection, a potentially redemptive faculty according to the gothic imagination, suggests that *some* lessons in life are learned only after prolonged reflection on bitter firsthand experience. Mr. Blunden's amazing story provides a compelling example. It also raises an important question concerning the extent to which an engagement with story, fictional or otherwise, can be instructive. Is forewarned truly forearmed? Can we truly learn from books? Clearly, the imaginative extension of human experience they afford is no substitute for personal experience. One the other hand, who can say with certainty that our vicarious involvement through the printed page is not a contributing factor in our decision-making process, or that it does not play a vital role in the way we ultimately come to understand those decisions (even if it does not enable us to avert their consequences)? It seems reasonable to surmise that the young are often as ashamed of their missteps as adults, perhaps more so in that they have not yet acquired the psychological armor of rationalization and denial that their elders have had time to burnish. They may therefore take comfort from an honest depiction of adult fallibility and its outcomes. Conversely, might not the elderly among us profit, as Scrooge does, from an occasional return to the seedtime of our own souls, a time when misfortune and disappointment was the exclusive province of others? In this sense as well, "Old age does not make childish, it merely finds us children still" (Goethe).

The day following Mr. Blunden's visit, the three members of the Allen family duly repair to the address that Mr. Blunden has supplied. They arrive at the offices of Blunden, Claverton, and Smith, only to be informed that the second Mr. Blunden in the firm's title is an aged invalid who could not possibly have traveled to Camden Town. Moreover, they are told, the job for which Mrs. Allen is applying has yet to be advertised. Though confusion reigns for a time, Mr. Blunden's inexplicable job offer is ultimately affirmed, partly on the strength of Mrs. Allen's obvious need, partly on the favorable impression made by her family, and partly because the last couple employed as caretakers mysteriously abandoned their post after a mere week on the job. Although Mrs. Allen senses that Mr. Smith, like the allegedly decrepit Mr. Blunden before him, is clearly telling less than he knows, she gratefully accepts his offer. Her decision ratified by both Lucy and Jamie. So ends part one of this four-part narrative.

Part two is set at the partially dilapidated Victorian mansion with Lucy roaming its deserted labyrinthine corridors, disused chambers, and musty attics. Her conversation with Mr. Blunden in Camden has primed her to expect a ghostly visitation, and her expectations are soon realized. While wondering through the overgrown shrubbery of an adjacent garden, she falls into a semi-trance. This trance is accompanied by an eerie silence broken only by the "warning note" of a blackbird. More than willing to heed this warning, she takes flight, running headlong into Jamie, who has eagerly anticipated a supernatural encounter of the sort that his sister has just averted—barely. He hasn't long to wait, as two Victorian children, "a tall girl in an old-fashioned dress and a little boy who came walking quite naturally along the path toward them" draw near (30). They introduce themselves as Sara and Georgie Latimer. More skeptical than his imaginative sister, Jamie challenges their ghostly credentials. Sara patiently explains that apparitions exist in the eye of the beholder. Seen from his point of view, Sara points out, she and her brother are indeed ghosts, but seen from their own perspective in time it is Sara and Jamie who are the specters. Jamie finds this argument unconvincing until he notices that neither Sara nor Georgie cast a shadow, thereby confirming that they are not of this world (or not of this time, at least).

The answer to Jamie's questions about his two ostensibly preternatural visitors hinges on the mystery of time itself. As it turns out, Sara and Georgie are not spirits from beyond the grave, but time travelers who have leapt ahead one hundred years in search of help. "Unless we can find someone to befriend us," exclaims Sara, "Georgie and I may soon be dead" (37). "Time", she explains, "is not as you think of it. You think of it as a straight line along which you move…But really it is more like a vast wheel turning and you two and Georgie and I are on different parts of the rim" (33). When pressed by Jamie, Sara notes that time travel is easier for children, who lose themselves more easily in the moment, than for adults on whom certain imaginative limitations take an unbreakable hold. These two observations express concisely two of the fundamental precepts of the cult of childhood already encountered in the writings of Dickens, Cooper, and Bradbury: First, that past, present, and future are fluid parameters rather than rigid and discrete categories and second, that children are closer to an understanding (or at least an acceptance) of such mysteries than adults. "The child," as Wordsworth says, "is father to the man."

The dilemma faced by Sara and her brother has to do with the sinister schemes of Mr. and Mrs. Wickens, recently appointed caretakers to the Latimer estate (in the Victorian era). Both are brutal alcoholics who have acquired their position of power over the children primarily owing to the negligence of Sara and Georgie's legal guardian, Uncle Bertie. This callow young aristocrat, meanwhile, has fallen hopelessly in love with Arabella Wickens, the caretaker's simpering daughter. Though regarded as attractive by Victorian standards—emphatically not shared by Jamie—Bella (formerly a dancer at a disreputable London music hall) is cloyingly immature. Following the untimely deaths of Sara's and Georgie's parents in a carriage accident—that parallels the car crash in which Mr. Allen was to die a hundred years in the future—Uncle Bertie and the family solicitor, Frederick Percival Blunden, are named as legal custodians of the surviving orphans. They are consequently entrusted with management of Georgie's eventual inheritance. Characterized by the fair-minded Sara as a foolish rather than an evil man, their uncle prefers the diversions of London to his responsibilities as a surrogate parent. Tragically, he decides to turn a blind eye to the abuse suffered by his two charges at the hands of the sadistic Mrs. Wickens and her hulking husband.

When Uncle Bertie's spendthrift lifestyle places his financial future and that of his greedy caretakers in jeopardy, Mr. and Mrs. Wickens decide to take matters into their own hands. By bringing about the "accidental" death of the children (thereby allowing Uncle Bertie to claim Georgie's inheritance), they hope to secure their own prospects. The day following their first encounter with the Victorian time travelers, the Allen family attends a Good Friday service at the local Parrish church. The kindly Vicar (whose sermons throughout this sacred season serve as a running commentary on the principal plot) announces that they are assembled to celebrate "a great victory "(45). He goes on to enjoin his parishioners to renounce "uncharitable thoughts," "corrosive indifference," and "acts of selfishness." The closing hymn speaks of "Chasing far the gloom and terror, brightening all the path we tread" (47). Lucy and Jamie, unaware that these words have a bearing on their immediate situation barely pay attention, eager for the service to end so that they can visit to the adjacent cemetery. There they hope to discover some clue as to the ultimate destiny of their newly acquired friends.

Upon discovering the poorly maintained gravesite of Sara and Georgie, they enquire as to its history of from the Parrish sexton who informs them that precisely a century earlier two children living in the very house they now occupy died in a terrible fire. The cause of this fatal conflagration, believed to have been started in the manor library, was never officially determined. Moreover, explains the kindly sexton, this tragedy claimed a third victim, young Tom Fletcher, the gardener's son. According to local folklore, Tom, who befriended the neglected children in their time of need, is thought to have fallen to his death while attempting their rescue. When Lucy examines the dates on the tombstone more closely, she is horrified to realize that Sara and Georgie will meet their fate the very next day, a hundred years previously.

Having promised to return with them to their nineteenth-century home, Lucy and Jamie have no option but to await Sara's and Georgie's next appearance in their own time. During the ensuing tense interval, Lucy expresses doubts concerning the feasibility of changing the "Pattern of the Wheel," i.e., reversing the harmful effects of the past. The always practical but honorable Jamie concurs, frankly stating his "common sense" belief that the past is immutable. When asked why then they should to risk the potential dangers involved in time travel, he reminds his sister that they have given their word and expresses a frail hope that they might at least be able to provide moral support during the ordeal that lies ahead. Sara finally appears without Georgie, who has been locked in the cellar for defying Mrs. Wickens. When Mr. Blunden materializes unexpectedly next to Sara, Lucy screams, though Sara, who is well aware of the old man's long remorse, finds his presence reassuring. He has come at this crucial juncture to explain both the conditions necessary to render the "Charm to Move the Wheel of Time" effectual and his own part in the events that are about to unfold. The charm itself is a potion, the recipe for which Sara discovers in a book on magic to which she is mysteriously directed by writing that appears on a frosted window pane in the library of the manor house (one of Mrs. Wickens's favorite detention centers).

According to Mr. Blunden, in order for this charm to bring about the desired effect three conditions must be met: First, Sara and Georgie must extend their forgiveness. Second, someone must once again be willing to trust him with their life, and third, the repentant malefactor must, by his own suffering, undo the past for which his negligence was largely responsible. Having died shortly after the fire of a heart attack brought about by shock and regret, he has spent the intervening century (as he had stated earlier) learning wisdom the hard way: "Once, a long time ago when I was alive," explains the sorrowing solicitor, "I made the wrong choice Not by chance, for that is easily forgiven, but through my own indifference, my own selfishness. I was guardian to Sara and George and I failed to guard them; I was their trustee but I was not worthy to be trusted. They came to me when they needed help, when no one else could help them, and I failed them. I would not listen to them and the result…" (60). At this point, Mr. Blunden abruptly breaks off, too overcome by emotion to continue. When he is again able to resume his narrative, he quotes from the Bible, "It were better for such a man that a mill-stone were hanged about his neck and he were drowned in the depth of the sea." This passage (from Mark 18:6) affirms Mr. Blunden's certain knowledge that his former selfishness, like that of Lord Voldemort in Rowing's saga, has resulted in a fate worse than death. Essentially Barber is here restating the theme of Marley's ghost in Stave One of Dickens's *A Christmas Carol*:

> Oh! Captive bound and double ironed…not to know that ages of incessant labour by immortal creatures, for this earth, must pass into eternity before the good of which it is susceptible is all developed. Not to know that any Christian spirit working kindly in its little sphere, whatever it may be, will find its mortal life too short for its vast means of usefulness. Not to know that no space of regret can make amends for one's life's opportunities misused! Yet such was I" (62).

Indeed, Antonia Barber's Lenten parable might more appropriately have been entitled *An Easter Carol*.

The reader's uncertainty as to the final outcome is greatly heightened when Jamie rashly retracts his offer to trust Mr. Blunden, despite repeated warnings that the Pattern of the Wheel can only be altered under the conditions stated previously. This uncharacteristic recanting of his earlier pledge comes when Jamie witnesses an attempt made by the Latimer children to alert Mr. Blunden (the self-important Victorian lawyer) to their danger. Their agonized pleas for assistance are, of course, ignored. When Blunden's remorseful *Doppelgänger* suddenly appears on the scene, the startled and confused Jamie offers to confront his former self on behalf of Sara and

Georgie. To this suggestion, the ghostly solicitor replies, "Yes there are two of us...though we are the same man. We are separated by a great gulf of time and knowledge. But he would not know you; it was I who brought you here...He would not hear you. He would not even see you. He is a shallow, insensitive man, incapable of visions. If it were not so, I would plead with him myself" (79). Again, one is reminded of Dickens: Marley's ghost informs the unregenerate Scrooge that it has been no light part of his penance to have sat invisible beside him many a day and the Ghost of Christmas Past compels him to witness his own irreversible folly. The difference, of course, is that Barber's universe in which the ill effects of human folly are indeed reversible, though only at a terrible cost.

Gothic literature for the young often toys with the conundrum posed by the following question: Is it theoretically possible to alter the past or do we inhabit what the philosophers refer to as a deterministic universe? Theologically speaking, the problem hinges on how to reconcile human free will with the concept of an omnipotent deity. If God's intentions can be thwarted, divine will is not omnipotent. If human intentions are predetermined, freedom of choice is an illusion (an ethical position that is difficult to square with the notion of moral accountability). Many theoretical solutions to this paradox have been proposed, most of which require the reader to abandon either a belief in divine omnipotence or human free will. The gothic narratives for the young discussed in this volume tend to accommodate both alternatives (indeed "both/and" rather than "either/or" might serve as a motto for the gothic imagination).

The essence of Christian cosmology is, after all, a conviction that the world (and everything in it) is the process of being restored, or redeemed, to a condition that is perfectly in accord with God's "intentional will," a term coined by theologian Leslie Weatherhead to distinguish between confusing and contradictory assumptions about divine providence. When conflated, these assumptions tend to diminish God's moral stature (to paraphrase Origen, there have always been "Christians" whose conception of the deity implied a creator ethically inferior to his or her more enlightened creatures). To avoid this pitfall, Weatherhead posits the existence of three quite distinct but related concepts (the use of the male pronoun in the following explanation is intended purely as a stylistic convenience): the "intentional" will of God, the "circumstantial" will of God, and the "ultimate" will of God. The first term refers to God's original plan spoiled by human folly and sin. The second refers to God's provisional will (an improvised adjustment made in light of human sin and folly). The last term attributes to God an ability to enfold circumstances contrary to His intentional will into the ultimate outcome of history. Weatherhead explains the ultimate compatibility of divine providence with human free will in the following passage:

> The omnipotence of God, you perceive, does not mean that by a sheer exhibition of his superior might God gets his own way. If he did, man's freedom would be an illusion and man's moral development would be made impossible. No 'end' which God has in mind can be imposed from without; for his end, the at-one-ment of all souls with him, must come from man's choice of God's way, not the imposition of God's will in irresistible might which leaves no room for choice. Power means ability to achieve purpose. Since the purpose is to win man's volition, any activity of God's that which denied or suppressed man's volition, in that it would defeat the purpose, would not be a use of power but a confession of weakness and an acceptance of defeat (34).

The application of this theology to Barber's narrative suggests that Jamie's confusion with regard to the possibility of changing a past that has already occurred, though understandable, is unnecessary. Human free will and its consequences are real, but so too is the ability of time and space to accommodate them. As Madeleine L'Engle observes, "We simply do not understand time...artists often have a more profound understanding of time than do scientists" (L'Engle, *Walking on Water* 94). While this statement is certainly true of the current scientific consensus, it is obviously less applicable to those quantum physicists who acknowledge the theoretical possibility of time travel as well as the existence of parallel dimensions, i.e., infinite variations on the space-time reality we experience in our own universe and time-line. Long before Einstein, however, theologians were compelled to deal with (or ignore) such science fiction scenarios in the Bible, often glibly excusing them on the intellectually insufficient grounds that "with God all things are possible."

Alluding to the New Testament narrative of the Transfiguration (during which Jesus allegedly breaks the time barrier by communicating directly with Old Testament prophets) L'Engle remarks in *Walking on Water*, "Here we are on the border of the tremendous Christian mystery: time is no longer a barrier" (L'Engle 80). One of the more interesting speculations to arise out of this welter of ideas relating to the puzzling concept of time in the post-Einstein era is the theory of "serial time" as proposed by aeronautical engineer John W. Dunne (and popularized by the English writer J. B. Priestley in books such as *Over the Long High Wall: Some Reflections & Speculations on Life, Death & Time*). According to Dunne/Priestley, human afterlife is devoted not to existence on a supernatural plane of reality but to an imaginative revision of our earthly timeline designed to undo the moral errors of which we have been guilty. Known as "serial time," this temporal theory allows for precognition (it was a precognitive dream that led Dunne to devise his theory) while addressing the central theological issues raised by theodicy, i.e., that branch of theology concerned with the question of how to reconcile divine providence with the claims of justice. In order to do so, it combines features of both Christianity (the doctrines of redemption and atonement) with the theme of reincarnation (usually associated with Eastern belief systems) into a scenario not unlike the fictional scenarios proposed by Barber, Cooper, and L'Engle. Based on this discussion, it seems fair to conclude that such notions are not only the stuff of gothic literature for children, but the stuff of serious modern scientific and theological speculation as well.

Jamie's final attempt to save the Latimer children, who lie asleep in the upper-floor library of the burning house after having been locked in and drugged by Mrs. Wickens, ends in an admission of defeat. Though he is able to rescue Sara, the fire advances so quickly that he can see no way to reenter the house in order to retrieve the unconscious Georgie. "Desolation filled him, "writes Barber, "a terrible feeling of helplessness. Tears stung his eyes and involuntarily he cries out, 'I would if I could! Don't you see that it just isn't possible!' as if addressing the unconscious child" (104). At that precise moment, the modern-day Mr. Blunden appears at his side telling him to grasp his hand and not let go. He reassures Jamie, who is still paralyzed by doubts as to his trustworthiness, that "it was not meant to be easy to change the Pattern of the Wheel" and that Jamie's unconditional trust is a necessary precondition for the ordeal they are about to undergo. He further reassures Jamie that so long as he does not relinquish his hold, "only I will suffer" (105). As they ascend the steps to the library through a blazing inferno, Jamie is, as Mr. Blunden predicted, immune to the flames. When he disobeys Mr. Blunden's injunction to look straight ahead, however, he find himself starring up at a face twisted with pain, and realizes with a shudder that, "just as the coolness flowed into him from Mr. Blunden's hand, so the pain he could not feel flowed back into the old man" (106).

Mr. Blunden's agonized journey through the purifying flames of memory and imagination underscores a literary gothic insight into this life at least as old as the *Divine Comedy*. Retribution, in Christian philosophy, is essentially transformative rather than punitive in nature. Dante's notion of *contrapasso*, whereby the consequence fits the crime is perfectly exemplified in the fate of Mr. Blunden. Painful though it may be, the ordeal through which he must pass is one that he undertakes voluntarily (just as he had voluntarily abandoned his responsibilities in his former life), not one that is imposed by a sadistic deity. The divine providence reflected in Barber's children's book, as well as Dante's allegorical epic poem, is one in which humans inescapably reap that which they have sown. According to this understanding, the wounds of Hell are self-inflicted as well as limited in scope and duration (provided conscience has not been utterly destroyed).

It is in this sense that the many biblical injunctions to live in awe of God—dubiously rendered as the "fear of God" in most instances—are to be understood. Fear is a hopeless emotion that will always fail us, always lead us into temptation and betrayal of better selves. Awe, on the other hand, implies a judicious awareness of human limitations in the face of a universe that is both Sublime (one in which humans are vulnerable) and morally conditioned (one in which we are responsible for siding with or against the demonic—both as individuals, and collectively as a society). Without that awareness, implies Barber, our thoughts and actions can indeed result in worse than death. In this connection, it is well to remember that no less an authority on Christian orthodoxy than C. S. Lewis points out that the Jewish claim to being God's chosen people is justified not by the tone and tenor of the Bible—much of which paints a picture of a vindictive people filled with fear, hatred, and an unabashed lust for vengeance—but by those moments in scripture when the uncharacteristic image of a God who is merciful as well as just shines through the corrupting influence of tribal fear, oppression, and brutality (Lewis *Christian Reflections* 116).

Such moments attest to the prophetic voice of Judaism. For example, the realization that a "repentant heart" (rather than a living animal or human being) is the sacrifice most acceptable to the Lord—growing perhaps out of God's having stayed the hand of Abraham against his son Isaac—is uncharacteristic given the kind of sacrificial rites routinely practiced by certain ancient near-Eastern religions. This fact has implications for our understanding of the cult-of-childhood's repudiation of coercive force in relation to such blatantly un-Christ-like conceptions as the Pauline doctrine of "substitutionary atonement" (God sent his only son to earth in order to be tortured and killed for our benefit as the only means of propitiating His wrath). Those who accept the plenary inspiration of Scripture, i.e., those who contend that every scriptural episode is a valid expression of God's intentional will—in contrast to those who see the Bible as a revelation mediated by the human fallibility of its authors—are obliged to square the circle of God's unlimited love and power with divine sanction for such fruits of fear and malice as blood feuds, militarism, and judicial murder—the ethic of "an eye for an eye," rather than that of "turn the other cheek."

The pederasty practiced by some modern Catholic clerics pales in comparison with the child abuse inflicted on his son by a heavenly father, according to those who insist on biblical infallibility. Such a hermeneutic—one that contradicts both character and conduct of Christ—is either a gross misunderstanding of what is supposed to be the "Good News" or else it is sufficient grounds for any sane human being to reject the Gospel. In equating the Kingdom of God with the least powerful inhabitants of a world dominated by Rome (it's children) Christ was clearly signaling very different conceptions of peace and power from those endorsed by Caesar (whose infamous *Pax Romana* was established through military conquest, maintained by a brutal army of occupation, and administered by corrupt puppet regimes indifferent to the welfare of their subjects). Children do not live by the sword (or the cross) and neither did Jesus. That there are times when one must risk one's well-being, even sacrifice one's life for the sake of others is affirmed throughout the pages of cult-of-childhood fiction as well as those of religious lore, but that such sacrifices are consistent with the intentional will of God is not.

A Wind in the Door

That tragic possibility a fate worse than death is also explored with original-ity and warmth in Madeleine L'Engle's time trilogy (*A Wrinkle in Time*, *A Wind in the Door*, and *A Swiftly Tilting Planet*). All three works concern the fate of two fictional families (the Murrays and the O'Keefes) tracked through several generations. In *A Wrinkle in Time*, we are introduced to Charles Wallace Murray, a precocious youngster, and Meg, his intelligent but impetuous teenaged sister as they "tesseract," i.e., travel through a worm hole in space/time, to the benighted planet of Camazotz. Their mission is to rescue their scientist father, who has been imprisoned there. In the process, they seek to rehabilitate a society sapped of vitality and individuality by IT, a sinister force bent on the negation of all love, creativity, and compassion. They are guided in this undertaking by three supernatural entities (Mrs. Who, Mrs. Which, and Mrs. Whatsit), an eccentric and dowdy trio reminiscent of the fairy-godmothers in Walt Disney's animated version of *Sleeping Beauty*. At the heart of Camazotz (a corruption no doubt of the Arthurian utopia Camelot) lies Central Central Intelligence, home to IT (a. k. a. the "Black Thing"), a bastion of governmental secrecy, deception, and soulless conformity. Any resemblance in name or function to a certain Cold War institution created in 1947 by the National Security Act is presumably intentional.

While there, Charles Wallace, who has been routinely ostracized and bullied by his peers on earth, is temporarily possessed by IT, in the form of a pulsating, disembodied brain evidently borrowed from the cinematic thrillers of science fiction depicted by Hollywood during the 1950s. IT seduces Charles Wallace with flattery and vague promises of shared power. In the course of this adventure, Meg first learns of the excruciating pain that the forces of negation, i.e., the demonic, are able to inflict on those who would resist their influence: "Without warning Meg was swept into nothingness again. This time the nothingness was interrupted by a feeling of clammy coldness such as she had never felt before. The coldness deepened and swelled all about her and through her, and was filled with a new and strange kind of darkness that was a completely tangible thing, a thing that wanted to eat and digest her like some enormous malignant beast of prey" (92). Her nearly fatal encounter with the Black Thing leaves her feeling vulnerable, frightened and, above all, betrayed by a father who she assumed would somehow make everything all right once found. Resentful of the responsibilities imposed upon her (prematurely from her perspective), Meg lashes out verbally at Mr. Murray, accusing him of indifference to the danger in which he has placed youngest son, Charles Wallace. This petulant (and inaccurate) outburst prompts a rebuke as well as an apology from the extraterrestrial nurse (Auntie Beast) who has supervised Meg's recovery from her devastating encounter. "Don't judge her too harshly," pleads Auntie Beast, "she was almost taken by the Black Thing. Sometimes we can't know what spiritual damage it leaves even when physical recovery is complete" (171).

As in the imagined fantasy worlds of Cooper, Bradbury, and Rowling, L'Engle's universe is one in which characters are required (though never coerced) to jeopardize their security and sense of well-being in order to respond to threats not even perceived by more "sensible" types (often including their less imaginative peers, respected mentors, and even beloved family members). The positive path of the Gothic hero toward transcendence and maturity, as in the three writers just mentioned above, entails an irreducible measure of loss and alienation. Sometimes (as in the case of Meg's father) authority figures—even when they are not actually implicated in the evils they are supposed to prevent—are nevertheless powerless to protect against them. In short, Meg inhabits a world that is neither as it appears to be nor as it should be, one in which she is free to grow and deepen but also to fail

Camazotz, home to IT as well as the CCIA, is obviously a dark, mirror image (a *Doppelgänger*) of the constitutional democracy enshrined in America's foundational documents. Indeed, while inside Central Central Intelligence the children resist the influence of IT by chanting familiar passages from the Declaration of Independence, passages that affirm a distinction the disembodied brain of Camazotz is unable or unwilling to grasp. In response to Jefferson's "All men are created equal," for example, IT protests, "But that is exactly what we have on Camazotz. Complete equality. Everybody exactly alike" To which Meg replies triumphantly that, "*Like* and *equal* are not the same thing at all" (146)! Though published prior to the social traumas of the 1960s, L'Engle's political Gothic subtext clearly resonates to the paranoid political witch hunts of the MacCarthy era, i.e., the irrationalities of a nuclear "balance of terror," and the creeping police state tactics employed by a "shadow government" committed to advancing its Cold War agenda against an enemy that it increasingly came to resemble.

In the end, realizing that she and she alone can save Charles Wallace, Meg lovingly accepts the risks involved in exposing herself once more to the terrors of nothingness, thereby transcending her own terrible fear and indecisiveness. In fact, like Harry Potter in J. K. Rowling's saga, whose loving nature is ultimately what distinguishes him from Lord Voldemort, Meg's epiphany comes when she realizes in a flash of introspection that her innate capacity to love is "what she had that IT did not have" (187). In the spirit of the fifth century church father St. Augustine, who said "Love and do what you will," Meg finally learns to trust that only by shunning evil means however expedient (i.e., by faithfully acting on the assumption that the power of love is ultimately stronger than that of coercion) can she hope to procure just ends. She also learns that security, personal as well as collective, is paradoxically dependent on letting go of fear, calculating self-interest, and denial. These same lessons, implicit in *A Christmas Carol, The Halloween*

Tree, The Amazing Mr. Blunden, and *A Wrinkle in Time* are further developed in the second volume of L'Engle's trilogy, *A Wind in the Door.*

As this exciting (more sophisticated) sequel opens, a somewhat older Charles Wallace—the precocious youngest son of the Murrys—is seriously ill. Claiming that he has seen dragons in the back garden of their rural New England home, he convinces Meg to investigate. Her concern over his psychological well-being is exacerbated by her knowledge of his steadily worsening relationships at school. "Why," asks Charles Wallace, plaintively—at the end of another school-day in which he has been subject to ridicule from his teacher as well his classmates—"do people always mistrust people who are different" (20)? This most recent incident has to do with his outspoken admission of interest in the microscopic world of mitochondrion and farandolae, an interest sparked by his parents's scientific research into a possible connection between events transpiring at both the sub-atomic level within individual human cells (Mrs. Murry's area of expertise) and at the cosmic, galactic level of outer space (Mr. Murry's specialization). "A human being is a whole world to a mitochondrion," explains Charles Wallace to his sister, "just the way our planet is to us" (23). He goes on to speculate that the minute farandolae live within mitochondria much as mitochondria live within each human cell and that if anything bad happens to the farandolae, the mitochondria get sick, as does its human host.

Meanwhile, their scientist father is consulting with the government on an inexplicable phenomenon in the distant galaxies of space whereby several stars have simply vanished emitting in the process a detectable sound characterized by the *Times* as "a cosmic scream" (37). Needless to say, Charles Wallace's interest in such matters more than qualifies him "different" in the eyes of his peers and mentors. When Meg, who is unusually close to her brilliant brother, had earlier in the day pleaded angrily with his elementary school principle, Mr. Jenkins, to intercede, an impassive and seemingly unsympathetic Mr. Jenkins dismisses her concerns as exaggerated and coldly berates her impertinence in advancing them (particularly as she has skipped school to do so). Against this backdrop of school-related tensions as well as domestic tensions related to uncertainties concerning the state of the world, Charles Wallace's contention that he has encountered a mythical creature in the family's vegetable garden merely adds to the recent strangeness of Meg's already uncertain world: "Like everything else," protests Meg as she contemplates the botanical disarray of the family garden by moonlight, "it's falling apart" 44.

At that moment Mr. Jenkins, or rather a *Doppelgänger* of Mr. Jenkins, appears inexplicably in the garden. His ostensible excuse for this sudden appearance is that he has come to offer an apology for his earlier behavior, but when Louise the Larger (a quasi-pet snake who is in reality a benign supernatural being) appears coiled to strike, this simulacrum of Mr. Jenkins rises into the air like a great flapping bird, leaving behind a nauseating stench as well as "a rent, an emptiness, a slash of nothingness" (46) suggestive of the cosmic tare in space with which Mr. Murray is currently preoccupied. In L'Engle's post-Einstein vision of reality, space and time are relative concepts. If any event is likely to act on every other in such a way that the providential pattern can be impacted locally at any point (in time or space), size and distance are illusory. In L'Engle's relativistic cosmos, the familiar charge that Christianity is anthropomorphistic is meaningless because the health of the cosmos is as likely to hinge on the fate of a small child (or a single-cell organism) as on that of a distant galaxy. To put it another way, if God is omnipresent, the center of the universe is every place at every time.

Following the startling disappearance of the false Mr. Jenkins, Charles Wallace, Meg, and Calvin O'Keefe (a schoolmate and Meg's future husband, who by this time has joined the two Murry children in the garden) are confronted by the even more startling appearance of two angelic creatures, Blajeny and Proginoskes. The latter proves to be the winged cherubim that Charles Wallace had understandably misperceived as a dragon. As unlike the chubby Hallmark angels as possible, Progenoskis conforms to certain Old Testament depictions of the angelic hosts in that he has multiple wings and eyes, an indistinct form, and (like a dragon) emits little spurts of flame and smoke. Though undoubtedly familiar to some modern readers, it might be helpful at this point to review the hierarchy of angelic beings postulated by the sixth-century theologian Dionysius the pseudo-Areopigate. In his *Celestial Hierarchy*, Dionysus distinguishes nine choirs, or ranks, of extraterrestrial intelligences. They are (from lowest to highest) seraphim, cherubim, thrones, dominions, virtues, powers, principalities, archangels, and angels (Adler 44). It follows from this traditional ranking that Progenoskes belongs to a comparatively less exalted choir while Blajeny belongs, in all likelihood, to one of the higher orders—a circumstance that, by extension, underscores the vocation of all educators as a "high calling" (66). In this, as in other matters pertaining to Christian theology, L'Engle demonstrates a knowledge that lends substance and mythic resonance to her narratives—

which no doubt accounts, in part at least, for their popularity among informed adults as well as younger readers.

The former of the two angels (Blajeny), a majestic creature with what is described as a "cello-like voice," announces his approach in the accepted biblical manner with the words, "Do not be afraid," i.e., fear not, and identifies himself as a "Teacher." Here the author (Madeleine the Angel) introduces a theme traceable theologically to the Church Fathers of second and third century Alexandria, Clement and Origin, who spoke of life as a school and God as a master pedagogue. Needless to say, the Jewish word *rabbi*, frequently applied to Christ, translates as "teacher." This conception of life's journey as an educational process is, of course the central metaphor of J. K. Rowling's Harry Potter saga as well. When asked by Calvin, "Where's your school," Blajeny replies, "Here, there, everywhere. In the schoolyard during the first-grade recess. With the cherubim and seraphim. Among the farandolae ...My school building is the entire cosmos" (63).

It would be difficult to conceive of a metaphor more calculated to impress upon young minds the importance of learning as a lifelong pursuit or to inculcate a clearer understanding of the larger context from which schooling (in the sense of a formal education) derives its legitimacy. With her former penchant for looking to an outside authority figure to solve her problems, Meg looks to Blajeny to take over and make everything all right with regard to her ailing brother. Instead, Blajeny shifts the weight for her brother's welfare from his/its shoulders onto hers and those of her new cosmic classmates, Calvin and the Progenoskes (though he hasn't any shoulders). At one point when Meg looks to the cherubim for guidance, he reminds her that as a being new to her planet it is *she* must tell *him* what to do next. "This is too much responsibility," protests Meg. "I'm still only a child! I didn't ask for any of this" (90). Though reluctant at first to join forces with such an immature earthling, Progenoskes (Progo, as he is affectionately known from this point on in the story) quickly recants; recognizing that if Blajeny wishes him to collaborate with Meg, he must have something to learn from this petulant adolescent. "A cherubim" Progo reflects, "is not a higher order than earthling, you know, just different" (62). Nevertheless, Meg's resentment at having been kicked out of the nest and expected to fly prematurely is entirely understandable. It is not only the young who experience life as "too much responsibility," though it is potentially helpful to be reminded of the unique anguish the young feel at the traumatic potential of a hard landing.

The Importance of Being Named

Blajeny next assigns three tasks or trials, a common fairy-tale motif appropriate to L'Engle's *Kunstmärchen*. First, Meg—confronted by three alternate versions of the school principal—must "name" the real Mr. Jenkins (who will play a decisive role in future developments). To "name," is a crucial concept in Madeleine L'Engle's thought-world. It means to affirm in the unique potential and worth of another. When Adam confers names upon God's creatures in Genesis, or God names the stars in the heavens, these acts are understood by L'Engle to legitimize and fix their value within the harmonious pattern of creation for all time (L'Engle *Walking on Water* 60). Meg and Calvin are "Namers" whose function is to "know who people are and what they are meant to be" (97). The second task has to do with entering the body of Charles Wallace at a cellular level in order to persuade a rebellious adolescent farandole named Sporos to "deepen," i.e., to mature by leaving the frenzied tarantella of his fellow adolescents and join in a more sedate but profoundly joyous cosmic dance appropriate to the "Music of the Spheres." This microscopic entity, though not a human child, represents a spirit of selfish irresponsibility that belongs to the literary tradition of James Barrie, whose Peter Pan is the archetypal narcissistic child. The "tune in, turn on, drop out" mentality of the Woodstock counter-culture of the 1960s is clearly mirrored by this character, whose unwillingness to "deepen" threatens the survival of Charles Wallace and, ultimately, the survival of the cosmos itself. The third and final task requires Meg to risk her own life in order to rescue Mr. Jenkins from the blandishments of the Ecthroi, i.e., those who are engaged in un-Naming, i.e., "making people not know who they are" (98). Essentially, the Echthroi (derived from a Greek word meaning "enemy") are a more sophisticated representation of the forces of negation ("IT") featured in *A Wrinkle in Time*. The outcome of these trials, if successfully performed, will be the restoration of Charles Wallace—and by extension the universe—to a condition of health and providential order.

It is in the final two trials that L'Engle sharpens her focus on the archetypically gothic theme of sacrificial love. As Progo explains to Meg, "Love...that's what makes a person know who they are" (99). In order to love, however, one must sometimes risk actions normally regarded as sinful, including murder and suicide. Here, L'Engle does not refer specifically to the ritualized murder of warfare—though "Echthroi are always about when there is war," states Progo, "They start all war" (97). Her outlook, when it comes to such issues, defies such easy categories as "pro-life" and "right to choose," as attested by her adult novel, *The Other Side of the Sun*. Through its pages, L"Engle chronicles the life of the Renier family in South Carolina during the heyday of the Klu Klux Klan. Greatly simplified, its plot concerns a brilliant Oxford educated African-American (Ronnie) and a young Englishwoman who has recently married into the Renier family. Stella (the Englishwoman) cultivates an innocent friendship with Ronnie, unmindful of the fact that in doing so she is defying the reconstructed South's crusade against racial equality and tolerance.

In consequence, the Riders (a provocatively recurrent motif in gothic literature) eventually demand that Aunt Olivia, who is sheltering Ronnie from the wrath of the Klansmen, yield him up to their evil designs. Stationed on her front porch—a shotgun ominously perched across her lap—the frail old woman refuses to comply. Ronnie, whose hiding place is inevitably discovered, is unceremoniously dragged out to face a hideous death. Before the Klan's established ritual of torture and humiliation can be implemented, however, Aunt Olivie pulls the trigger, aiming her gun directly at Ronnie's heart. She thereby thwarts the cruel intentions of his captors, but only by defying the laws of man and God. By obeying the dictates of her conscience, she not only ends Ronnie's life but inflicts painful damage on her own soul. Her intention, of course, is to spare a man she deeply respects spiritual as well as physical degradation. Redemption for this paradoxically loving murder, implies L'Engle, can only be intuitively glimpsed on "love's terrible other side"

Similarly, there are circumstances, suggests L'Engle in which suicide may be understood as a sanctified act of spiritual affirmation. Conditioned, as we all are, by Hamlet (to say nothing of orthodox Christianity) to regard suicide as either the act of one too cowardly and indecisive to face up to his or her obligations or else as a blasphemous usurpation of a divine prerogative, we are primed to regard the self-negation of suicide as reprehensible. Once again, L'Engle's imaginative narrative challenges this pat assessment, contending that a sentient soul is indestructible once "named" by the unfathomable love of God and that suicide, under certain circumstances, is preferable to the evil represented by beings such as IT and the Echthroi. In short, she suggests that self-destruction can, under certain circumstances, be justified.

As at the conclusion of *A Wrinkle in Time*, in *A Wind in the Door* Meg is once again called upon to sacrifice herself for another. This time it is her erstwhile nemesis, Mr. Jenkins who must be rescued. He has exposed himself to the danger of being X-ed by the Echthroi in his attempt to per-suade the rebellious farandole Sporos to "deepen." The Echthroi who play skillfully on Mr. Jenkin's long habit of self-loathing are close to persuading him to surrender his identity to the nothing. At the crucial moment, Meg overcomes her own sense of dread in order to save Mr. Jenkins, who had earlier saved her from a similar fate. Just as they (Calvin, Mr. Jenkin, Progo, and Meg herself) are on the point of being "X-ed," Meg finds it within herself to "name" the Echthroi—thereby passing the final test and saving Mr. Jenkins as well as Charles Wallace. On the heels of this ordeal, she suddenly finds herself standing at the bedside of her brother—whose condition is greatly improved—along with Calvin, Mr. Jenkins, and her parents (from whom she learns that the condition of the galaxy, formerly indicated by "cosmic screams" from space, has mysteriously improved as well). In order to escape the Ethroi, however, another sacrifice is required. When she enquires after the fate of Progo, she learns from Calvin that the loving and lovable Cherubim has made the ultimate sacrifice, i.e., he has "X-ed" himself on their behalf. "But where is he," demands Meg, to which Calvin replies, "As Pro might say he is Named. And so he's all right. The Echthroi did not get Progo, Meg. He X-ed of his own volition…Proginoskes is a Cherubim, Meg. It was his own choice" (209). Is Progo's decision to end his own life a sin or is it an expression of transcendent love? At the very conclusion of the story, a strong wind (often a symbol of the divine presence in biblical lore) inexplicably blows open the kitchen door. Could this be a cryptic sign from Progo attesting to his survival? That question, like the previous one, is left to hang ambiguously in the air as L'Engle's narrative draws to a close.

Apart from whatever ethical, moral, or doctrinaire objections one might have to such a conclusion, it is—on the face of it—remarkable that she has chosen to grapple with such painful and unsettling issues in a piece of literature for children. Addressing this issue head on in *Walking on Water* L'Engle explains that, "When I am grappling with ideas which are radical enough to up-set grown-ups, then I am likely to put these ideas into a story that will be marketed for children because children understand what their parents have rejected and forgotten. Because I am a struggling human being; trying to make sense out of the meaninglessness of much of life in this century…it is unlikely that I will ever want to write novels of pessimism or porno, no matter how realistic my work" (110). In defense of her methods, in other words, L'Engle invokes the definition of the gothic imagination which seeks to give expression to life's painful and darkly mysterious experiences by treating them as a potential source of insight and transcendence.

The moral vision of both Madeleine L'Engle and Antonia Barber is similar in that both writers are informed by their shared commitment to a Christian (though not an evangelical) perspective that does not shy away from ethically complex dilemmas. In many respects, though not all, that perspective and the gothic imagination are inseparable. Both focus on an archetypal hero who is typically unconventional, rebellious, isolated, burdened by a private or secret sorrow, gifted with access to alternate realities, and often deemed dangerous or simply demented by his less courageous and determined contemporaries. Both presuppose the existence of an alternate order (or orders) of reality, both see the humanity as existing in dialogue with a Mysterious Other (sometimes identified with "God" or with a "transcendent moral authority"), both attempt to make sense of human pain and suffering by placing them within an educative, i.e. redemptive, rather than a nihilistic, i.e., punitive, context, both regard memory plus imagination as the primary redemptive faculty, and both see a capacity for loving self-sacrifice as a power that is ultimately stronger than that of either fear or force.

In both stories, characters are called upon to remember a dismembered and broken world, i.e., to restore a lost providential order or pattern. Though both affirm the reality of free will, Barber's chronicle of redemption and human folly is portrayed as a natural consequence of pride, ambition, and selfishness. In effect, Barber interprets evil negatively— in the tradition of Plato and St. Augustine— as the absence of goodness, whereas in L'Engle biblically inspired fantasy, the demonic is a positive force that actively works to promote violence, cynicism, and denial. Both are narratives of personal transformation with Blunden's long purgatory of remorse and self-recrimination leading to regeneration and Meg Murry's ordeal leading to a process of "deepening" not unlike that of the farandole, Sporos (L'Engles commentary on the narcissistic children, personified by Peter Pan, who refuse the demands of adulthood to the detriment of themselves and others). In noting these parallels, one is reminded that the historical origins of the term "gothic," are inextricably linked to an ecclesiastical style in architecture. That style encoded a set of core values in stone and mortar that would in time—with the emergence of the nineteenth-century cult of childhood—come to be identified with children as secular symbols of spiritual attributes essential to any civilized society. One of those spiritual attributes is the wisdom to understand, as Dumbledore tells Harry in *The Deathly Hallows*, "There are far, far worse things in the living world than dying" (721).

5 Rendering Unto Caesar: *The Sword of the Spirits* Trilogy

English author Samuel Youd (a.k.a. John Christopher, Jonathan Christopher, Stanley Winchester, Hilary Ford, William Godfrey, Peter Graaf, Peter Nichols, and Anthony Rye, all literary pseudonyms) is perhaps best known for his *Tripod Trilogy* and its prequel (*The Coming of the Tripods*). The latter is a quartet of adolescent science fiction that recounts the subjugation of earth to a technologically advanced race of aliens who bestride the planet in walking machines reminiscent of those featured in H. G. Wells' *The War of the Worlds*. Like the *Tripod Trilogy*, *The Sword of the Spirits* is a continuous science fiction narrative spread over three volumes. It tracks the political rise and fall of Luke Perry, son of a commoner who attains to the rank of nobleman, though at an inordinate cost to himself and others. John Christopher, the literary alias under which this trilogy is published, excels in portraying the inner life of his characters, i.e., their complex triumphs and tribulations, as well as the interior and interpersonal conflicts to which such complexities inevitably give rise. In this regard, his political gothic science fiction for younger readers illustrates the psychological gothic genre at its best. As with all first-rate gothic literature, however, the principal genres of the gothic imagination (supernatural and political as well as psychological) are merged into a compelling synthesis.

Like the other cult-of-childhood stories discussed in this volume, the *Sword of the Spirits* trilogy is a meditation on the transvaluation of all values relating to "common-sense" understandings of power. It lays bare the cost of worldly power and explicitly champions its alternative, referred to aptly by Canon C. K. Robertson as "the violence of love." In the kingdom of childhood, as in that of heaven, suggests the gothic imagination in children's literature, those who are first shall come last and our spiritual fate will be ultimately determined by how lovingly we treat the littlest and least among us. Considering the scope of modern, violence, political and otherwise (Gerald L. Schroeder, an MIT trained physicist, estimates that eighty million humans were murdered by their fellow human beings during the twentieth century), it should come as no surprise to discover a decidedly pacifist vein in modern cult-of-childhood novels, particularly when the unintentional (though no less cruel) slaughter of children is a routine occurrence in modern warfare. The commonly accepted military parlance for such high-tech slaughter—engaged in equally by democracies and dictatorships—is "collateral damage." The secular adjective frequently used in conjunction with this euphemism is "Orwellian." I would prefer a religious alternative…"Satanic," which, to my way of thinking, conveys the evil as well as the sophistry of such language.

The first volume of Christopher's trilogy gives us the background of Master Luke Perry, a commoner from the walled city of Winchester who aspires to membership in the elite warrior caste within his rigidly hierarchical society—a society consisting of a militant aristocracy supported and informed by a religious establishment known as the Seers. This militant ruling class is served by "polymufs," a caste of menials dwarfed and deformed since the days of the Great Disaster. The lowest run of the social ladder is occupied by Christians, a small and marginalized group of pacifists, politically disenfranchised and widely viewed within their combative culture as an eccentric cult of cowards.

The story of Luke's rise to the very pinnacle of power and the personal price he pays is a convoluted tale of blind ambition, treachery, and deception. It entails reversal into the opposite (enantiodromia) whereby a courageous and well-intentioned youth gradually transforms into a brutal conquistador willing to embrace any means to advance a political agenda that is not even his own. As the story unfolds, the Seers, who ostensibly serve as mediums for the transmission of messages from the spirit world, prove to be a conspiracy of scientists (remnants of the technologically sophisticated society that was destroyed by the Great Disaster). Their covert mission is to restore the old order by manipulating a post-apocalyptic culture modeled on medieval feudalism. Seizing upon Luke as their vehicle, the Seers orchestrate his political ascent in accordance with their own hidden agenda on behalf of science and technology.

As in Rowling's novels, though without the supernatural gothic trappings that figure so prominently in her work, the primary narrative belongs to the political gothic genre with its overarching themes of abusive power, hidden history, and conspiracy. The tragedy of Prince Luke (like that of Tom Riddle, Severus Snape, Arcturus Black, and Albus Dumbledore) is essentially a subversive narrative whereby the individuals we are led to perceive in black-and-white terms as "good" or "bad" are eventually exposed as complex, many-facetted characters seduced and ultimately blasted by over-reaching ambition, even Lord Voldemort's background and final fate elicit a certain degree of pity. By the end of Rowling's saga, the Dark Lord is reduced to the abject status of an abandoned infant beyond the ability to inspire love or attract attention. Like a combination of Snape and Voldemort, Prince Luke ends up alone, disillusioned, and bereft of hope with distempered dreams and memories as his sole companions. Unlike Riddle, however, Luke Perry stops short of committing the crime that would have destroyed his soul utterly.

The process of corruption experienced by Luke entails a series of tragic, personal losses. His unprecedented elevation over the others in line of succession to the throne (occupied by Prince Stephan who has disappointed the Seers by resisting the blandishments of war for five long years) sets in motion a chain of tragic consequences resulting in a failed arson plot hatched by the ambitious mother of the heir apparent, a foiled plot that results in capital punishment, a practice that is opposed only by the Christians who, deprived of worldly power themselves, have reverted to the non-violent resistance against the encroachments of a coercive state that had marked the earliest Christian stance toward the *Pax Romana* of imperial Rome. As Luke comments, "The only trouble came from Christians. They opposed the taking of life, even in battle or the execution of murderers, and always made a nuisance of themselves on such occasions...The Christians, it was well known, were all mad, and no one took them seriously" (Christopher *The Prince in Waiting* 109). The ancient Roman imperium was a system of nominally secular government premised on the theocratic notion of a leader (or Caesar) who enjoyed the status of demi-god, i.e., a human conduit of divine revelation. As in Christopher's post-apocalyptic city-state of Winchester the will of the leader was conflated with that of divine providence in such a way as to suggest that public policy is the outcome of divine guidance. Ironically, in the case of Winchester, the invisible hand dictating policy proves to be that of a secular conspiracy, one that conceals its cloak-and-dagger methods and purposes behind a pious façade of spiritualism.

In the Potter saga, though there is no comparable religious conspiracy, there is nevertheless a Ministry conspiracy to hide the reality of Voldemort's return from the wizarding public. Its effect is to render the Ministry more susceptible to manipulation and infiltration, to engender a matrix of officially sanctioned opinion and denial on the part of a public only too willing to be reassured by its complicit news media, and to create an intellectual climate in which contrived political theater, e.g., the Wizengemot trial of Harry in the *Order of the Phoenix*, replaces legitimate discourse with empty partisan disputes designed to deflect public attention from the true sources of unrest and danger within the wizarding world. Once again, some might see in this conspiratorial formula (which includes a carefully orchestrated campaign to discredit anyone who skirts too near the truth) a distant mirror of the current political dilemma of Muggledom.

As Luke falls prey to intrigues hatched by rival families within Winchester, enemies in surrounding city-states, and the Seers (who inveigle him with the promise that he will inherit the invincible Sword of the Spirits provided he pledges unquestioning obedience), he is led ever deeper into an ethical maze, like that of the Tri-Wizard Tournament, in which his own identity is imperiled. The invincible sword motif, which derives from Arthurian legend, figures prominently in Rowling as well. Not only does the Sword of Gryffindor play a significant role in Harry's fortunes, but the Wand of Destiny (a slight variation on the theme of invincible power) leads to Vodemort's downfall. Though the Seers ultimately make good their promise, Luke's path to the throne of Winchester proves to be both arduous and circuitous.

The likelihood that the High Seers will ever fulfill their end of the bargain seems remote in as much as Luke's enemies have seemingly prevailed, exiling him to the so-called "Burning Lands," a desert wilderness long since blighted by the Great Disaster that is said to be inhabited by mutant monsters known as "polybeasts." This Wilderness Journey, reminiscent of Harry's forays into the Forbidden Forest as well as his period of wandering in search of horcruxes following Dumbledore's death, is a mythic symbol of the gothic hero's (or anti-hero's) "dark night of the soul," an inevitable brush with despair at a time when his or her prospects are at their lowest ebb. Banishment to the Burning Lands is as good as a sentence of death, and indeed, Luke is at the point of death when he is recued by the Seers, who still have need of him to fulfill their master plan. Let in on the true nature of the Seers' conspiracy, Luke is told that his status as the Chosen One will entail a life of deception. "I will serve your ends as far as I can," replies Luke, "but my honor comes first," thus drawing an ethical line in the sand that will lead him (as followers of Dumbledore are led in Rowling's story) to a crucial moment of choice between what is right and what is expedient or easy.

Prior to his banishment, Luke had been compelled to serve Prince Peter, his half-brother. At the time of Peter's assumption of the throne, Luke had been enjoined by a public pledge that, if fulfilled, would secure the throne to Peter's offspring and forever bar his own path to power. Such an outcome would, of course, undermine the plans of the Seers who consequently arrange for Peter's gentle Christian wife, Alice, to be killed. As predicted, this covert murder plunges Peter into a depression from which he is unable to recover personally or politically. In fact, the bereaved prince comes increasingly under the influence of a Christian priest who, like his wife, abhors war and leads Peter inexorably toward the realization that he (Prince Peter) is confronted by an inescapable dilemma. Should he continue to reign over a system premised on waging war or should he embrace his deceased wife's faith and resign his office accordingly.

This dilemma is, in a sense, one that is as old as Christianity itself. Since the time of Constantine, the first Caesar to embrace Christianity as the official state religion of Rome, the church has renounced its original commitment to pacifism, pursuing instead an uneasy but expedient arrangement with secular power. The documented practice of the earliest Christians was to reject military service as contrary to their commitment to one true Lord. By extension, some would argue, any system of social organization that rests its authority on its war powers will necessarily pose a fundamental dilemma for any authentic Christian (one is reminded of the exchange between New Orleans District Attorney Jim Garrison and the mysterious Mr. X in Oliver Stone's film *JFK* in which the latter claims that the organizing principle of *any society* [emphasis mine] is for war).

Citing the essential ethical options offered by human history, peace through military might or peace through justice, i.e., the non-coercive power of love, one prominent theologian writes, "The Christian Bible forces us to witness the struggle of these two transcendental visions *within its own pages* and to ask ourselves as Christians how we decide between them. My answer is that *we are bound to whichever of these two visions was incarnated by and in the historical Jesus.* It is not the violent, but the nonviolent God who is revealed to Christian faith in Jesus of Nazereth" (Crossan *God & Empire* 94–95). Clearly, Crossan sees these options as being mutually exclusive. If Mr. X, J. K. Rowling, and John Christopher are correct, it follows that the pacifist vision of the Kingdom of God preached by Jesus represents a radical trans-valuation of all political values, one that does indeed threaten to unravel the very fabric of the social contract as it has existed since the demise of Christendom (which promoted, however hypocritically, a theoretical restraint on the Death-Eater precept that "Magic [i.e., coercive power] Is Might." So radical a notion not only flies in the face of common sense, but in the guise of gothic literature for children, it flies under the radar of media scrutiny. Therein lies the subversive potential of cult-of-childhood literature.

Like Lord Voldemort, proponents of the Muggle war system don't bother to understand that which they regard as beneath their notice, including the radical call to non-violence embedded in much of the twentieth-century's most beloved story-telling for adolescent and pre-adolescent readers.

The Wages of Sin

After struggling to make their way back to Winchester, where they expect a hero's welcome, Luke finds himself instead placed under arrest and tossed unceremoniously into prison. As he subsequently discovers, the charge is complicity in a plot hatched by the Seer, Ezzard, to murder his half-brother's pregnant wife, Princess Ann. Believing at first that his brother has simply gone mad, he hotly repudiates this charge, justly claiming that he knows nothing of any conspiracy against the throne. When he learns the exact nature of the plot, however, he realizes that his brother's suspicions, though unfounded, are incriminatingly plausible. It seems that Ezzard, fearing that the offspring of Peter and Ann would permanently thwart the High Seer's plan by forestalling the coronation of the Prince in Waiting, decided to take matters into his own hands by devising a means of electrocuting Ann as she bathed. When his scheme was discovered, Peter's nascent Christian faith in the existence of a caring God is shattered. Sentencing Luke to a traitor's death by fire, the only opposition faced by the traumatized Prince comes, predictably, from the non-violent Christian community.

On the day the execution is to be carried out, their attempts to plead with Peter for Luke's life are blocked by an angry mob. Luke, still proclaiming his innocence, pronounces his half-brother a coward and angrily challenges him to personal combat, taunting him with recollections of how the former prince Stephen, unlike the "usurper," Prince Peter, had exhibited the courage to honor such a challenge. Inflamed by this taunt, his physically superior brother accedes to Luke's proposition. Using the machine-made sword that Edmund (his only friend in the crowd) manages to slip him during the combat, Luke, on the point of prevailing, makes a last, desperate attempt to reason with his crazed sibling, offering to take himself and his friends into exile. Spurning the offer, Peter, maddened by grief, and disillusionment, throws himself upon Luke's technologically superior Sword of the Spirits. Thus the prophecy of the Seers is realized as the prince in waiting is elevated to that status by popular acclamation. In his first official act, Luke sentences the Seer of Winchester, Ezzard to death for his treachery. Lanark, one of the

High Seers, arranges an audience with Luke during which he explains that his Spiritualist Order knew nothing of Ezzard's criminal intentions: "We want a better world than this, Luke," says Lanark. "Science and human knowledge are not ends in themselves. We use tricks and maneuvers, but we do not murder the innocent" (214). As volume two of Christopher's trilogy concludes, the world-weary Luke is left to ponder the devastation wrought to his own life by the Machiavellian "tricks and maneuvers" of the Seers.

Luke the Bayomet Slayer

The final stage in Luke Perry's essentially negative gothic journey begins with an expedition across the Bosch-like terrain of the Burning Lands with the apathetic Prince Peter to Klan Gothen, a "Wilch" settlement strikingly different from Winchester in its customs, social organization, and political priorities. In this comparatively hedonistic culture, bright apparel, an appreciation of the fine arts, and a taste for luxury are the order of the day. Hunting is viewed as a sport to be conducted with the aid of machines, the Royal Perfumer is a respected and influential public official, men and women fraternize on terms of equality, polybeast is accepted fare, and dwarfs (along with other outcasts in Winchester society such as polymufs) mingle freely with one another as well as with royalty. Based on commerce, Klan Gothlen seems to be a portrait of a liberal, pluralistic democracy of sorts (though ruled by an affluent elite) reminiscent of modern America.

Luke, who finds this diverse culture strange as well as offensive, is nevertheless strongly attracted to King Cymru's beautiful and accomplished daughter, Blodwen. A free spirit, Princess Blodwen challenges all of Luke's presumptions and prejudices concerning relations between the sexes and the militaristic values of Winchester and its neighboring city-states. On a recreational hunting expedition, Luke manages to slay a grotesque and fearsome polybeast known as a Bayomet (no doubt a corruption of the biblical Behemoth). Though severely wounded, Luke returns to Klan Gothlen a hero. In recognition of his achievement, King Cymru publicly announces the betrothal of Luke to the princess. Unfortunately, Blodwen's heart is already committed elsewhere. This complication is exacerbated by the fact that Luke's rival happens to be Edmund, an erstwhile political opponent who has become one of his best, most trusted friends from Winchester.

Not unlike the estrangement between Ron and Harry that is precipitated by Ron's unwarranted jealousy, Luke's brother-like love for Edmund turns to hatred when Blodwen confirms his all-too warranted suspicions by eloping in defiance of both her finance and her father.

Can Unjust Means Ever Produce Just Ends?

Luke's introspective mood is quickly dispersed by the demands of his office as *The Sword of the Spirits* (the final volume of Youd/Christopher's trilogy) gets underway. Michael, Prince of Petersfield (the city annexed to Winchester by Luke's father in defiance of historical precedent) has murdered an emissary sent by the new prince, thereby declaring his intention to rebel against the rule of Winchester. Luke, intent upon establishing a reputation as a strong leader, mounts a new campaign, against the wishes of the Seers who caution patience. Meanwhile, Luke honors his pledge to the dwarf Hans by conferring upon him the rank of warrior, an innovation resented in some quarters as a dangerous break with tradition. In an even more controversial decision, Luke orders his men to lure Prince Michael's army from its impregnable stronghold by setting fire to the wheat fields outside of Petersfield (thereby destroying its population's winter food supply). Edmund, shocked at Luke's disdain for time honored rules of engagement, protests against so dishonorable a tactic; but Luke proudly defends his decision reflecting that one is justified in breaking rules if by doing so they can ensure victory. Noting Luke's new-found dedication to the principle that the ends justify the means, Christopher comments laconically, "And ruthlessness followed on from ruthlessness" (22).

At this point, Luke's other friend and confidant from his boyhood, the acolyte Martin, who has become an aspirant to the priestly caste of Seers, re-enters the narrative. Appraising Luke of the fact that the Christians seek to erect a new cathedral on the alleged site of the old one dating from Winchester's pre-Disaster days—a prospect that he contemplates with bemused tolerance as a tacit acknowledgment of Winchester's political importance and preeminence. When Luke objects that in choosing a seat of power and riches on which to build, they are contradicting their supposed commitment to austerity, Martin replies, "They would probably say power and riches are good when they are means to an end: to guide men's minds to what they think is truth." Luke replies that, "It is a vastly different truth from the one you seek. They have no interest in Science" (38). Moreover, warns Luke, their religion appeals to polymufs, whom they treat as equals. Martin confidently brushes aside his concern, saying that irrational beliefs will never appeal to any but the irrational, an opinion that, in retrospect, proves to be ironic.

Like Rowling and L'Engle, Christopher struggles to envision a synergy between the legitimate claims of expediency as those of idealism. "Slavery is evil," says one of L'Engle's characters, "but so is war." The Dumbledore-Harry contingent, while they seldom express ethical qualms about using violence on the violent, nevertheless champion force only as a last resort, in distinction from the Grindlewald/Voldemort contingent who embrace it ruthlessly. For Death-Eaters, such as Bellatrix, inflicting pain is pleasurable. Where Christopher differs from both L'Engle and Rowling is in his willingness to make allowance for the possibility that the only way to short-circuit violence and the war-system that supports it is through a radical commitment to uncompromising pacifism of the sort endorsed by a remnant of authentic Christianity.

Prior to eloping with Edmund, Blodwen pays a visit to Winchester where she makes the acquaintance of the Christian Bishop of Winchester. The ensuing exchange of views proves illuminating as well as consequential. The Bishop, an imposing man of considerable stature, imparts something of the forgotten history of Winchester as a once important center of Christendom. At Blodwen's prompting, he relates the essentials of his faith—without evangelical fervor—weaving them into compelling and convincing narrative that downplays the miraculous. When Martin, Luke's friend and prospective Seer, angrily denounces this redacted version of Christianity declaring that "Truth does not surround itself with lies," the Bishop counters, calmly and not without a tinge of humor, by asking if the deceptions practiced by the Seers in their Séance Halls is quite consistent with Martin's idealistic defense of the unvarnished truth (57).

Noting that truth can be ugly, a proposition that Martin hotly denies, the Bishop asks whether it would not be preferable to withhold the full truth under the circumstances. To do otherwise, he suggests, would be cruel, and where there is cruelty, maintains the Bishop, there can be no beauty. In direct contradiction to the prospective Seer's implicit faith in knowledge (technological and scientific) as the key to rehabilitating civilization, the Bishop proposes an alternative perspective: The machines that had rendered men capable of "killing a thousand men a thousand miles away," had blunted the ethical implications of their murderous deeds. "What men do matters more than what men know" (58). As to the outcome of this debate, Martin later confesses to Luke that he has decided to remove himself from the sham magic of the Séance Hall by removing himself to the underground Sanctuary of the High Seers. When his incredulous friend and sovereign expostulates against this decision, stating that no healthy-minded young adult could tolerate such deprivation, Martin replies, "I cannot stay here. I cannot go on with the trickery and deception and lies in the Séance Hall. The end may be good but I cannot tolerate these means" (63). In short, just as Luke is on a gothic journey that will lead him potentially to a tyrant's fate, Martin's decision to repudiate unjust means will lead inexorably to a quite different but equally unanticipated outcome.

Camelot Redux

As Blodwen's visit unfolds, so does the flowering of her illicit relationship with Edmund. Struggling to contain his awareness of the truth behind a wall of denial, Luke confronts Blodwen and Edmund separately, confessing his suspicions and enjoining them to obedience. When they each refuse to surrender their love for one another unconditionally, he places them both under arrest, threatening to send Edmund into exile. This is Luke's decisive and irreversible moment of *enantiodromia*. Knowing full well that this course of action represents an abuse of his power he nevertheless persists: "By fighting," Luke admits to himself, "I must lose everything in the world that is worth having, and gain nothing. But I could not go back" (98).

In short, Luke (like Scrooge, Mr. Blunden, Mr. Jenkins, Lord Voldemort) is complicit in his own self-destruction and that of everyone and everything they most cherish. He is led over the brink of temptation into a spiritual abyss not by unavoidable circumstances but by his own unreasoning pride and habitual failure of imagination. While some, like Dumbledore, stop shy of the abyss, Luke rushes headlong toward his own undoing. Dante's universal law of *contrapasso*, according to which the punishment is an inseparable concomitant of the crime, he is afforded ample opportunity to repentent, but like Tom Riddle who declines Harry's eleventh hour reprieve, Prince Luke shuns remorse and declines the counsel of a wiser man. The Christian Bishop pays Luke a visit hoping to dissuade him from his reckless course of action. Warning Luke that he is acting from a pride that could destroy him, the Bishop says, "She has done you no wrong...And if you wrong her, you will wrong yourself far more" (101). Predictably, the Bishop's well-intentioned words fall upon deaf ears.

Under the influence of ungovernable jealousy, a misguided sense of honor, and an even more misguided sense of his political destiny, Luke reflects that if Blodwen and Edmund are unfaithful, justice no longer matters: "If they were not honest the whole world was a stinking ruin, broken and slimed like the village which the Bayemot overran. And I had killed the Bayemot" (83). Lacking the essential humility to accept responsibility for the circumstance in which he finds himself, Luke, by lashing out at his two friends, is in reality lashing out against a projection of his own pride and folly. Predictably, the monster he slays this time (like Dorian Gray stabbing at his own corrupted image in Oscar Wilde's *The Picture of Dorian Gray*) is the Beast Within himself. In this episode, Christopher depicts the psychological dangers of denial and selective memory. Cut off, i.e., dismembered, at the crucial moment from his own experience and former scruples, Luke is unable to summon them precisely when they are most needed.

From this point on, the narrative pace quickens, leading Luke to a belated realization that in pursuing victory to its bitter end, he can only contribute to his own defeat. Before this devastating moment of self-reckoning, however, he experiences a seemingly fatal reversal of fortune: Luke's throne is usurped by two long-standing rivals. The deposed prince convinces the conspiracy of scientists known as the High Seers, to arm him (in defiance of Winchester's most cherished traditions) with the automatic rifles that they call "Sten guns." With these, he intends to recruit an army from Klan Gothlen, mount an attack on his own city, and rout the usurpers.

En route to the realm of King Cymru, Luke is beset by a pack of mutant hounds endowed with "signs of more intelligence than a beast should have" (145). These cunning creatures are soon able to gauge the range of the Sten guns and mount a patient campaign to pick off their prey one by one. Just when they are about to succeed, help arrives in the form of a tribe of peaceful primitives known as the People of the Bells, so named on account of their passion for the silvery ornaments that adorn their clothing. This egalitarian tribe, which has long since learned to live in peace, is a Utopian community, fundamentally immune to the ravages of disease, hunger, greed, and envy. While there, Luke experiences a happiness and contentment that almost cures his lust for power and revenge (which the tribe views as a disease). Though tempted, Luke declines an offer of permanent sanctuary among the People of the Bells. Sending him on his way, a spokesman for the tribe leaves Luke with these prophetic words, again reminiscent of Harry's final appeal to the Dark Lord, "Go in what peace you can know. Maybe in the end you will heal yourself; but you will suffer for it" (158).

Upon arriving in Klan Gothlen, Luke tells his story to Cymru, who is outraged by his daughter's disobedience. Pledging his support, the King (reminiscent of King Lear in Shakespeare's tragedy) renounces Blodwen saying that, "In our country, when a man makes an enemy it is forever" (162). Commenting on the latent steak of sadism exhibited by his new ally, Luke observes, "I think he would have watched her die with a smile on his lips," an observation that exposes the brutality at the heart of Klan Gothlen's ostensibly liberal civilization. For all its sophistication and apparent superiority to the feudal order of Winchester, suggests Christopher, Klan Gothlen is a barbarian civilization (just as our own unacknowledged greed and barbarism are shielded by a self-congratulatory veneer of economic and political freedom). Faced with the grim prospect of a protracted war of attrition, Luke wavers until one of the High Seers offers a solution to his dilemma. In exchange for a promise to promote the restoration of science and technology, the Seer promises another new weapon (a mortar) guaranteed to bring down the city walls, though at a considerable cost in terms of human life. Agreeing to this Faustian bargain, Luke promises to restore science to its former prestige.

The mortar is delivered accordingly, and though success is not immediate, the Seer estimates that the city will fall by noon of the following day. That night, Luke receives another unexpected visitor, Martin the Acolyte who, to Luke's astonishment, comes to him not on behalf of the Seers but as a spokesman for the Winchester Christians. When asked about his earlier intention of joining the High Seers at their primary Sanctuary near the ruins of the ancient southern City of London, Martin says that after undertaking this arduous pilgrimage, he had unexpectedly discovered the truth he was seeking where he had least expected to find it, namely in the creeds and practices of the despised Christian cult. Luke refuses to budge on his conditions of surrender, and taunts his former comrade with the following sarcastic question, "Will your stable-god who worked such miracles work one here?" "It may be," answers Martin, "through the weak bodies of his servants" (204).

Bringing to the mind the words of the Christian Bishop ("Machines put a distance between men"), Martin reflects that Luke is not a cruel man, merely blind. When the time arrives, a human bulwark comprised of the freedom-loving citizens of Winchester (Christians, polymufs, and dwarfs along with the rest) line the V-shaped opening blasted into the city walls by yesterday's bombardment singing Christian hymns. "Give the order to fire whenever you choose," shouts Martin. "But this time you will not be blind. This time you will see what it is you do" (206). His latent conscience finally aroused, Prince Luke of the Three Cities relents. That night, he dreams of younger and happier days in the company of Edmund and Martin. The scene shifts as the radiant Blodwen stands at his bedside following his struggle with the Bayomet. In his dream, he is finally able to say to Blodwen the simple words that in real life he could not bring himself to utter, words that might have changed everything.

Luke awakens to find his pillow drenched with tears. Upon returning to Klan Gothlen, where he has been picked to succeed Cymru, he lives to witness the reinvention of motor cars, railroads, and flying machines. Softened by time and personal disappointment, i.e., more tolerant of human differences, he even comes to respect the once despised Klan Gothlen Bishop. The pacifism of the Winchester Christians, however, he cannot embrace. Confidently anticipating future military campaigns against the southern cities, he reflects, "We shall conquer them because we represent the strength of the future, and they the past which must always bow to it…But I shall have no son" (212). With this sorrowful reflection on the futility of power, Christopher concludes his three volume saga of a neo-feudal world that resembles our present and might yet become our future.

Is the New World Order the Old World Order?

It was in the same decade in which John Christopher published *The Sword of the Spirits* trilogy that historian Barbara Tuchman penned *A Distant Mirror*, highly regarded her cultural and political history of fourteenth-century Europe. In providing this magisterial survey, she sought to underscore certain parallels between the late Middle Ages in Europe and the modern world during the Cold War era. I suspect that prior to the 1960s, such parallels would have made little sense to most of its American readership. Until that watershed decade, America was typically portrayed as a bastion of freedom whose citizens regarded themselves as proud custodians of an unbroken tradition extending from the signing of the *Magna Carta* to the *Declaration of Independence*. The Middle Ages, on the other hand, were widely portrayed as a period of incessant warfare and political savagery—the very antithesis of a representative democracy.

In light of the political horrors of the twentieth century, that portrayal seems decidedly naïve in retrospect. It was only in the 1960s—primarily as a result of serial political assassinations, an interminable and unjust war in Southeast Asia, and the overt corruption of the Watergate scandals—that many ordinary Americans began to notice a growing discrepancy between an American Dream that envisioned a peaceful, open, and law-abiding society promoted by representative leaders from Jefferson to Kennedy and an alternative vision—promoted by post-war conservatism—of a country sometimes referred to as "Fortress America." How was the baby-boomer generation to respond? Was modern America a mirror image of the feudal, post-democratic world order described by Tuchman? Finally, and perhaps most importantly, what did this transformation imply with regard to the civic and ethical obligations of the average citizen? These were the still unad-dressed questions that preoccupied that increasingly disillusioned genera-tion—a generation that took to the streets with confidence, courage, and, above all, an authentic patriotism informed by the tenets of Anglo-American liberalism. As popular wisdom correctly observes, however, it is the winning side that writes history. The winning side since 1963 has been the side bent on victory at any cost. The peace-loving, childlike spirit of the "flower children" was no match for those Bob Dylan identified as the "Masters of War." It was nevertheless closer to both the Holy Spirit and the Spirit of 1776 than the recurrent, widely publicized images of strung-out hippies and flag-burning rabble-rousers would have us believe. The "greatest generation" may well have saved us from the enemy at the gate, but it was the much vilified counter-culture of the 1960s that sounded the alarm (or tried to at least) when that same enemy entered by a back door.

As we embark upon what promises to be another interminable war (this time the enemy is "terror"), how are subsequent generations to distinguish between the legitimate and illegitimate use of power? Do new threats necessarily render old democratic values obsolete? Do old biblical values still apply to new political and social realities? If so, which ones and in what way? Is our late-twentieth century transformation into an imperial super-state, (comparable in many respects to the ancient Roman Empire) irreversi-ble, or is there a viable alternative to the post-Kennedy era *Pax Americana* advocated (or at least tolerated) by so many on both the Right and the Left? Christopher's *Sword of the Spirits*, which raises many of these questions implicitly, provides some intriguing answers. It is for this very reason that I have discussed its plot in some detail. This cult-of-childhood trilogy, though no longer readily obtainable, is more pertinent today than when it was first published.

Like our own world, the militarized society envisioned by Christopher, is a civilization that stands on the threshold of significant change. Whereas the modern world might be described as a *de facto* anarchy of nation states none of which is sovereign over all, the political *status quo* inherited by Robert and Luke Perry is a similar anarchy of small, independent city-states. Can such a patchwork quilt be unified under a central authority without loss of basic human rights and freedoms? Should it be, and if so, is Luke right in his conclusion that superior force is the only glue that can unite and regulate the new world order envisioned by the Seers? The resources of this unstable social structure, human and material, are organized around the principle of perpetual warfare and competition for limited food and energy sources. Its leaders are a class of warrior-statesmen whose authority is ratified by a priesthood of technocrats whose influence, supposedly conferred by supernatural forces known as the Eternals, rests in reality upon a secret knowledge of science and history.

In effect, the Hobbesian/Darwinian world inhabited by Luke Perry is, to a considerable degree, governed from behind the scenes by a cabal that withholds its true nature and social agenda from everyone, including the warrior-statesmen. The High Seers comprise a covert power-elite, an invisible government bent on the restoration of science and technology. One of the most powerful tools used by this conspiracy is its knowledge of the hidden history of the great Disaster. According to the consensus history promoted for their own purposes by the High Seers, this Disaster was caused by the now forbidden machines. The Seers, however, know that in reality it was triggered by purely natural causes—an ironic twist of fate considering the pervasive fear of nuclear holocaust during the Cold War era. They also secretly seek to promote the very evils they decry.

The hidden political agenda of the High Seers calls for the unification of the city-states under a sovereign authority favorable to the reintroduction of scientific and technological knowledge. Luke has been chosen to accomplish this goal by establishing an imperial hegemony over his neighbors—a strategy not unlike that recommended by a neo-conservative think-tank in the now infamous document entitled Rebuilding America's Defenses prepared by *Project for the New American Century* (see Griffin *The New Pearl*

Harbor xvi). In doing so, he is led step by step to abandon the chivalrous traditions of limited and just warfare (thereby waging total war in which civilian populations and their food supply are targeted, and the use of mechanized weapons confers an unfair advantage). As time-honored codes of combat are sacrificed to the demands of political and military expediency, Luke gradually transforms into a cruel tyrant, a political monster who places his own insatiable lust for power ahead of the welfare of his subjects, the rule of law, and the transcendental moral authority to which princes and subjects alike are ultimately held accountable. Whenever this happens, according to the political gothic imagination, the result is an asymmetrical power arrangement in which the interests of one party are advanced at the expense of every other. It was precisely to forestall such an outcome that the system of checks and balances advocated by Anglo-American liberalism was originally advocated.

Christopher's political gothic parable would seem to suggest that imperial means, even those motivated by ostensibly democratic ends, i.e., the restoration of lost knowledge or the spread of democracy, undermine and ultimately subvert their own rationale. Long before Luke has succeeded in laying the political foundations for the scientific renaissance desired by the High Seers, he has lost the moral authority to implement it. As a British citizen aware of the consequences of British imperialism in the nineteenth and early twentieth centuries, Christopher was perhaps able to assess the budding imperial aspirations of modern America with a degree of objectivity that many of her own citizens seemed to lack (and still do). Luke's negative journey follows the prescribed pattern from trauma (the Disaster and his own unanticipated rise to political preeminence) to denial (the failure to recognize his own overweening pride) to projection (of sinister or unworthy motives unto all those who would defy or attempt to deflect him from his self-destructive course) and finally to the *enantiodromia* (reversal into the opposite) of his willingness to contemplate the mechanized murder of his former subjects.

Perhaps the most controversial and intriguing question raised by Christopher's political gothic parable has to do with the question of whether or not there is any alternative to the seemingly unbreakable cycle of coercive power wielded by the modern state. Christopher's answer is ambiguous. On the one hand, he anticipates the eventual success of Luke's imperial ambitions. On the other, he posits the tactics and philosophy of a politically marginalized sect of Christians as an effective check on Luke's power. Throughout history there have been Christians, from Tolstoy to John Dominic Crossan, who have interpreted the central teachings of Christ as a non-violent alternative to the reigning *Pax Romana* of the time in which he lived (as well as its long and illustrious history since his death). For centuries the biblical injunctions to "obey the authorities" and "render unto Caesar" have been cited to condone Christian participation in war and the Church's endorsement of a political system based on violence. Indeed, a great many prominent Christians from Augustine to C. S. Lewis have accepted, without apparent qualm, dual citizenship in the City of Man and The City of God. Periodically, however (as during the rise of Hitlerism in Germany) the Church—a portion of it at least—is obligated to choose between the earthly Kingdom of Caesar and the eternal Kingdom of God.

Clearly the Christian community of Winchester in Christopher's trilogy has reached such an impasse. Unable to prevail against either the sham religion of the High Seers or the militant secular culture with which it is allied, it embraces a pacifist alternative regarded as irrational by both factions. The problem with Luke's proposed *Pax Winchester* (as with its historical counterparts in ancient Rome and modern America) is well-expressed by a Caledonian Chieftain quoted in David Ray Griffin in *Christian Faith and the Truth Behind 9/11*, "The Romans rob, butcher, plunder and call it 'empire'; and where they make desolation they call it 'peace'" (Griffin 109). In part, Luke's proud denial and projection stem from his conviction that he has been divinely chosen to fulfill a mission, i.e., that his power has been conferred by the Great Spirit. That this conviction remains unshaken even by the revelations he experiences while a guest at the Sanctuary, attests to the accuracy of the Winchester Bishop's perception that what motivates Luke finally is neither patriotism nor piety, but ego and unbridled political ambition.

Luke's conflation of state authority with a transcendent moral authority is the essence of Caesarism. In the Ancient Rome of Augustus Caesar (ruler of Palestine during the lifetime of Jesus) the Emperor was venerated as divine. To defy him was therefore to defy God. The current leadership of our own society is clearly laboring under a similar and equally sanctimonious delusion (a part of it is, at any rate). Just as clearly, from the gothic perspective, those on the Christian Right who have embraced its policies are guilty of rendering unto Caesar that which belongs to God alone. The specific name for this particular heresy is "American exceptionalism." Its history can be traced to America's theocratic origins which are rooted in a Calvinist belief in a monarchical God who rewards the faithful with affluence and political advantage—despite a prophetic tradition in the Bible that links worldly prosperity with corruption and temptation.

The northern Wilsh city of Klan Gothlen, in Christopher's trilogy, comes closest to representing the kind of hedonist, commercial culture that modern corporate capitalism seeks to establish on a global scale. Cymru, its King—though ostensibly more sophisticated than his southern counterparts—is fundamentally a barbarian posing as a cultivated man of the world. Proud, unforgiving, and ruthless, he kills for sport and brooks no opposition, even from a "beloved" daughter. Moreover, the cozy relationship between church and state practiced in Klan Gothlen accurately mirrors the kind of "culture Christianity" practiced in today's world by those for whom the attractions of religion are primarily aesthetic. The King values Christianity primarily for the quality of its music, while the Bishop (typical of the stereotypical corpulent clerics of medieval Christendom) has no difficulty accommodating his belief system to the requirements of the secular power elite. The crucified Christ—who sided with the powerless, defied the might of Rome as well as his own religious establishment and would rather endure than inflict suffering—is nowhere to be found in this parasitic alliance of church and state. From pulpits across the land, prayers go up each Sunday on behalf of our gallant troops abroad, and in many churches the American flag and denominational flags are proudly displayed side by side.

Christ's radical message of pro-active love and non-violent resistance supported by a culture founded on values such as compassion and self-sacrifice (rather than nationalist self-interest backed by military might) is lost to the citizens of Klan Gothlen, as it is apparently lost on many of today's evangelical super-patriots. It is among the great ironies of modern history that the recent revival of evangelicalism, which began as a protest against culture Christianity, has ended by becoming a willing tool of those whose devotion to war and clandestine political activity on behalf of a *Pax Americana* so closely resembles the devotion of those responsible for the very *Pax Romana* under which Jesus was sentenced and crucified. If the political gothic imagination in children's literature requires a utilitarian rationale, Christopher's fictionalized exploration of the political intrigues of the 1960s and his prescient contextualization of their subsequent impact on society, i.e., a toxic blending of religion and tribalism, arguably provides one.

Young minds at sea in a political tempest are provided by Christopher with a political and moral compass with which to navigate in waters churned up by perpetual war, conspiracies designed to promote a system based on perpetual war, and the cover-ups of those who seek to hide their brutal agenda behind a smokescreen of democratic and religious platitudes. According to today's radical neo-conservatives, America—a nation that seems scarcely able to rule itself—deserves, to rule the world in recognition of its divinely appointed status as a Christian nation, i.e., its "exceptionalism." This blatant repudiation of Jeffersonian ideals acknowledges no conflict between the practice of torture and the rule of law (including, presumably, those international laws established at Nuremberg against the commission of war crimes). Civilian surveillance, unwarranted official secrecy, de facto media censorship, and military sponsored civilian death squads are all justified in the name of national security. Though conspiracy theories and those who advance them are either ignored or condemned by proponents of this hybrid blend of religious and political ideology, the kind of cabal depicted by Christopher is arguably the norm of modern history. In this regard, the fact that Christopher's post-apocalyptic society is the product of a Machiavellian invisible government comprised of pseudo-religious technocrats and militarists who conspire to deceive both the leadership and the citizenry of Winchester is worth emphasizing.

By 1972, when *The Sword of Spirits trilogy* first appeared, speculation was rife that a generation of democratically elected leaders (all of whom were liberal in outlook) had been disposed of by a dark network of power that had coalesced to thwart their progressive agenda. Those today who suspect this same conspiratorial network of being behind the terrorist attacks of 9/11 (adherents of the so-called "9/11 Truth Movement," derisively referred to by its detractors as "the controlled demolition crowd") are pilloried by those who set the parameters of legitimate public discourse; but what, I wonder, might defenders of the *status quo* in Christopher's fictional realm have said about anyone rash enough to accuse the High Seers of conspiracy (or to expose the Death Eater conspiracy in the wizarding world)? Actually, Rowling leaves her readers in no doubt that the full weight of the political and journalistic establishment has been brought to bear against both Dumbledore and "Undesirable Number One." If, at some future point, those who see the covert intelligence operation in Dallas in 1963 and the "false flag" operation in New York, Washington D.C., and Pennsylvania in 2001 as being linked are vindicated, citizens of the present social order, no less than those of Winchester and Klan Gothlen, will be compelled to realize that their way of life, for the past half-century at least, has been founded upon a comforting delusion. We are not, as most of us pretend, living in an open society under the protection of a benign ruling order. On the contrary, we are subjects of a de facto totalitarian state, a plutocracy devoid of either democratic intentions or legitimacy. Our exoteric form of government, as in Winchester and Klan Gothlen, has become a mere camouflage for a hidden (esoteric) political-economic order that operates beyond the legal restraints of constitutional checks and balances or the ethical restraints of common law and custom.

Despite the phalanx of propaganda from the reactionary right, the moderate middle, and the radical left in support of the current ruling order, the young are increasingly impatient with of parameters of "responsible' political discourse and open to alternative perspectives. Such openness stems less, I suspect, from youthful credulity and inexperience than from the fact that they find *ad hominem* attacks unsupported by rational arguments unpersuasive in light of the disturbing nature of the world in which they live (it cannot be overstated that in the mainstream media—along all points of the ideological spectrum—conspiracies and conspiracy theorists are indiscriminately lumped together, or that otherwise respected scholars, such as David Ray Griffin and Peter Dale Scott, have been denied a public forum from which to defend their positions). Perhaps that is why many of these "buffs" such as Oliver Stone have dedicated their efforts to the young "in whom the spirit of truth lives on"—a clear echo of the romantic cult of childhood.

According to the current "realist" consensus, idealism is the exact opposite of realism. An idealist, according to this consensus, is little better than a fool, i.e., someone who is deluded into seeing the world as they wish it to be rather than as it truly is. On the contrary, suggests the gothic imagination as well as the cult of childhood, idealism and realism must complement each other. Only an idealist can perceive reality accurately, just as only a realist can hope to approximate his or her ideal. John Kennedy is said to have identified himself as "a realist without illusions." If so, he was identifying himself as an idealist. When properly understood, the widely shared delusions of what passes today for political realism is a clear indictment of our present system of governance and those who wittingly or unwittingly support it: When the youthful Beethoven, prior to his epiphany at Heilegenstadt, claimed that his morality was that of power, he was proclaiming the philosophy of Grindelwald, Voldemort, and the youthful Albus Dumbledore. Only after his ethical transformation (under the gothic influence of spiritual distress) from "strong man" to "authentic hero" did he come to understand the true nature and purpose of his artistic powers.

As in art so in politics, the *only* legitimate use of power is, paradoxically, the renunciation of power. Luke Perry is forced to a point where he can no longer hide from this timeless dilemma. Either he must condone the slaughter of innocence or he must end his siege. Being a decent man, at heart, he makes the appropriate choice. When Harry renounces his hard won right to wield the Deathly Hallows, he does likewise. In both instances, conscience and sound character prevail over ruthless ambition. The question remains: would the most callous practitioners and enablers of power in either the Muggle World (most recently Adolph Hitler and his Nazis) or the Wizarding World (Lord Voldemort and his Death-Eaters) relent under any circumstances, however inhumane. The answer is not as obvious as one might think. Grindelwald and Dumbledore—who started down the path that Riddle perused to its inevitable conclusion, but stopped short—did live to experience the remorse upon which redemption is contingent. Had Hitler been opposed rather than appeased in his own time, had a guilty political establishment listened to its idealists rather than its realists, who can say with certainty what would have become of Hitler's evil ambitions?

The astounding corollary of this observation is that appeals to self-defense (even against a ruthless adversary) are ethically insufficient to justify the use of coercive force. Why, because "those who live by the sword shall die by the sword." The one indisputable Christian in human history—a man who allegedly embodied the moral authority of the universe—submitted to an agonizing and humiliating death rather than resort to using the means of his enemies. That, and not some arcane ritual of self-sacrifice necessary to placate the "Deep Magic" invoked by C. S. Lewis in his *Narnia Chronicles* (and preached from church pulpits since the time of St. Paul), is the true meaning of John: 3: 16. Violence, whether "defensive" or "offensive" (in the end, they come to the same thing) perpetuates an unbreakable cycle that conceals its evil means behind any number of plausible ends, e.g. self-defense, protection of the weak against the strong, the maintenance of law and order, a posture of readiness etc. As long as there are those who make collective security dependent on invincible might, the Dark Lord and his Muggle counterparts will rise again. "What kind of peace do we seek," asked President Kennedy rhetorically, in a speech promoting universal disarmament shortly before the war-system conspired to end his presidency and his life. His answer, utterly discordant within the context of the prevailing Cold

War ideology: "Not merely peace for Americans but peace for all men and women—not merely peace in our time but peace for all time" (Schotz *History Will Not Absolve Us* 42). Paradoxically, it is only by questioning the misguided patriotism of the willing warrior and discrediting the mock Christianity of the flag-waving Evangelical that either patriotism or faith can ever advance the angelic proclamation of Peace on Earth.

Perhaps too, that is why Samuel Youd, a.k.a. John Christopher, chose to hold up his distant mirror to an audience of adolescent readers. "Whether a story is to be marketed for grown-ups or for children," writes L'Engle, "the writer writes for himself, out of his own need...There is no topic which is of itself taboo; if it springs from the writer's need to understand life...if it is totally honest and unselfpitying, then it will have the ring of truth" (L'Engle *Walking on Water* 109). In the next chapter, we will look more closely at Madeleine L'Engle's literary efforts to locate our present societal drift toward violence and *enantiodromia* with unselfpitying honesty. Before doing so, however, it would be well to address directly the central issue raised obliquely by this discussion. Is cult-of-childhood literature a particularly insidious form of religious and/or political propaganda?

Cult-Of-Childhood Art and Propaganda

Though ludicrous on its face, this question does arise naturally from the parallels drawn thus far between children's literature and contemporary religious and political controversies. One might infer from them that J. K. Rowling, along with several other authors, considered in these pages are purveyors of a particularly insidious form of propaganda aimed at indoctrinating impressionable young minds into the tenets of Christian pacifism and left-wing conspiracy theories. Indeed, much of the criticism on the right leveled against Rowling has come from conservative Christians who accuse her of glamorizing the occult. Though Rowling's politics have not generated the same degree of ire as her alleged religious heresies, one entire section of a recently published collection of essays devoted to the Harry Potter series (see *Harry Potter and History* edited by Nancy R. Reagin) focuses on such issues as whether or not Dumbledore is a libertarian and Voldemort's Death-Eaters are Nazis.

In truth, all successful art is necessarily successful propaganda in that all art presents a compelling point of view (or at the very least, a number of compelling points of view). The distinction between art and propaganda is therefore not always clear cut. Essentially, it has to do, once again, with the issue of means and ends—this time applied to the realm of aesthetics. An artist is not someone who sets out to preach a sermon or deliver a polemic, but rather someone who sets out to explore a unique, previously uncharted creative space. Whatever messages (ethical, political, or religious) that might emerge from this exploration are incidental the story the artist is telling. To paraphrase a familiar passage from Shakespeare, the play might indeed catch the conscience of the king, but it was not conceived with that purpose in mind.

Propaganda, as distinct from art, may call upon a high level of literary craftsmanship to illustrate its message, but the polemic, rather than the play, is "the thing,' (i.e., the central focus and rationale that motivates the story-teller). Propaganda, in other words, uses art as a means to an end extrinsic to itself. The point of propaganda is not to become a medium through which situations arise in the course of which characters emerge and interact, sometimes in ways the author herself may not have anticipated, prodding the narrative toward unforeseen, and even undesirable ends from that author's point of view. The point of propaganda is precisely to shape the means in order to produce a desired end, i.e., to tell a story that leads both the author and the reader to a pre-determined outcome. Obviously, as stated above, there may be stories that defy, or altogether elude, this distinction (though on the whole, I find it to be valid). In my opinion, the allegory of C. S. Lewis, for instance skirts dangerously close to this dividing line (between "Christian" art and propaganda) much closer, indeed, than the far more explicitly Judeo-Christian mythology of Madeleine L'Engle. Christopher's trilogy, by way of comparison, preserves throughout a certain "negative capability" that allows him to empathize with the differing ethical perspectives of his characters (including those of the "willing warrior," the secularist, and the Christian pacifist) without committing to any of them. Finally, Rowling's polemic (both religious and political) is easily enfolded within her sensibility as an artist and story-teller. While her religious and political outlook is clearly liberal in its orientation, and while she may reflect obliquely on contentious issues such as "conspiracy theories," she is first and foremost a story-teller *par excellence.*

To the extent that modern cult-of-childhood literature is rooted in reality, it will necessarily touch upon contemporary issues. To the limited extent that religious and/or political orientations are shaped by exposure to books, such literature will no doubt factor into an adult's mature perspective. Nevertheless, cult-of-childhood literature is not an example of what David Ray Griffin has recently referred to as *Cognitive Infiltration* (the title of his most recent contribution to the unsettling controversies surrounding the events of 9/11). That is to say, it is not an insidious form of indoctrination. Young readers are not expected to extrapolate from conspiracy theories concerning the Ministry of Magic or the Seers of Winchester to real-world conspiracy theories. They may, however, find themselves better equipped as adults to engage such controversies with an open mind as result of childhood exposure to stories not premised on indiscriminate bias or childish (not child-like) religious doctrine. According to the gothic imagination, such stories are an act of faith—in both a religious and a political sense. As seen through the eyes of future historians, today's world will, I expect, bear little resemblance to the consensus reality that many of us have been conditioned to accept (at a conscious level, at least).

The second half of the twentieth century will be remembered not as an era in which a great liberal democracy arose phoenix-like, from the ashes of its totalitarian enemies (the Axis powers and the former Soviet Union) but as a time of global fascism during which a patchwork quilt of warring nation-states, including America, vied for possession of the earth's ever-dwindling reserves of fossil fuel. It will be remembered as a hinge moment in history when a country once committed to peace, social justice was tragically seduced by the blandishments of wealth and power into pursuing an empire—a time when anti-communist hysteria led a nation once secure in its liberal principles to adopt the means of its enemies until the distinction between itself and them was no longer discernable. It will be seen, in other words, as a barbaric, neo-feudal time not unlike that depicted by John Christopher. Under fascism, whether nationalistic or global, citizens are reduced to the status of children dependent upon a paternalistic state. Unable to effect change, they become of necessity mere spectators of a political drama designed to distract and entertain rather than to empower. Most thoughtful and honest readers will, I venture to suggest, recognize themselves in this rather pessimistic portrait. When asked, as one such spectator, what can be done to save America (and the rest of the world) from itself, my answer is the same as that given by exponents of the cult of childhood from Charles Dickens to J. K. Rowling: Change, if it is to come, will be effected by individuals willing to act with the faith of children in might only when used in the vindication of what is right...and perhaps not even then.

6 Coping With the Unthinkable: The Political Gothic Imagination of Madeleine L'Engle

After what seemed a brief hiatus following the collapse of the former Soviet Union, children everywhere, but particularly here in the United States, were once more thrust into a world of apocalyptic expectations and anxieties following the events of September 11, 2001. Despite frequent official pronouncements that everything had changed as a result of those events, to those of us who came of age during the Cold War the climate of terror engendered by 9/11 has seemed like *déjà vu* all over again. The "Better-Dead-Than-Red"/"We Will Bury You" brand of zealotry that shaped political discourse when I was first peering over the rim of adolescence into the adult world is abroad once more. Then, as now, a clash of civilizations that could well end in the collapse of civilization as we have known it was the stuff, not of science fiction or religious lore, but of the daily headlines. Then, as now, the voice of reason was routinely dimmed by the din of an obsessive and largely irrational noise generated by a vociferous far Right and a timid but less zealous Right-of-center (there is not now, nor has there never been a genuine Left in American political culture).

Never was this irrational climate of opinion more noticeable than during the so-called Cuban Missile Crisis of October 1962, when President Kennedy and Soviet Premier Khrushchev confronted one another over the surreptitious installation Russian nuclear missiles on the island of Cuba. For thirteen tense days and nights, Americans young and old, went to bed (like Ray Bradbury's ancient Egyptians) wondering if the setting sun would be resurrected the following morning. The "unthinkable" had become, for those thirteen days, the probable. These events, though altered somewhat, form the starting point for the final volume in Madeleine L'Engle's political gothic sci-fi trilogy. Several years have passed since the self-sacrificing cherubim Progo intimated his survival by a mysterious wind in the door. Meg, who is expecting, and Calvin O'Keefe are now married. Charles Wallace is fifteen years old and the entire Murry clan (except Calvin who is attending a medical conference abroad) has assembled to celebrate Thanksgiving, a social ritual that—under the circumstances—only serves to underscore the sense of disquietude shared by the entire group. This group includes Calvin's sullen, habitually churlish mother.

Mr. Murry, Meg's physicist father, who is well-connected in Washington political circles, has just received a phone call from the President of the United States informing him that the intractable South American dictator of Vespugia, "Mad Dog" Branzillo, a.k.a. *El Rabioso*, is threatening nuclear war and that military confrontation seems unavoidable. Outside the Murrys' rural New England residence, gothic weather, i.e., a slashing rain driven by bitter northeasterly winds, mirror the spiritual turbulence felt by those within the Murry household. It also provides a fitting backdrop to the events unfolding in "This Fateful Hour" (the title of the opening chapter). "There's something wrong with the weather," observes Meg who quickly shifts emotional gears to a cosmic level, "There's something wrong" (L'Engle *A Swiftly Tilting Planet* 9).

Megan's mother, a Nobel Prize winning micro-biologist, reminisces about a similar time of trouble, clearly referencing the Kennedy era: "I remember my mother telling me about one spring, many years ago now, when relations between the United States and the Soviet Union were so tense that all the experts predicted nuclear war before the summer was over. And Mother said she walked along the lane wondering if the pussy willows would ever bud again. After that, she waited each spring, for the pussy willows, remembering, and never took their budding for granted again" (15). This passage sets the stage for L'Engle's imaginative exposition of the interdependence of all times, places, and peoples existing in a precarious synergy, a synergy that is threatened by cosmic entities known as Echthroi (i.e. the enemy). These Death Eater-like beings thrive on selfishness, greed, envy, and lust for power.

When the Murry twin brothers, Sandy and Dennys, suggest that the destruction of the planet could set off a chain reaction with unforeseeable consequences to the galaxy, Meg, whose instincts are more those of the religious mystic than the Newtonian scientist, corrects them: "More than that. Interdependence. Not just one thing leading to another in a straight line, but everything and everyone everywhere interacting" (17). Obviously, the beleaguered planet in L'Engle's title that is swiftly tilting out of control (ethically, politically, and spiritually) is our own. The apparent independence of phenomena is not what it seems to be, nor is the earth that we have exploited (unmindful of the universe's complex but precarious synergies) as it should be. "You know my dears," comments Meg's father, "the world has been abnormal for so long that we've forgotten what it's like to live in a peaceful and reasonable climate. If there is to be any peace or reason, we have to create it in our own hearts and homes"(26).

The key to fending off the ultimate triumph of the negative energies abroad in the world proves to be an ancient rune recited aloud while in a trancelike state by Mrs. O'Keefe, known by her nickname as Bezzie.

She no sooner completes her halting recitation of this long-forgotten rune than Charles Wallace opens the curtain to discover that the menacing gothic weather by which the Murrys were recently beset has transformed into a beautiful blanket of snow that Meg not only interprets as a sign of hope but links to the mysterious rune. "Really, Meg, be reasonable, "protests her sensible older brother, Sandy. "Why, "responds Meg, "We don't live in a reasonable world. Nuclear war is not reasonable. Reason hasn't got us anywhere"(22). Sandy objects once again, pointing out that Branzillo epitomizes precisely the kind of irrationality that Meg seems to be defending. Meg readily admits (with a characteristic and engaging capacity for self-criticism) that she has reacted impulsively against the kind of scientific progress that seems to have led humanity into a nuclear cul-de-sac. At which point, Mrs. O'Keefe, addressing Charles Wallace with unaccustomed familiarity as "Chuck," charges the youngest Murry with stopping Mad Dog Branzillo, enjoining him to use the rune. (23) Meg finds Mrs. O'Keefe's outburst inexplicable, but later that evening her precocious adolescent sibling cautions against dismissing the old woman too readily. "Mother always said there was more to her than meets the eye," he reminds his impatient sister (32).

Mrs. Murry's intuition with regard to her usually laconic sister-in-law is amply justified by subsequent events. As a young girl, Mrs. O'Keefe, whose maiden name was Branwen Zillah Maddox, simultaneously lost a beloved brother and a loving grandmother to a brutish stepfather named Duthbert Mortmain. One night at the dinner table, Mortmain, the brutish proprietor of a country general store, had behaved abusively to the children's mother, who had married him (more from a desire to provide for her children than out of love). When the grandmother dared to rebuke him for his crude and inappropriate conduct he suddenly erupted in a fit of ungovernable rage. Interposing himself between his insensate stepfather and the frail old woman, Chuck— the brother with whom Mrs. O'Keefe had apparently confused Charles Wallace at the Murrys' Thanksgiving celebration—took the full weight of the blow leveled by the cowardly Mortmain. In consequence, the young boy was mentally impaired for the remainder of his short life, much of which was spent within the walls of an asylum.

Accordingly, the *Ananda*, as L'Engle calls it (i.e., an East Indian term for "the joy in existence without which the universe will fall apart and collapse") went out of the bereaved sister with who had been as close to her brother as Meg is to Charles Wallace. (38) Indeed, brother and sister had shared an exceptional empathy amounting to a sixth sense (as do the Murry siblings). Both, for example, possess a paranormal ability to *kythe* (L'Engle term for a heightened state of mental and emotional telepathy). "Beezie," explains Meg at the conclusion of L'Engle's time trilogy "must have married Paddy [Calvin's brutish, low-brow father] for more or less the same reason that her mother had married Duthbert Mortmain. Furthermore, she learned not to feel, not to love, not even her children, not even Calvin. Not to be hurt. But she gave Charles Wallace the rune, and told him to stop Mad Dog Branzillo. So there must have been a little of the Old Music left in her" (275–276). Her allusion to the "Old Music, is a reference to the transcendental Music of the Spheres, a poetic representation of cosmic harmony dating from the time of the ancient Greek philosopher and mathematician Pythagoras, that is one of L'Engle's central metaphors.

Traveling to a New When

The temporally convoluted plot of *A Swiftly Tilting Planet* recounts the adventures of Charles Wallace, who on the back of a unicorn named Gaudior ("more joyful") rides the winds of time, retracing the historical origins of a fratricidal conflict between two genealogical lines. These lines consist of generations of characters with confusingly similar names—like the genera- tions in Emily Brontë's *Wurthering Heights*—that serve to further compli- cate the narrative. Unless altered, these biological strands will lead to Mad Dog Branzillo and the imminent threat of nuclear annihilation. As in the case of John Christopher's adolescent sci-fi trilogy, it is important to follow recurrent conflicts through shifting timeframes in order to fully appreciate the cosmic scope of L'Engles vision. For this reason, I have chosen to provide another plot synopsis that may appear at times overly elaborate. My purpose is to convey something of the novel's Bach-like texture. L'Engle's narrative goal (marvelously realized in my view) involves the creation of an intricately contrapuntal texture of times, settings, characters, imagery, and interpolated tales into which is woven a conception of God's intentional will for humanity. A less elaborate re-telling would, I fear, effectively reduce a five-part fugue to a two-part invention. Analysis of the various strands of that majestic tapestry and how they converge to produce a literary Music of the Spheres will follow in due course.

Together, Charles Wallace and Gaudior witness the formation of the earth and the various evolutionary stages through which it has passed leading to the establishment of a primitive, though recognizably human, habitation. When, upon arriving at their first destination, Charles Wallace asks where they are, Gaudior impatiently explains that their location (the familiar star watching rock located in the Murrys' backyard from which they had departed) has not changed. They have traveled, says the unicorn, to a new *When*, not a new *"Where."* He goes on to explain that owing to Charles Wallace's proven ability to *kythe*, he has been chosen by forces that promote cosmic harmony to identify and alter those crucial junctures in history (Gaudior refers to them as *Might-Have-Beens*) that have led to the present world crisis.

The first assignment undertaken by Charles Wallace in hopes of altering the current time line finds him *kything* within Harcels of the People of the Wind, a Rousseauite tribe of noble primitives who inhabit a Golden Age before the cosmic order is corrupted (on the natural level) by envy—a hatred and envy fuelled by on a supernatural level by Echthroi who embody the cosmic forces of negation. In each of her three volumes L'Engle begins her exploration of the discrepancies between the world as it is and as it should be by presenting the reader with a verbal portrait of an Utopian order in which peaceful cooperation rooted in a genuine, almost instinctive, regard for the interdependence of all life is normative. "Everything that happens within the created Order, no matter how small, has its effect," explains Gaudior. "If you are angry, that anger is added to all the hate with which the Echthroi would distort the melody and destroy the ancient harmonies. When you are loving, that lovingness joins the music of the spheres." (61)

Through the character of Gaudior, L'Engle invokes an Edenic image of innocence in the animal kingdom reinforced by the image of Harcels riding the back of a dolphin-like creature named Finna as well as an eagle-like bird (Eryn), both creatures perfectly adapted to their surroundings and perfectly at ease with human companions. The tribal world to which Harcels belongs thus exemplifies Isaiah's prophetic vision of a nature that is not yet "red in tooth and claw," a nature restored to a condition "where darkness was the friend of light" (one in which in which lambs and lions, i.e., the gentle and the fierce, exhibit a synergy lost to the natural order with the mythic Fall of Adam and Eve, as recounted in the biblical Book of Genesis). This dynamic equilibrium is, however, already threatened—as attested by the tribal "Teller of Tales" who informs Harcels that he too has ridden the back of a creature like Eyrn to the habitation of a neighboring tribe where he secretly witnesses a murder. When Harcels innocently asks why any man would want to kill another, the Shaman answers, "Let us hope that you will never have to know" (64).

In order to save Harcels from such bitter knowledge, Charles Wallace, shortly after this exchange, interferes with his host's intention to gain first-hand knowledge of his murderous neighbor's strange ways. In so doing, Charles Wallace both changes the course of history and incurs the enmity of the Echthroi, who seek to preserve the existing time line. Though Harcels, owing to this timely intervention, is spared the spiritually devastating spectacle of brother turning against brother, Charles Wallace is not. Indeed, his mission is to discover the hidden history of humanity's long propensity for war and violence by tracking the Cain and Abel–like conflict between two brothers from its primitive beginnings through subsequent generations.

Cain and Abel Revisited

No sooner has Charles Wallace refreshed his spirit by means of his visit to Harcels's uncorrupted world then he and Gaudior are blown off course into a *projection*, i.e., "a possible future the Echthroi want to make real" (68). They find themselves in a devastated landscape similar to John Christopher's Burning Lands, about to be attacked by a mutant monster reminiscent of the Bayomet, a fearsome creature with a scabrous and suppurating face, "a great blotched body, short stumps for legs, and long arms, with hands brushing the ground" (70). Barely escaping the ravenous maw of this irradiated, post-nuclear war aberration, they soar into the starry night to the accompaniment a celestial music characterized by Meg (who remains in telepathic communica-tion with her brother throughout his adventure) as "more real than any music I've ever heard" (73).

When they again touch ground, having arrived at a new *When* (i.e., an-other time shift, accompanied in this instance by a shift in location as well), Charles Wallace finds that he is now within a different host—a seventeen year old prince of Cymru in what would later be known as Wales. His new host's name name is Madoc (Son of Owain, King of Gwynedd). His bride to be is Zyll, daughter of Reschal (Old One of the Wind People) and this is their wedding day. We learn that Madoc had left his native land hotly pursued by his evil brother Gwydyr in order to avoid a fraternal quarrel over who would succeed to the throne of Cymru. "For brothers to wish to kill each other for the sake of power," proclaims Madoc, " is to anger the gods...I left Gwynedd to prevent the horror of brother against brother" (80). Here again, we find L'Engle's central theme of fratricidal murder being played out in an ancient Celtic setting. The Celtic heritage shared by Meg and Charles Wallace (as well as their ancestors) is significant in that it lends plausibility to the ESP they exhibit. Such legendary abilities figure prominently in Celtic folklore and in various genres of English literature associated with including Arthurian tales, romantic novels, and cult-of-childhood *Kunstmärchen*.

Believing his power hungry brother to have been killed by a snake subsequent to the shipwreck that brought both of them to the People Across the Lake, Madoc is prepared to renounce his former life. He feels morally obligated, however, to first seek out the grave of his brother who was hurriedly buried by the People Across the Lake somewhere deep within the forest, or so he believes. It was while searching for the site of his brother's burial plot that Modoc became lost, was rescued by Zyll, and brought to the shores of the People of the Wind, a peaceable tribe that inhabit the shore opposite that of the People Across the Lake. The implication is that Gwydyr (who, as subsequent events will prove, is not dead), and his surviving companions have fallen in with offspring of the same tribe that the Teller of Tales in Harcels's world had spied in the act of committing murder. The stage is accordingly set for an inevitable confrontation these between two disparate cultures, one committed to peace and amity, the other to conquest and war. At its heart lies a feud between brothers who, like Cain and Abel, represent a complex gothic duality within each of us, a potential for either self-actualization or self-destruction. Referring to the People on the Far Side (a.k.a. The People Across the Lake), Reschal explains, "They fear the dead and try to escape the ancient terror." When asked to elaborate, Reschal defines "the ancient terror" as "that which went wrong," bringing with it blight to crops, flood, and most importantly, the fear of death (81).

Amazed by Madoc's clear blue eyes and pale skin, genetic markers of his Welch origin, The People of the Lake seek to proclaim Madoc a god, an apotheowsis that the level-headed youth stoutly refuses saying to his father-in-law Reschal, "I will not be worshipped, nor will I be king" (85). No sooner has he made this declaration than the People of the Wind spy a flotilla of Indian canoes moving across the lake toward them. It is led by the blond, blue-eyed figure of Gywydr. Overjoyed to discover him alive, Madoc warmly embraces his supposedly dead elder brother. His joy is short-lived, however, for Gywydr has not come to reunite with family but rather to state terms of surrender as the newly self-appointed King of the Two Tribes. Those terms include marriage to Zyll as well as an exorbitant ransom in fish and game. Rather than involve Zyll and her people in what is essentially a family feud, Madoc challenges his power-mad sibling to mortal combat *mano a mano*. Gywdyr accepts but only on condition that he is allowed the choice of weapons. When Zyll's aged father challenges his right to set such terms, Gywdyr ruthlessly shoves him to the ground.

As he does so, Madoc catches sight of his brother's reflection in a pool of clear water referred to as a *scry*. Lapsing into a precognitive trance, Madoc sees a black-haired woman cradling in her arms an infant who she addresses as follows, "You shall be great, little Madog, and call the world your own to keep or destroy as you will" (91). As the scene shifts, the face of the baby transforms into that of a man saying, "We will destroy then, Mother," followed by images of bombs falling from the sky, enveloping the earth in great bulbous clouds "raging redly and driven wild by wind." These dark forebodings of Mad Dog Branzillo are then supplanted by a more hopeful vision of another woman cradling another infant whom she refers to as El Zarco, or "Little Blue Eyes," whispering as she does so, "Your eyes are an omen, a token for peace. The prayer has been answered in you, blue for birth, blue for mirth"(94).

Calling upon the powers above to come to his aid, Madoc intones the words of the old rune that would be recited centuries later by Mrs. O'Keefe on Thanksgiving Day and flings himself at his brother. The two of them wrestle at the lake's edge until Madoc, forcing Gywdyr's head beneath the water and holding it until his body goes limp, orders his brother's men to return across the lake with their leader and refrain from ever again sounding the drums of war. Though he eventually recovers, Gywdyr is forced to leave the People Across the Lake in disgrace, immigrating eventually to South America. Thus, the first fateful *Might-Have-Been* is averted and the odds that the evil Projection of the Echthroi, experienced momentarily by Gaudior and Charles Wallace, will ever be realized are significantly reduced.

When Charles Wallace emerges from within his host, Madoc, he reflects with amazement upon what he has just experienced. Noting a recurring theory that Welsh sailors came here before Leif Ericson, he struggles to remember a book that he had encountered somewhere having to do with this improbable legend. Suddenly, he recalls that according to this same legend, Gywdyr ends up in Vespugia, a country that includes Patagonia, the province in which Mad Dog Branzillo was born. Thus, a direct link is established between the modern dictator and the ancient Welshmen thought to have visited the New World long before it was first colonized by European. Later, when Charles Wallace's *kything* sister Meg approaches Sandy, the Murry family's history buff for additional information, she learns that a party of immigrants left Wales in 1865 (a pivotal year in United States history) to resettle in Vespugia. This information prompts Meg to comment, "So maybe Mad Dog Branzillo has some Welsh blood in him" (102).

Hysterical Evangelicalism and American Theocracy

In researching this matter more deeply, Meg learns that 1865 was also the year in which Matthew Maddox's first novel, *Once More United*, was published. This apocryphal piece of fiction, penned by an ancestor of Zyll's Madoc, proves to be an early attempt at science fiction based on the paranormal theory of FIP (future influencing the past), as is Madeleine L'Engle's *A Swiftly Tilting Planet*. Passionately anti-war, *Once More United* and one other subsequent volume entitled *The Horn of Joy* were to be Matthew Maddox's sole claims to literary distinction. By means of these stories-within-a-story, L'Engle creates a self-referential effect—narrative surfaces reflecting one another in such a way as to impart depth and resonance to her primary narrative. Charles Wallace, of course, recognizes immediately the significance of these discoveries to his mission and asks Gaudior if they can travel to the year 1865. Before they can reach their destination, however, they find themselves once more under attack from their dreaded enemy, the Echthroi, who seek to prevent Charles Wallace from *going within* anyone else who might provide a vital clue as to the *Might-Have-Beens* that must be altered if El Rabioso is to be stopped. When, in order to escape the Echthroi, the time travelers arrive at a different "When," Charles Wallace discovers that his third host, Brandon Llawcae, is a twelve year old Puritan living in seventeenth-century New England. Brandon (a.k.a. Bran) is in the middle of an earnest conversation with his graceful sister-in-law, Zylle, a blue-eyed, native-American maiden from a peaceful tribe known as the People of the Wind. This uncharacteristic physical trait (clear blue eyes) is a recurring literary metaphor suggesting clarity and purity of vision. It is also genetic marker that can ultimately be traced to the Welsh brothers (Madoc and Gwydyr) whose destinies are intimately connected with past and current events. The full extent of that connection is, of course, not revealed until the conclusion of the novel.

Zylle is married to Bran's older brother Ritchie. The main topic of conversation is Bran's strange visionary powers, powers that are feared by his own people, including his brother, but embraced by the People of the Wind. Zylle, who possesses similar powers, tells Bran that her people would regard him as a Seer (113). Zylle, who is about to give birth, is regarded with suspicion by the settlement on account of her Native American (i.e., "savage heathen") heritage, her incongruous blue eyes, and her paranormal powers. She shares with Bran the legend current among her people of a golden haired prince who came to the New World from across the great ocean long ago, a blue-eyed man of peace and courage. Looking down into a stream, Brandon sees a vision (similar to that seen earlier by this legendary prince Madoc) of a dark-haired woman cradling an infant whose face transforms into that of a military man consumed by cruel and violent thoughts, a man whose image is obliterated by a raging fire (119). When Zyll's birthing time arrives, the Llawcae's call upon the services of the local midwife, Goody Adams. It was she who referred to the People of the Wind as "savage heathens." As a representative of the theocratic political order of the early American colonies, the midwife and her like-minded ally Pastor Mortmain are voices of religious intolerance, racism, and a dour, legalistic brand of Christianity memorialized in the fiction of Nathaniel Hawthorne.

By introducing this episode, L'Engle, like Hawthorne before her, is taking aim not at the past but at the present. Her target is a form of contemporary Evangelicalism that during her lifetime would increasingly come to conflate a hard-line, ultra-reactionary political agenda with the will of divine providence. The theocratic America of seventeenth-century Puritanism was steeped in the doctrines of Christian triumphalism and American exceptionalism, both of which tended to see material prosperity as a mark of divine favor and the New World as a New Garden of Eden. As to the second of these contentions, its exponents were perhaps more right than they realized. The fate of the original inhabitants of Eden was sealed when their grasp for power exceeded their legitimate reach. Writing of Hawthorne's literary classic, *The Scarlet Letter*, a renowned critic has summarized Hawthorne's cautionary tale as follows: "In the seeming Eden of the New World, a man and a woman who are still essentially the old Adam and Eve, deceive

themselves for a moment into believing that they can escape the consequences of sin" (Fiedler 233). This reading is, in itself, rather Puritanical in
that it misses Hawthorne's deeper message concerning the ambiguities of
good and evil. Is the adultery of Hester Prynne and Rev. Arthur Dimmesdale
more or less egregious then the "demonic," i.e., domineering and harshly
self-righteous, theocracy that condemns them?

The second half of the twentieth century, when L'Engle was writing her
political gothic novels, would rehabilitate these theologically and ideologically questionable doctrines premised on a belief in America's unique status
as a chosen people in the service of an anti-communist/pro-capitalist *Pax
Americana*. The ardent Cold Warriors (progenitors of today's Post-9/11
culture of neo-conservatives) have, warns L'Engle, promoted a domineering
and harshly self-righteous social agenda in the name of a religion of peace
and tolerance—like their Puritan forebears. When she came to link the
mindset of Pastor Mortmain with that of Mad Dog Branzillo, her memory of
the comparatively recent anti-Communist "witch hunts" of Senator Joseph
McCarthy were no doubt still fresh.

In *A Swiftly Tilting Planet*, Zyll and Brandon are ultimately denounced
for practicing witchcraft and Black Magic. Zyll's healing ways with indige-
nous herbs, her inter-racial marriage, her emotional restraint during childbirth, her Welch heritage, her closeness to Bran, and her "heathen"
spirituality all form parts of the indictment. As tensions mount between the
Mortmain faction and the Llawcaes, Brandon and his family are increasingly
shunned by their neighbors. Mortmain himself threatens Brandon claiming,
"There is evil under your roof," referring obviously to Zyll. "You had better
see to it that it is removed." When Ritchie hears of this threat, he accurately
points to the psychological projection of which the cleric is guilty saying,
"The evil is in Mr. Mortmain's own heart" (132). Finally, Mortmain and his
son Duthbert confront Zyll herself, subjecting her to an informal inquisition
in order to challenge her credentials as a Christian.

When Duthbert claims that all Native Americans are pagans, Zyll responds by saying that while she does not understand that term, she recognizes Christ as one who "knows the ancient harmonies" and "sings the true
song." The Mortmains are shocked and outraged at this aesthetic characteri-
zation of Jesus. Zyll's lamentable lack of orthodoxy, in their view, is further
attested by her stubborn devotion to the inter-racial legend of the Welch
prince whose love for her people transcended doctrinal considerations and
social taboos. "Scripture says that God loves every man," protests Zyll. That

is in the Psalms. He loves my people as he loves you, or he is not God."
Mortmain's counters with a fiery denunciation of story-telling as the devil's
work, a denunciation that Zyll refutes by pointing out that "Jesus taught by
telling stories" (133–135). At the core of Mortmain's brand of what Fiedler
characterizes as "hysterical evangelicalism," lies a disdain for the aesthetic as
well as the intellectual and sensual dimensions of life. "Inherent in their
position," he writes, "is a fear of art that cuts as deep as the fear of sex, and
there is therefore, no possibility of literature developing out of their low-
brow, plebian Puritanism" (Fiedler, 430).

Modern writers of gothic literature for children, such as L'Engle and
J. K. Rowling, have had to endure similarly vitriolic attacks from later-day
exponents of "hysterical evangelicalism" within the modern Christian
conservative movement, such as Laura Mallory (see Melissa Anelli, *Harry, A
History* 177–201). It follows, one could argue, that educators intent on
nurturing the seeds of civil society in their classrooms may want to use such
literary sources as a springboard for discussions about the role of story-tellers
and other artists in a free society, the aesthetic dimension of religious lore,
the distinction between critical thinking and proselytizing in the classroom,
the benefits of cultural diversity and pluralism, the importance of racial
tolerance, and the dangers to an open society posed by today's resurgent
Duthbert Mortmains.

Provoked beyond endurance by Zyll's unorthodox views, Pastor Mortmain proclaims her a witch and, sentences her to death by hanging. When her
loved ones refuse to assist in erecting her gallows, they are warned that,
given the present "witch-hunting fever" their lack of cooperation may
imperil their entire family. Richard Llawcae replies, "There was another
carpenter once, and he would have refused to do this thing. Him I will
follow"(139). Like Hawthorne, L'Engle comes down on the side of Grace,
rather than that of Law. In doing so, she endorses Dominic Crossan's Christ-
centered hermeneutic (mentioned earlier) whereby in choosing which of the
diverse, often conflicting, strands of scripture one will follow, the decisive
factor is the example of Jesus. Relying on the People of the Wind to interfere
with the execution, a contingency foreseen by Mortmain, the execution goes
ahead as scheduled. What Mortmain has not foreseen, however, is the power
of the ancient rune that Zillo (Zylle's Native American father) has taught
Brandon. At the crucial moment, Brandon calls on "all Heaven with its
power." Duthbert Mortmain is struck by lightning just as he is about to fire

his rifle at a group of "pagans" concealed in the nearby darkness of the surrounding forest. At that instant the church bursts into flames as well.

Richie, seizing his opportunity, addresses the following rebuke to the citizens of the settlement: "Do you think all power is of the devil...Your church is burning because you tried to kill an innocent woman." Turning on pastor Mortmain he continues: "Our friends and neighbors would never have consented to this madness if you had not terrified them with your fire and brimstone" (144). As the assembled crowd watches the church belfry collapse ("a belfry erected more to the glory of Pastor Mortmain than to the glory of God" observes L'Engle), Richard comments to Zillo that the ways of the Lord are mysterious and His gifts, as manifested by Brandon, need not be understood in order to be validated. Having first extracted a promise from the abashed settlers that no such incident will ever be repeated, Zillo and his people return peacefully to their forest homes while Richard, Zylle, with their new baby, opt to begin a new life together in the Llawcae's native land of Wales. First, however, Brandon and Maddok participate in a ceremony whereby they are declared brothers that, as Brandon says, no one can part. "No one" rejoins Maddok, "and perhaps you will marry one of the People of the Wind. And perhaps our children will marry, so that our families will be united until eternity" (148).

In this episode, L'Engle underscores the morally corrosive influence of fear on otherwise decent and caring humans. She also underscores the readiness with which some, including civic leaders such as Pastor Mortmain, are willing to wield fear as a weapon with which to advance their own sacred or secular agendas. Obviously, the doctrines of Manifest Destiny (political imperialism) and Christian triumphalism (cultural imperialism), are twin heresies, according to L'Engles understanding of Christianity. They represent a corruption of both the authentic American dream premised on belief in cultural diversity and human equality, as well as the authentic Christian dream of a non-violent community premised on universal brother-and-sisterhood that Dr. Martin Luther King once characterized as "the beloved community." Though one may question the credibility (as well as the theology) of L'Engle's *deus ex machina* resolution, she certainly leaves no doubt in the mind of her readers as to which brand of Christianity (Zyll's or Mortmain's) providence endorses. Those who today advocate for guns and the Bible rather than guns or the Bible are the ideological descendants of Mortmain.

In preventing the hanging of Zyll (through inspiring Brandon to recite the rune at just the right moment) Charles Wallace has once again thwarted the evil design of the Echthroi by altering, however minutely, a pattern of history that would have culminated in nuclear war (151). Clearly, L'Engle, like Dickens before her, subscribes to a belief that the work of redemption may hinge on the seemingly slight contributions of those who are content to work in humble ways for the betterment of humankind. It is at this point in the narrative that Charles Wallace makes the connection between the name Madoc (as well as its variants) and "Mad Dog," the sinister nickname assigned to the twentieth century Patagonian dictator who is holding the world hostage to the threat of nuclear Armageddon. (150) He decides accordingly to aim for Patagonia in the year 1865. It was in that year that Maddok's Welsh group arrived in South America. Tying himself to Gaudior's back as a precaution, the two time travelers are attacked almost instantly by the enemy (Echthroi). Consequently, they find themselves not in nineteenth century Patagonia but back at the Murry's Star Watching Rock during a pre-historic era when the entire region was swallowed by an Ice Age sea. Meg sends a warning message to Charles Wallace, enjoining him to recite the rune, which he does. Immediately, the two of them, boy and unicorn, are lifted by a propitious wave unto dry land.

The Tragedy and Triumph of Bezzie

The final two episodes of *A Swiftly Tilting Planet* provide the remaining strands of L'Engle's contrapuntal tapestry. The first of these relates the tragic back-story of Mrs. O'Keefe—one that proves to be as surprising and decisive to the fulfillment of the protagonist's mission, i.e., the thwarting of Mad Dog Branzillo's demonic intentions, as is J. K. Rowling's back-story of Professor Snape to the thwarting of Lord Voldemort. The other weaves together the tragedy of Bezzie (Mrs. O'Keefe's youthful nickname) and that of her long dead brother with the fate of two other siblings during the era of the American Civil War. Having narrowly averted drowning and missed there destination once again, a distraught Charles Wallace is forced to conclude that, "Every time I've tried to control things we've had trouble" (160). Loosening the protective ropes that are now cutting painfully into their flesh, they set out to explore what proves to be a "hatching ground" for unicorns, i.e., Gaudior's birthplace. Charles Wallace quenches his thirst by sucking on a "moonsicle" (Gaudior refreshes himself with a draught of pure starlight) and together they relieve the pain of their rope burns with the healing properties of the surrounding snowfall. Shortly thereafter they encounter a new-born unicorn. Gaudior teaches it to dance as Charles Wallace and his clairvoyant sister look on, captivated by the innocent grace and beauty of this spectacle. As mentioned previously, both L'Engle and J. K. Rowling (*The Sorcerer's Stone*) draw upon the medieval iconography of unicorns as a mythic symbol of purity and innocence. When his traveling companion expresses a longing that the security and peace of the moment could continue indefinitely, Gaudior admonishes him, saying, "You human beings tend to want good things to last forever. They don't. Not while we're in time" (169). Typically, in L'Engle's narratives periods of trauma are punctuated by episodes of respite in which her protagonists are permitted to recoup their spiritual energies. In this way her young readers (as well as her fictional characters) are alerted to the inevitability of loss, conflict, pain in a world tossed by winds of time and change. Likewise, they are instructed in the need for occasional periods of withdrawal to allow for both recuperation and the contemplation of an implicate orders of reality untouched by life's debilitating traumas.

Apropos of his hard-won determination to trust in a power greater than himself to guide his progress, Charles Wallace travels next not to 1865 but to a time much closer to his own. There he encounters "a modern Brandon Llawcae" dressed in jeans and a T-shirt along with his golden haired, blue-eyed younger sister. Chuck and Bezzie Maddox (recognized immediately by Meg) are direct descendants of the Llawcaes. Speaking in a tangy rural New England dialect the two children plead with their Grandma to recount the familiar story of their genealogy from Queen Branwen, taken from her British home by an Irish king who did not love her, to Zillah, the Native American princess descended from the children's Maddox forbears. This lineage explains the young girls name, Branwen Zillah Maddox, a name that registers on Meg with a shock of realization (Bezzie, Maddox, her mother-in-law's maiden name, is a corruption based on the opening initials of Branwen Maddox's first and middle names). Chuck, Bezzie O'Keefe's brother, with whom she had apparently confused with Charles Wallace on that fateful Thanksgiving on which she had recited the ancient rune, becomes the third *within* experienced by Charles Wallace.

Bezzie and Chuck's father, a country merchant lacking in business sense, regales his children with the remainder of the family legend as recounted in the second science fiction novel, *The Horn of Joy*, by their illustrious forbear

Matthew Maddox. Based on the story of the power hungry Welsh Prince Gwydyr and his peace-loving younger brother Madoc, from whom Bezzie and her family are descended, this early science fiction novel—like L'Engle's primary narrative—"plays with time" and features a unicorn. In the course of these revelations, we learn that, prior to his father's unexpected death (which forced him to assume responsibility for the general store) Mr. Maddox aspired to being a writer. "I never had a chance to prove whether I could be a writer," laments Mr. Maddox, "but I'm a failure as a merchant"(182). Chuck, who helps out at the store, has inherited his family's sixth sense, which manifests itself in his case in premonitory dreams, clairvoyant flashes, and a unique ability to literally smell the approach of trouble. In one such clairvoyant moment, while delighting at a magical display of fireflies, he suddenly gasps, "Oh Bezzie! I felt as though the earth had tilted...It made me dizzy" (184)! A short time later, Mr. Maddox experiences a heart attack from which he does not recover, a tragedy that certainly becomes a tilting point in the dark destiny of his two children. This recurrent motif of an episode of cosmic significance accompanied by sensations of dizziness and nausea is obviously linked to the book's title.

Emerging from her *kything* trance, Meg Murry seeks out her mother-in-law in order to confirm what she has just learned. When confronted by Meg, Mrs. O'Keefe protests (out of a denial that has become her habitual defense against the traumas of her youth) that the past is best forgotten. She proceeds to hand Mr. Murry the yellowed manuscript of a letter dated November, 1865 from Bran Maddox in Vespugia to his literary brother Matthew. In this family epistle, Bran Maddox confirms the existence of a Native American branch of the family headed by a blue-eyed descendant of a Welsh prince named Gedder. Underscoring the connection even further is the fact that Gedder's sister, though not blue-eyed, is named Zillie. As Mrs. O'Keefe points out to the astounded Murry clan, "The names Bran. Zilla. Zillie. Put them together and they aren't far from Branzillo" (193).

The letter concludes by encouraging Matthew and his sister Zillah, to whom he is betrothed, to join Bran and his sister Gwen in Vespugia. As Charles Wallace inches closer to his goal of changing history, Meg realizes that not only has a clearly documented connection between Wales and Vespugia been established but that the interconnections between the legend of the two warring brothers of old, the mad South American dictator Banzillo, and her own family history are far greater than any of them had originally suspected. Still, the mystery of precisely how the O'Keefe family history relates to the current political crisis remains obscure. As Meg ruminates, "Then the Matthew he wrote to must be the Mathew Maddox who wrote the books. There's something in that second book that matters," she concludes, something that the Echthroi are attempting to conceal from them (196).

Following the untimely death of their father, Bezzie, Chuck and their Grandma discover a locked chest containing letters and artistic sketches, as well as a journal from their Civil War era descendants that elaborate further on the family's history revealed in the letter from Bran to Matthew. The first journal entry, which pre-dates the letter, is penned by Brans's seventeen-year-old betrothed, Zillah. In it she laments the psychological impact that the Civil War has had on Bran, who has returned home suffering from post-traumatic stress syndrome. In it she reveals her love for both brothers, the emotional support she has received from Matthew during Bran's recuperation from "the ghastly war wounds of his mind and spirit," and her suspicion that were it not for Matthew's "accident" (a cryptic reference not explained in the entry) it might have been he to whom she would have been betrothed. In a later entry, Zillah, who by this time has migrated to Vespugia, situated in a part of South America known formerly as Patagonia, expresses her distaste for Gedder who is romantically interested in Matthew's sister Gwen. Acknowledging that his insights into the practical necessities of survival in their new homeland have proven invaluable, she nevertheless distrusts his dour nature, sensing in his inability to laugh, the seeds of a cruel and morbid sensibility.

In the meantime, the O'Keefe family fortunes continue to deteriorate as Mrs. O'Keefe (Bezzie and Chuck's mother) is courted by and ultimately wedded to Duthbert Mortmain—a descendent of the seventeenth-century religious bigots who were nearly responsible for the murder of Bezzie's Indian forebear, Zylle. The children's new stepfather is clearly tainted by the same cruel strain that marked his Puritan lineage, a strain that can be traced all the way back to Madoc's ruthless and ambitious brother Gwydyr. Resentful of the children who are not his and of the grandmother who befriends and defends them, he discourages their laughter and easy rapport. The mother, caught in the middle between her love for her offspring and her desperate financial need, is powerless to protect them from the emotional and physical abuse that Mortmain visits with increasing frequency, especially upon Chuck, who defies his authority. This volatile situation comes to a head one evening at the dinner table when Duthbert makes inappropriate sexual advances toward his teenage stepdaughter. When the grandmother intercedes on Bezzie's behalf, Duthbert aims a violent blow at her head that is intercepted by Chuck, who tumbles down a steep flight of stairs. When Bezzie reaches his crumpled body she finds him staring vacantly past her muttering an incoherent warning from distant time: "Gedder pushed me. He pushed me. Don't let him marry Gwen, Zillah, don't let Gedder, don't let..." (209)

Unbeknownst to his distraught family, Chuck is attended by Gaudior, whose depleted powers of healing prove insufficient to mend the fractured skull that will leave him permanently disabled. "He could not cure Chuck," comments the unicorn whose birth Charles Wallace and Gaudior had witnesses on the Ice Age planet following their first skirmish with the Echthroi, "though he kept him from dying—and that may not have been a kindness" (213). This harsh assessment is a reflection on the quality of life that Chuck is destined to experience from this point in time forward. He frequently confuses past and present, muttering dark warnings that neither his sister or his mother can comprehend, e.g., "Gwyn shouldn't marry Gedder. Gwydyr's children shouldn't marry Madoc's" (218). The grandmother, like her son before her, succumbs to a fatal heart attack brought on by Mortmain's viscous assault. For Chuck and his remaining family, the planet has indeed tilted beyond their control or understanding. What Bezzie and her mother have no way of realizing is that Chuck's inchoate, seemingly random statements are, in fact, insights derived from his access to a "shifting universe" of time. The key to a correct understanding of Chuck's warnings (as the kything Meg realizes) lies in a knowledge of the two infants that were glimpsed in the scry by both Madoc and Brandon Llawcae, one of which ("little Madog") belongs to a family tree that will ultimately bring forth Mad Dog Branzillo (a. k. a. El Rabioso, "the rabid one"). Conversely, the other ("El Zarco," "little blue eyes") bodes well for the future peace of humanity. A clear answer to which brother should prevail, reflects Meg, lies between the pages of a novel that Charles Wallace is being prevented from discovering by the Echthroi.

Paddy O'Keefe, a loutish, hulking athlete who has had his amorous sights set on Bezzie since their days together in high school, has dropped out of school to assist Duthbert Mortmain at the general store. Together he and Mortmain, who each have their own reasons for wanting to dispose of him, conspire to have Chuck institutionalized. Eventually, they succeed, as Charles Wallace learns from Gaudior after emerging from within the injured O'Keefe sibling. At this point in her narrative, the remainder of Bezzie and

Chuck's tragic story is deferred until the missing final pieces of L'Engle's complicated puzzle is completed. Then, and only then, does the reader grasp the full scope of the cosmic synergy she envisions. "Not just one thing leading to another in a straight line," as Meg had commented on Thanksgiving day, "but everything and everyone everywhere interacting". "Bezzie," reflects Meg sorrowfully toward the end of the novel, "must have married Paddy for more or less the same reasons that her mother had married Duthbert Mortmain. And she learned not to feel, not to love, not even her children, not even Calvin [Meg's husband and Mrs. O'Keefe's son]. Not to be hurt. But she gave Charles Wallace the rune, and told him to use it. So there must be a little of the Old Music left in her" (275). With this final allusion to the Pythagorean music of the spheres, inseparably linked in her imagination with the eternal *logos* of Greek philosophy, the cosmic Word of God identified with Christ in the Gospel of John of Patmos, and the East Indian notion of *Ananda*, L'Engle gathers together the diverse stands of her spiritual vision.

In making the tragedy and triumph of Mrs. O'Keefe the core of her political gothic narrative of planetary redemption, she also underscore's the central point of the psychological gothic genre, which is that each of us (no matter how imperfect or damaged by our passage through life) are beings of infinite potential—a potential that is often hidden from our neighbors and even from ourselves (though not, according to L'Engle, from God). What saves this insight from triteness is the emotional realism with which she is able to envision the concrete circumstances that so often defeat God's intentional will. In L'Engle's writing, there is no glib avoidance of the implications of her theological vision: That pain without which insight and transcendence are impossible can be devastating as well as heuristic, occasionally leaving some (if not all) of God's crucified children to wonder why they have been forsaken. Tragically, the same fire that lights or path may burn and the resulting pain—which the gothic imagination interprets as a potential catalyst for spiritual growth and enlightenment—may (as in the case of Bezzie) sap us of the very joy (*Ananda*) that is our best defense against the Enemy (as well as our most compelling clue as to the existence and nature of that which the Enemy seeks to destroy).

Preventing the Crucial Might-Have-Been

Following his sojourn within Bezzie's beloved brother, Charles Wallace and Gaudior arrive, at long last, in the year 1865, though not without first being diverted into a sinister *projection*, i.e., yet another alternate timeline in which they glimpse armed men wearing gas masks as they patrol a largely deserted city square, a mercifully brief encounter intended, no doubt, as a reminder of the Apocalyptic consequences should the two time travelers fail in their mission. As Charles Wallace embarks upon his fourth and final "Within," his first reaction is one of excruciating physical discomfort, intense back and leg pain. This experience is quickly followed by the equally great emotional discomfort. A muscular, though crippled young man (confined early in life to a wheelchair by a riding accident provoked by Echthroi, without his knowledge of course) is addressing Zillah Llawcae—the woman he loves but cannot have, a woman pledged to marry his twin brother Bran (to whom he is equally devoted). It was Bran, as Charles Wallace's new host tells her, who stood by and helped him to eventually overcome his bitterness and resentment in the aftermath of his accident: "It was Bran," Matthew confides to Zillah, "who brought me back to life" (231). The speaker is the innovative author of *Once More United* and *The Horn of Joy*, Matthew Maddox. Bran, who currently lies in a hospital tent suffering from a gunshot wound sustained in battle, is shortly due to be bivouacked home. Matthew, who has experienced a clairvoyant episode forewarning him of Bran's condition, tells Zillah and the other members of his own family that Bran's Civil War wounds go much deeper than those to his body.

His prediction is soon vindicated as Bran, realizing that he will be partially crippled for life, asks Zillah to be released from their engagement, for her sake. Determined to return the service Bran had rendered him in his time of need, Matthew attempts to persuade, cajole, and, if necessary, shock his traumatized brother out of what Zillah refers to as his John Bunyan-like "Slough of Despond." While discussing Bran's resistance to his methods one evening, Matthew confides in Zillah that his sister, Gwen seems to be falling in love with a burly but brutal assistant at his father's general store. As his name (Jack O'Keefe) suggests, he is both a descendant and a harbinger of the Paddy O'Keefe who will marry Bezzie a century later. Shortly thereafter, Bran confides in Matthew concerning the Civil War in which he has recently participated.

"The only positive thing war did for me, "says Bran, "was confirm my enjoyment of travel. I like adventure," he says, "but not killing. And it seems the two are seldom separated" (242). Prior to his debilitating accident, Matthew and Bran had both dreamed of joining other members of their Welch family in Patagonia, a dream that his war-weary brother has revived, though not in connection with Matthew whose physical condition debars him from so strenuous an undertaking. Realizing that his father's expectation that he assume responsibility for the family store when the war is over are not in accord with his own wishes, Bran confesses to Matthew that he never did want to take over the business. Opening up further, Bran goes on to recount the horrors of his wartime experience, finally giving full vent to his pent-up emotions in the compassionate embrace of his crippled brother:

> I went to war thinking of myself as Galahad, out to free fellow human beings from the intolerable bondage of slavery. But it wasn't as simple as that. There were other, less pure, issues being fought over, with little concern for the souls which would perish for nothing more grand than political greed, corruption, and conniving for power. Matt, I saw a man with his face blown off and no mouth to scream with, and yet he screamed and could not die. I saw two brothers, and one was in blue and one was in grey, and I will not tell you which one took his saber and ran it through the other. Oh God, it was brother against brother, Cain against Abel all over again. And I was turned into Cain. What would God have to do with a nation where brothers can turn against each other with such brutality...There were many nights during the war when God withdrew from our battlefields. When the sons of men fight against each other in hardness of heart, why should God not withdraw? Slavery is evil, God knows, but war is evil too, evil, evil. (243–247)

When Bran announces his intentions at the dinner table to a gathering of both his own family circle and the Llawcaes (Zillah and her physician father), his own father seconds the plan—much to Bran's surprise. Dr. Llawcae, however, who insists that his seventeen year old daughter wait until she comes of age to marry Bran, is not so obliging. Bran, accordingly, has no choice but to embark on his own accompanied only by his sister Gwen (who having being caught kissing Jack is sent packing, against her wishes, to South America by her irate father).

Though mail service between the two continents is slow, Matthew is apprised of his brother's progress through their shared ability to *kythe*. Indeed, Bran's adventures form the basis of his second novel. What he learns is that the new colony has been materially assisted by Gedder and his sister Zillie, whom he (Gedder) treats cruelly "as though she were his slave and inferior"

(253). Gedder, it turns out, is a Native American descendant of the greedy, power-mad, and vengeful Welch prince Gwydyr whose blood feud with his gentler brother Madoc initiated the long cycle of fraternal violence that now threatens to engulf the entire world. Bran's closest friends prove to be descendants of the branch of the Llawcae family that migrated to Vespugia to escape the theocratic intolerance the Rev. Mortmain in colonial New England at the time of the Salem witch burnings. Richard Llawcae's son, Rich is enamored of Gwen who, much to her brother's distress, only has eyes for the cruel and domineering Gedder. Gedder's sister, meanwhile, is in love with Zillah's fiancé Bran.

As Bran and Zillah grow more desperate to be reunited, Matthew, (recognizing through Charles Wallace that the complex web of emotional attachments forming in Vespugia threatens to advance the cause of the Echthroi) intercedes in their behalf. Setting caution aside, he confronts Dr. Llawcae with the accusation that his resistance is based not on a genuine concern for his daughter's welfare but on a selfish desire to force her into the unnatural relationship as the emotional substitute for the wife he has long since lost. Dr. Llawcae, bound by social custom from striking a cripple, storms out of Merioneth (the name of the Maddox residence); more determined than ever that Zillah will not follow Bran to South America. Realizing, through the time-honored instincts of an artist (the modern-day equivalent of shamans and tribal story-tellers) that the future of humanity depends, in some rationally inexplicable way on the union of Bran and Zillah, Matthew arranges her passage from funds garnered by the sale of his increasingly acclaimed literary efforts. As his health steadily declines from overwork on his new book and the residual effects of his boyhood accident, Matthew experiences a series of prophetic dreams communicated by Charles Wallace. In these dreams, he is repeatedly warned that Gedder must not prevail over Rich in their common bid for the affection of Gwen and that the baby (El Zarco) must come from Madoc's line not the "tainted" line of Gwydyr, "a genealogy which could go in two different directions, a like a double helix, writes L'Engle" (258). In one direction there is hope (El Zarco); in the other, disaster, i.e., El Rabioso.

In another visionary dream, Charles Wallace (within Matthew) envisions Rich and Gedder poised precariously on the verge of a high cliff overlooking the settlement, quarreling over Gwen. Gedder draws a knife and in the process of lunging at Rich, who is unarmed, hurls himself off the cliff as Zillie looks on horrified. This final phase in the long struggle between forces that promote peace and reconciliation and those that promote violence, vengeance, and war proves to be the time line that Charles Wallace was sent to avert. As he whispers in Meg's ear at the conclusion of the novel, "When Mathew sent Zillah to marry Bran, and when Gedder was killed, that was the *Might-Have-Been.* El Rabioso was never born. It's always been El Zarco"(277). Shortly after completing his manuscript for *The Horn of Joy*, Matthew is released from his pain racked body and Rich and Gwen marry. Unable to remain in the colony after what has happened, the two of them return to Merioneth where Rich eventually takes charge of the family store, thereby fulfilling the role once reserved by Mr. Maddox for his younger son, Bran.

The setting undergoes one more kaleidoscopic shift back to the modern Murry household. Meg rushes downstairs to confirm the conclusion of Beezie's sad story as detailed above, insisting that Charles Wallace, in tracing the interconnected family histories of the Maddoxes and the Llawcae's has somehow altered the course of world events. Her practical, narrowly rational twin brothers (Sandy and Denny) protest the impossibility of such a claim, whereupon Mrs. O'Keefe (Beezie) suddenly demands to see "Chuck" (Charles Wallace). They find him unconscious, stretched out upon the family "star-gazing rock" that figures prominently in much of L'Engle's adolescent fiction. Having barely emerged from the dying Matthew Maddox in time, Meg's extraordinary brother is rewarded by Gaudior for accomplishing his mission with a final ride through the galaxies during which Gaudior underscores the relativity of time and space by variously transforming the two of them into creatures as small as dragonflies and as large as constellations—creatures that are, for a time, permitted to join a cosmic dance to the joyous strains of celestial music.

Charles Wallace's enigmatic assertion that "It was always El Zarco" is confirmed by the letter from Vespugia that Mrs. O'Keefe in this changed time line holds out to Mr. Murry to read aloud. It proves to be a letter from Bran to Gwen and Rich in response to an earlier missive informing her and Bran of the death of Mr. Maddox. In it, Zillah reports on the growth of their young son, Matthew who has acquired the nickname of "Banzillo," (a combination of Bran and Zillah) bestowed by the South American children. Owing to the commitment and rare courage of generations of peacemakers (including the Murrys) everything is changed. The dark *projections* experienced directly by Charles Wallace and Gaudior (and vicariously by Meg Murry) will remain unrealized. Moreover, the threat of nuclear war that—in the changed timeline—was never relayed by a phone call from the President of the United States to one of his trusted scientific advisors is replaced by one in which that same President reports on an important South American peace initiative spear-headed by El Zarco, an enlightened third world leader who has succeeded in prevailing over the more militant members of his cabinet. As for Mrs. O'Keefe, whose utterly unexpected recitation of an ancient rune set all of these changes in motion, her days are numbered as she suffers from a congenital heart condition, diagnosed by Meg's medically trained brother, Denny. "I hate the thought of losing her," says Meg to her mother...just as we're discovering her...You're more right about Mom O'Keefe...than any of us could have imagined. There's much more to her than meets the eye" (278).

The Politics of Hope

In *A Swiftly Tilting Planet*, Madeleine L'Engle offers her readers, young and old, a complex and serious meditation on the psychological and spiritual roots of war. Nowhere in adolescent gothic literature does one find a more compelling blend of feminine warmth, unflinching psychological realism, and visionary prowess. The common experience of adolescence, e.g., a longing for family, a paralyzing sense of awkwardness and inadequacy, frustration, and an impatient lack of perspective, the painful search for identity and visibility, the emotional vulnerability and violent mood swings, are addressed, but within a cosmic context that satisfies another seldom recognized yearning of the young for heroic endeavor. The question posed by Charles Dickens at the beginning of his autobiographical novel *David Copperfield* is the question posed by each of us as we gaze over the rim that separates youth from adulthood: Will I become the hero of my own life? Time and circumstance teach us soon enough to temper our expectations and eventually to confront the dreadful possibility that we may become its victim or even is villain. Nevertheless, hope and heroism are the rightful prerogatives of youth. The heroic mission assigned to Charles Wallace is nothing less than a mandate to change the course of human history. To accomplish this, he must travel through time in search of critical junctures, i.e., *Might-Have-Beens* in the history of two families, both of which at various times in the near or distant past had occupied the New England site that is his home.

The supernatural-gothic elements of L'Engle's religious science fiction include the existence of mythic creatures such as unicorns and Echthroi, otherworld journeys to alternate realities known as *projections*, paranormal forms of communication such as *kything*, and the invocation of cosmic forces summoned by the recitation of a powerful ancient rune at strategic moments throughout the narrative. Indeed, the entire context of her story, though it avoids stock religious rhetoric, is premised on the Judeo-Christian conception of a dualistic universe wherein the earth is portrayed as a planet under siege from supernatural agencies vying for the souls of men. In such a struggle, neither size nor distance matter. As in *The Amazing Mr. Blunden*, *The Dark is Rising*, and the *Harry Potter* saga, time itself is a malleable medium of change not subject to the Newtonian laws of cause and effect. FIP (Future Influencing the Past), a concept much discussed in popular expositions of quantum physics and paranormal studies, becomes the basis of L'Engle's fantasy in that the twentieth-century teenager, Charles Wallace Murry, eventually alludes the distractions and obstacles set in his way by Echthroi to preempt an occurrence that was already a century old when he was conceived.

For L'Engle, as stated earlier, time is no less relative than space and size. That the fate of the world may hinge as easily on the fate of a poor carpenter's child as on a king is consistent with a mystical vision common to Christian mystics, nineteenth century romantic poets, and twentieth century quantum physicists. L'Engle draws inspiration from the Old Testament story of Cain and Abel, two brothers locked in a tragic and deadly conflict, as a means of personalizing the story of all human conflict from the beginning of time. Why do some men (and now some women) organize to slaughter one another even when faced—as today they unquestionably are—by the unprecedented prospect of mutual annihilation? In her timely exploration of this human dilemma, L'Engle merges all three primary genres of the gothic imagination (supernatural, psychological, and political).

The psychological gothic emphasizes aberrant mental states including various modes of duality, internal and inter-personal conflicts, and (at the personal level) asymmetrical relationships in which one individual is clearly dominated by another, without authentic regard for the well-being of the subservient party. In L'Engle, the psychological gothic exploration of individual consciousness can easily overlaps with political gothic narratives (as it does in J. K. Rowling and John Christopher) in that memory is to the individual as history is to the tribe. In other words, according to the gothic imagination, only through a spiritually informed, often perilous reexamination of the past is moral progress possible, on either a personal or a political level. Is it not simplistic one might ask (and, by implication, invalid) to reduce the complexities of world affairs to the subjective level of personal melodrama, to extrapolate from the subjective realm of story-telling to the objective realms of political science and history? Might not L'Engle, in identifying the causes of international conflict with tabloid motivations such as greed, ambition, and lust, be accused of trivializing and sensationalizing religion as well as politics—thereby reducing both to a rickety framework on which to hang a liberal soap opera laced with platitudes? No one, I think, who has engaged her work with even a modicum of impartiality could possibly affirm such an uncharitable assessment. L'Engle, like the Inklings before her, is an exponent of "Romantic Christianity" (a term coined by mystery writer and Dante-scholar Dorothy Sayers with reference to novelist Charles Williams). Williams understood romanticism as a capacity to see the extraordinary in the ordinary or to make "the ordinary extraordinary" (Hadfield viii). What prevents L'Engle's work from sinking to anything like sensationalism is precisely her sacramental vision, a vision that lifts the ordinary to the level of the extraordinary, baptizing the imaginations of her readers in the process (an observation that applies equally to the work of Barber and J. K. Rowling).

Though utterly dissimilar in tone and atmosphere, L'Engle and Christopher share a common perception of Christian pacifism as a radical alternative to politics as it has been practiced throughout human history. For both, but especially for L'Engle, the Kingdom of God (which Christians are enjoined to realize on earth) is organized according to values that are diametrically opposed to those touted not only by today's exponents of God and gunpowder, but by the worldly wisdom of virtually every civilization in recorded history. To cite the motto of the opening chapter of Crossan's study of this topic cited earlier "There is no document of civilization which is not at the same time a document of barbarism" (*God and Empire* 7). What exponents of the historical status quo fail to take into account, according to the cult of childhood, is the existence of an alternative, Otherworldly wisdom that stands in radical opposition to the normative world order. The world, as the gothic imagination continually reminds us, is not as it should be. The norm (from the perspective of romanticism, the gothic imagination, the literary cult of childhood, and authentic Christianity) is, in other words, abnormal. The Bible commends what Crossan refers to as equal but irreconcilable modes of divine power—"peace through victory" and "peace through justice" (Crossan 94). These strands co-exist from one end of the Bible to the other, in both

Old and New Testaments, insists Crossan; but in light of the teachings and example of Christ, one must be dismissed as a potentially murderous misunderstanding of God's character and intentional will. L'Engle apparently agrees. Historically, the outcome of these conflicting perspectives is deftly observed in a saying usually attributed G. K. Chesterton, "Christianity has not been tried and found wanting. It has been found difficult and left untried." This remark was more applicable to his own brand of orthodoxy than he apparently realized. For Chesterton, the contradictions between the non-violence preached by Christ and the violence often practiced or condoned by the church was not a contradiction but a paradox attesting to the balance and wisdom of the latter. He writes, "There must be some good in the life of battle, for so many good men have enjoyed being soldiers" (Chesterton 103). Unfortunately for him, Christ was manifestly not one of those men. The "difficult" possibility that the non-violence of Christ was to be taken seriously by his disciples and that the Good News of the divine *logos* was fundamentally an absolute refutation of the logic according to which evil ends can only be averted through adopting evil means.

What L'Engle achieves in *A Swiftly Tilting Planet* is a politico-religious parable in which war itself is stripped bare of its pseudo-patriotic tinsel as well as its pseudo-Christian aura of righteous heroism. She reveals the very act of war, regardless of the cause on behalf of which it is fought, as a negation of the teachings and example of Jesus, as it is the negation of America's historical commitment to reasoned dialogue, compromise, and consensus building as the appropriate goals of enlightened statesmanship ("Slavery is evil, God knows, but war is evil too..."). In an age when far too many armchair warriors equate patriotism with a willingness to kill on behalf of whatever half-baked rationale the current powers-that-be deem politically expedient, L'Engle offers a valuable reminder that peace and the strenuous avoidance of war (as necessary pre-conditions for a democratic and open society) constitute a patriotic as well as a religious obligation. In this regard, it is worth noting that pundits on both ends of the political spectrum positively trip over one another in their eagerness to extol those who "serve" in the military. Similarly, Sunday morning services often include prayers of supplication for the "success of our military and political leaders" without reference to whether or not such a dubious blending of church and state is consistent with either the Constitution or the Gospel. Participation in the Vietnam debacle, for example (one of the most indefensible wars in American history) has become a golden highway to success in politics for an entire

generation of veterans, much as our current wars in the Middle East promises
to become for future generations. At a time when no one seems willing to
point to war as a positive evil, is it any wonder that pseudo-patriotism trumps
authentic Christianity? To speak in these terms of the trans-personal evil that
is the foundation of warfare is to be reminded of the Kings-Cross-station
exchange in *The Deathly Hallows* between Dumbledore and Harry Potter
(which we will have reason to consider again later in another context): "Tell
me one last thing," says Harry, "Is this real. Or has this been happening
inside my head?" Of course it is happening inside your head, Harry, "responds Dumbledore, "but why on earth should that mean that it is not real"
(723)? The "demonic" ideologies we concoct between our ears do most
certainly lead to real, often tragic, outcomes.

Apropos of the meaningless distinctions insisted upon by the simplistic
literal-mindedness of modern Evangelicalism, L'Engle's traditional Christian
humanism (which reminds us that to be "pro-life" is necessarily to be anti-
war) provides an antidote to the poisonous mentality of those who would
have us "Support Our Troops" by condemning them to a pointless death and
"Remember Who Put the Christ in Christmas" by endorsing a grotesque
inversion of *The Sermon on the Mount*. It would seem that like the poor, the
children of Cain will always be with us—though, as Madeleine L'Engle and
the cult of childhood strongly suggest, it is the descendants of Abel who are
ultimately destined to prevail according to the founder of Christianity.

7 Another Side of the Inklings: Smith of Wootton Major

An undisputed landmark of fantasy literature, Tolkien's *Lord of the Rings* trilogy is perhaps the only modern work of its kind, prior to J. K. Rowling's *Harry Potter* saga, to achieve cult status among young and adult readers alike. Numerous books and articles have been lavished both on it and the *Narnia Chronicles* of C. S. Lewis, Tolkien's academic colleague; though critical consensus suggests that Tolkien's longer three-part epic outdistances Lewis's seven part narrative qualitatively as well as quantitatively. Both works, familiar though they are, have recently reached a wide movie going audience as well, which is why this chapter will focus instead on one of the lesser known literary products to arise from that informal fraternity of medievalists, Christian polemicists, and modern exponents of *Kunstmärchen* known collectively as the Inklings. Tolkien's 1967 short story, entitled *Smith of Wootton Major*, unlike *The Lord of the Rings* or Lewis's *The Lion, the Witch and the Wardrobe*—both of which culminate in a pitched battle between the forces of good and evil—takes up a familiar heroic theme, the Spiritual Quest of Everyman, but couches it in more intimate, decidedly less epic terms.

With regard to Lewis (who has become the darling of the religious far Right) it is worth noting that this one-time atheist did not attend church regularly. He was also a frequent and unabashed imbiber of alcohol. Furthermore, as a literate Christian, he did not expect Jesus to come equipped with a knocker when his Bible likened him to a door. Similarly, as someone knowledgeable about the various literary genres represented in scripture, he did not equate the factual accuracy of a story about a whale that swallows a man (like the story of Jonah or Pinocchio) with that of a story about an omniscient god incarnate as a human infant. In short, C. S. Lewis was a Christian who could be counted on to tell the difference between a tall tale with a pig's tail, a metaphor and matador—unlike some of his more literal-minded members of today's Christian Coalition. Writing at a time when a belief in orthodoxy was itself unorthodox in more intellectual circles, Lewis defended a supernatural worldview against that of scientific empiricism (which was very much in vogue at the time). Neither he nor any of the other Inklings, however, would have countenanced the theological and political inanities swallowed whole by today's Christian conservatives. Though I regard the Lewis's concept of the "Deep Magic"—used in the Narnia series to sanction the necessity of the of Aslan's murder by minions of the White Witch (i.e., a metaphor of Christ's crucifixion at the hands of the Romans as a intellectual cop-out), I would never classify him as an Evangelical. As a devout Catholic (a heresy almost as reprehensible as occultism itself in the eyes of many Evangelicals), Tolkien, is similarly exempt. Like L'Engle, Rowling, and Cooper (as well as Tolkien), Lewis deals with witches, goblins, and other denizens of the nether-realms allegedly unacceptable to the religious Right. All in all, one might reasonably conclude that these Christian conservatives are as ill-informed and inconsistent in their choice of religious heroes as they are in their political preferences.

To an extent, the distinction referred to earlier (between more and less epic versions of hero's mythic quest) applies with more force to the film versions of Tolkien and Lewis than to the originals (just as the inevitable narrative compression imposed by cinematic time constraints ends up magnifying the bellicose aspects of both stories—to the point of distortion. In *Smith of Wootton Major*, there are no pitched battles, no monsters, and no evil sorcerers, i.e., no militant aspects to magnify. In one sense, of course, the war-like character of mid twentieth-century British fantasy reflects a century marked by political violence on an unprecedented scale. Perhaps the poignancy of both imagined realms (the *Shire* and *Faery*) in Tolkien's writings derive from his profound desire to escape the wholesale slaughter of Muggle civilization. The former (*Shire*), with its almost Dickensian coziness, and the later (*Faery*)—which is in reality an externalization of the realm of imagination that the life of the *Shire* makes possible—are inseparably linked. War, the nemesis of the contemplative life, inevitably threatens the peace that permits scholars, artists, and philosophers to venture into the *terra incognito* of human experience.

As the title itself suggests, the protagonist of Tolkien's parable of the artist's spiritual quest is a humble artisan, i.e., a smithy, who embarks upon a series of Otherworld journeys, not to defeat the forces of darkness (or escape them in the vulgar sense) but simply to experience wonders that exists beyond the perceptual range of his less gifted peers. In this regard, the smithy of Wootton Major is an archetypal romantic hero—a courageous but lonely sojourner through spiritual terrain hidden from others. He is both enriched and transformed by what he discovers there. Like Harry Potter, he wears on his forehead an ambiguous mark, one that ultimately leads to his alteration from a conscientious craftsman to an inspired artist whose work communicates something of *Faery* to those who might otherwise not so much as suspect its existence. Though Tolkien's Catholicism might suggest a comparison with Dante's cosmic excursion in the *Divine Comedy*, the latter's visionary landscape has more in common, according to Tolkien himself, with that of Magonia, the fabled "Perilous Realm" of elves and fairies.

The physical setting of *Smith of Wootton Major* is a quaint Medieval English village, inhabited (as are all human habitations in all times and places) by "a fair number of folk...good, bad, and mixed." (*Smith of Wootton Major* 9) The story itself concerns the fate of Smithson (son of the local smithy) who, while in attendance at a special celebration (the *Feast of Good Children*) that occurs only once every twenty-four years, swallows a magical token hidden within a piece of cake. This token proves to be a *fay-star*, a transformative agent that endows those who find it with a temporary passport to the Otherworld of *Faery*. Though in keeping with medieval literature, Tolkien stresses the undeniably fickle role played by Dame Fortune when it comes to the bestowal of special favors (noting that, "No doubt some who deserved to be asked [to the feast] were overlooked, and some who did not were invited by mistake, for that is the way of things, however careful those who arrange such matters may try to be" (10). He also makes it clear that the bearer of the *fay-star* is a "Chosen One" (to use the terminology that J. K. Rowling applies to Harry Potter).

Smithson was chosen by his grandfather (Rider), a former *Master Cook*. As a child, Rider, like his heir and beneficiary, had also been selected as the recipient of the magical favor. He was therefore in a position to request that this it be passed eventually to his deserving grandson. Why his grandson is deserving is an issue that is not explicitly addressed—though we do learn that at the *Twenty-four Feast* during which it was conferred, Smithson voluntarily surrendered one of several imbedded throughout the traditional cake by Nokes, who was *Master Cook* at the time (though not the special *fay-star* planted by the mysterious apprentice cook Alf). This charitable act is bestowed upon a disappointed young girl named Nell who is seated next to Smithson at the feast. She will eventually become his wife. Smithson's kindness (implies Tolkien) suggests a sensitivity and depth of character that—while it may go unrewarded in Wootton—is evidently prized in *Faery*.

Smithson's introduction to *Faery* occurs on his tenth birthday. Birthdays in cult-of-childhood narratives tend to be auspicious occasions on which to embark upon a spiritual quest—Harry Potter's first visit to Diagon Alley, for example occurs on his eleventh birthday. In Tolkien, as in Antonia Barber and Madeleine L'Engle, such journeys are frequently heralded by other-worldly music. Smithson's first visit to an alternate reality begins with the chirping of bird song that filled the land round the house and "passed on like a wave of music into the West, as the sun rose above the rim of the world" (22). Smithson himself breaks into song (a previously unknown tendency) and suddenly coughs up the *fay-star*, instinctively clapping it to his brow. Though visible only to attentive eyes, it remains there from that point forward (like Harry Potter's celebrated scar). This occurrence marks the beginning of Smithson's gradual progression from worthy craftsman to inspired artist—someone whose work acquires a reputation beyond the *Shire* for beauty as well as utility. Shortly thereafter, Smith—the "son" in his name is dropped following his father's demise—begins his exploration of the *Perilous Realm*, where he was guarded from both *Greater* and *Lesser Evils* (24). His access to this realm continues to the point in his life at which, having long since married Nell, Smith is old enough to father a child of his own (Ned Smithson).

Tolkien stresses that while on this quest, Starbrow (as Smith is known in *Faery)* "remained a learner and an explorer, not a warrior; and though in time he could have forged weapons that in his own world would have had power enough to become the matter of great tales and be worth a king's ransom, he knew that in *Faery* they would have been of small account. So, among all the things that he made, it is not remembered that he ever forged a sword or a spear or an arrow-head" (26). Though a committed Catholic, Tolkien's contributions to the literary cult of childhood (like those of Bradbury, Cooper, and Rowling after him) are not couched in the overtly religious language and iconography found in Barber, L'Engle, and his fellow Inkling, C. S. Lewis. Tolkien's gentle message and dualistic worldview are nevertheless consonant with his Christian orientation. In an episode that follows immediately from the omniscient narrator's observation that Smith's artistry was never lavished on implements of war, Starbrow finds himself terrified at the spectacle of eleven mariners dressed in military garb who lift their voices in a song of triumph leaving Tolkien's protagonist (who crouches on the ground as they pass) "shaken with fear" (28). The artist's way—which by implication is also Christ's way— is evidently not that of the warrior.

This moment of sublime terror is followed by another on the border of an extensive lake whose surface is unruffled. Catching a faint glimpse of strange, flame-like shapes below the surface, Smith, motivated by an innocent (or perhaps not-so-innocent) curiosity to take a closer look, attempts to dip his foot into the water only to set foot on a substance "harder than stone and sleek as glass" (30). He no sooner does so than he is driven by a *Wild Wind* from which he protects himself by latching on to a young birch tree. Left bowed and bleeding by the passing storm, the defoliated tree weeps. When asked if there is anything he can do to assuage the harm he has inadvertently caused, the remorseful explorer is enjoined to leave. "You do not belong here," exclaims the injured birch, "Go away and never return" (31)! Starbrow heeds this admonition for a time, though eventually his unquenchable need "to go deep into the land," i.e., to make contact with the most profound levels of spiritual and aesthetic reality, compels him to return.

Strarbrow ultimately penetrates the *Outer Mountains* to the *Vale of Evermorn* where, unbeknownst to him at the time, he encounters no less a personage that the Queen of *Faery*. Asking coyly if he does not fear the consequences of his presumption in having ventured as far as the *Inner Mountains* without first asking leave, Starbrow—unaware that he is addressing the Queen of Faery—merely acknowledges astonishment that the *fay-star* does not confer an unrestricted license to venture anywhere within the borders of the *Perilous Realm*. The beautiful maiden, partly pleased as well as amused at the audacity of this human interloper, withholds her true identity, inviting Starbrow to dance, an invitation he readily accepts. Before parting, she picks a magical flower reminiscent of the "ineffable blue flower" in Novalis (see below) as a memento of his visit. Upon his return to Wootton, his wife and son both notice that his face shines with a strange inner light. Ned, observing the shadow from the firelight that his father casts, comments significantly, "You look like a giant, Dad" (34). In terms of his father's spiritual stature, Ned's observation is perfectly correct.

On the eve of the next *Twenty-Four Feast*, Starbrow is summoned to *Faery* one last time. Brought before his erstwhile dancing partner, whose full majesty is revealed, he learns many things, wordlessly for the most part, "some of which gave him joy, and others filled him with grief." In the course of their telepathic communion, the Queen consoles her guest, bidding him to "not be too ashamed of his own folk." Referring to the ornamental Queen of *Faery* that adorns the *Great Cake* on the *Feast of Good Children* (a Disney-like vulgarization of the real thing insisted upon by Old Nokes) the Queen comments tolerantly, "Better a little doll, maybe, than no memory of *Faery* at all. For some the only glimpse. For some, the awakening" (37).

In this passage, Tolkien gives expression to the foundation on which his own conception of fantasy rests. In the first place, he rejects the notion that fairy tales are the exclusive province of childhood. In an essay entitled *On Fairy-Stories*, he asserts that, "Fantasy, the making or glimpsing of Other-worlds...is the heart of the desire of Faerie...If fairy-story as a kind is worth reading at all it is worthy to be written for and read by adults" (*The Tolkien Reader* 45). In this same essay, he goes on to say that the benefits of fantasy, which he enumerates as "recovery, escape, and consolation," are "all things of which children have as a rule, less need than older people" (46). While he endorses Andrew Lang's contention that, "He who would enter the Kingdom of *Faery* should have the heart of a child," he insists that "fairy-stories should not be specially associated with children" (42). This view not only echoes Christian parables having to do with of the Kingdom of God, it also implies the notion (promoted by the romantic cult of childhood) that the mind-set of children is a perspective of permanent value—as opposed to being a merely transient and immature stage of human development.

Fundamentally, Tolkien rejects the views on children and children's literature expressed by Andrew Lang, author of *The Green Fairy Book, The Violet Fairy Book* etc., whose "infantilization" (Tolkien's own term) of children's literature is based on an idealized notion of what childhood ought to be like. Admittedly, the tendency to regard childhood not as a "seedtime of the soul" but as a permanent sanctuary from the stresses associated with maturity—a tendency enshrined in James Barrie's classic story of a boy who never grows old—was a component of romantic thought generally and the cult of childhood in particular. Tolkien's opinion of it is clear: "Children are meant to grow up, and not to become Peter Pans" (44). Bradbury, Cooper, L'Engle, and Rowling clearly agree.

The high art of fantasy, i.e., the ability to create what Tolkien calls a "Secondary World," derives ultimately from our human status as images of the divine, or as Tolkien expresses it, sub-creators of a "Primary World" created by God. The legitimate function of all such secondary worlds, maintains Tolkien, is to recover a lost perception of the created order as it was meant to be, i.e., a perception of God's "intentional will." "Recovery," writes Tolkien, "(which includes return and renewal of health) is a re-gaining—regaining of a clear view... seeing things as we (or were) meant to see them and involve myself with the philosophers, though I might venture to say ' seeing things as we are (or were) meant to see them" (57). Elsewhere in *On Fairy-Stories* he writes, "Fantasy remains a human right: we make…because we are made: and not only made, but made in the image and likeness of a Maker" (55). As noted earlier by Crossan, this same capacity for secondary creation (corrupted by lust for power) also accounts for "the demonic" in human affairs. I suspect that he (Crossan) would agree, however, that such ambiguity in no way diminishes its potential as a redemptive faculty.

As to the charge that fantasy, and by extension all other genres associated with the gothic imagination, is inferior to less "escapist" forms of literature, Tolkien objects that in a fallen and painful world, the desire to escape is a healthy thing. "Why," asks Tolkien, "should a man be scorned if, finding himself in prison, he tries to get out and go home" (60)? Such an objection may seem inconsistent with the view that denial leads to "the reversal into the opposite; but there is no contradiction. As a temporary measure, denial can have therapeutic (even heuristic) value. The danger only arises when the need for escape becomes a permanent addiction—in which case rationalization usurps the legitimate role of reason. He counters the related accusation that fairy stories are archaic and unprogressive in their preference for medieval trappings (favored by Rowling, Cooper, and, of course, Tolkien himself) with a counter-accusation of the notion that dragons, castles, sailing ships, and bows and arrows may well be regarded as preferable to "things like factories, or the machine-guns and bombs that appear to be their most natural and inevitable, dare we say 'inexorable,'products" (63). He reinforces this protest against the brutality and mechanization of modern culture with an assertion that through fairy stories we may catch a glimpse of divinity understood as the right to power (as distinct from its mere possession) (25).

Drawing a further distinction between the healthy repudiation of coercive force and the unnecessary death to which it can lead and an unhealthy denial of death itself, Tolkien notes that, "It is one of the lessons of fairy-stories (if we can speak of the lessons of things that do not lecture) that on callow, lumpish, and selfish youth peril, sorrow, and the shadow of death can bestow dignity, and even sometimes wisdom" (45). Nevertheless, he goes on to speak of the consolation that such stories offer as being provided by what he refers to as their *Eucatastrophe* or "happy ending" defined as, "a sudden and miraculous grace: never to be counted on to return" This grace is inextricably bound up with what he calls "the oldest and deepest desire, the great Escape: the Escape from Death" (67). Once again, he draws a subtle distinction between a desire to escape *from* adult responsibility and a desire to escape *to* an affirmation of the world intended by a divine providence.

Eucatastrophe, writes Tolkien "does not deny the existence of *dyscatastrope*, of sorrow and failure," (i.e., of the irreducible gothic content of the human experience) contending that such possibilities are necessary to the "joy of deliverance" (68). Elaborating on this point, he goes on to say that this *Eucastrophe* "denies (in the face of much evidence, if you will) universal final defeat and in so far is *evangelium* [good news], giving a fleeting glimpse of Joy, Joy beyond the walls of the world, poignant as grief" (68). In keeping with both the German romantic and Christian historical origins of the literary cult of childhood and Tolkien's explicit references to Germanic literary genres such as the *Hausmärchen* (children's fairy-stories) and *Kunstmärchen* (artistic fairy-stories for adults), it is worth pointing out that the German language has a word (*Sehnsucht*) for this painful joy and longing. It is one that nineteenth-century German artists (such as Robert Schumann, the originator of the cult of childhood in music) use frequently. The bottom line for Tolkien and other practitioners of the gothic imagination in children's literature, seems to be that the glimpse of other worlds achieved through fairy-stories, however removed it may be from the source, is better than no memory at all.

Though related in obvious ways to medieval spiritual-quest literature such as Dante's *Divine Comedy*, Tolkien's fantasy more closely resembles that of the early Romantic German fantasist Friedrich von Hardenburg (better known by his pen name Novalis), chronicler of Heinrich von Oftendingen's quest for the "ineffable blue flower") and George MacDonald (author of *Lilith* and *Phantastes*), another nineteenth-century purveyor of novellas in the style of German Märchen, than with the doctrinaire poet laureate of medieval Catholicism. While among the Inklings it may have been C. S. Lewis who paid explicit homage to romantic literature as a source of inspiration, it is Tolkien, in *Smith of Wootton Major*, who comes closest to duplicating the refined spirit and vivid, Otherworld imagery of German fantacists and tone poets such as Eichendorff, E. T. A. Hoffmann, and Robert Schumann. Like these once celebrated visionaries, Tolkien, sought to promote a post-Enlightenment reconciliation between the secular and the sacred.

In his thought-provoking survey of nineteenth-century thought and literature entitled *Natural Supernaturalism*, literary critic M. H. Abrams argues that romantic artists sought to assimilate religious categories of thought to their own secularist agenda by denuding them of supernatural content (hence the clear privileging of the natural over the supernatural in the title of his book). Conversely, others have maintained that the aim of the most representative romantics was to revive the Greco/Judeo/Christian tradition by translating it into a post-Enlightenment language intelligible to their contemporaries. These artists sought to rehabilitate supernaturalism not naturalize it. Though this counter thesis to that of Abrams is impossible to prove (since an identical body of evidence points with equal plausibility in opposite directions), to my mind it accounts more credibly for the conversion, late in life, of poets such as Wordsworth and Coleridge, who began as anti-Christian iconoclasts but ended by seeking refuge within the Church. It also makes more sense of the overtly religious polemics of influential figures such as painter Casper David Friedrich, theologian Friedrich Schleiermacher, and the pro-Christian novelist and essayist Novalis.

In *Smith of Wootton Major*, Tolkien (like Rowling several decades later) achieves with Hoffmannesque ease, a seamless transition between this world and an adjacent realm of wonder and mystery. In E. T. A. Hoffmann's celebrated *Kunstmärchen The Golden Pot*, his acknowledged masterpiece in this genre, Anselm (the tale's protagonist) is a university student as likeable as he is awkward—a nineteenth-century precursor of the nerdy, adolescent heroes of later cult-of- childhood masterpieces such as the *Harry Potter* saga). Anselm slips casually, almost accidentally, in and out of a Philistine world of municipal bureaucrats—men who are blind to any reality outside their own narrow sphere of influence. The alternate reality in which Anselm finds himself is inhabited by shape-shifting salamanders, sensuous female serpents who morph into beautiful maidens, and other quasi-mythical creatures derived from the alchemical lore of Hermeticism. In this respect, it is interesting to note John Granger's extended discussion of the influence of the hermetical tradition on J. K. Rowling (see *Harry Potter's Bookshelf* 248–255).

Hoffmann's core theme, like that of Tolkien and later Rowling, is the sublime revelations and opportunities for personal growth that await those chosen to enter what Tolkien refers to as a "Secondary World." Such otherworldly revelations, reserved for those who are temporarily privileged as well as burdened, prove, in Tolkien's novella, emanate from a transcendent dimension of reality that parallels the Christian Kingdom of God. Despite its affinity with early German romantic literature, Tolkien's secular allegory of the extraordinary enfolded within the ordinary is grounded in a characteristic English attitude: "There is something," writes a prominent medievalist, "very English about this conviction that the little people of the medieval world were heroic too" (Cantor, 232). Needless to say, such a conviction shades easily into a genre of literature in which children (the least powerful, most vulnerable of the little people who inhabit any era) play a central role.

Returning to Tolkien's tale, the Smith Smithson is charged by the Queen of *Faery* with delivering a cryptic message to her consort, the King: "The time has come. Let him choose" (38). She informs Starbrow that as this is to be his final sojourn in the Perilous Realm it is time for him to surrender the *fay-star*. Kneeling before her, he finds himself "both in the World and in *Faery*, and also outside them and surveying them, so that he was at once in bereavement and in ownership, and in peace" (38). In recognition of his willingness to sacrifice his gift, the Queen consents to his valedictory request that he be allowed to personally deliver the token to the King. After she departs, he finds himself alone in a high field where he stood feeling empty in the knowledge that his way forward would take him back to bereavement (38).

Upon encountering a tall stranger on the border between Wootton and *Faery*, Smith suddenly remembers the message he has been asked to deliver. Thinking he has missed his opportunity, he inquires of the stranger if his journey will lead him through the *Perilous Realm* and, if so, would he mind relaying a message to its King. The hooded stranger turns out, on closer inspection, to be none other than Alf (former Prentice to Old Nokes, the Master Cook whom he has long since replaced). Smith's secret ally of long ago agrees to this request. At this moment, the smith notices, to his astonishment, that the Prentice seems not to have aged since the day they had participated together in the *Feast of Good Children*, the fateful day on which Smith first discovered the *fay-star*.

Lightly touching the star upon his forehead, Alf asks his companion gently if it is not time for him to relinquish it. Affronted and surprised by this unwelcome reminder of his recent encounter with the *Great Lady*, Smith replies heatedly that the star is his to keep. Alf reminds him that some gifts are lent rather than conferred outright, suggesting further that there are others beside himself who might have need of this particular gift. Feeling inwardly uneasy "for he was a generous man and remembered with gratitude all that the star had brought to him," Smith dejectedly acknowledges the justice of Alf's words (41). Brightening suddenly at the prospect of returning one last time in fulfillment of his commission from the Queen, he asks if he shouldn't return it to either one of the *Great Ones of Faery* or to the King. His hopes of revisiting *Faery* are quickly dashed, however, when Alf suggests that he could simply surrender the *fay-star* then and there. Realizing the difficulty of what he is asking, however, Prentice relents, suggesting that the two of them travel back to the village together so that Smith can replace the star in the spice drawer from which it was originally taken. Along the way, the smith asks to whom the star will be passed, but does not receive an answer.

As the *fay-star* drops from his forehead to his hand (Alf having accompanied Smith all the way to the *Great Hall*) Tolkien's protagonist is constrained to ask Prentice to place it back into the drawer for him—remarking, with touching reticence, that he cannot see clearly. Moved by his evident distress, Alf asks he would still like to know who will inherit the star. The worthy artisan replies that he would, naming as a possible though unlikely candidate his nephew, Nokes of Townsend (grandchild of Old Nokes). "You gave me the star freely," states Alf, "It shall go to anyone that you appoint" (48). At home, Starbrow is greeted by his son, Ned, who on noticing his father's weariness asks if he has travelled far, to which the father replies with allegorical significance "All the way from Daybreak to Evening" (48). Taking from his wallet a tiny stem of a wondrous flower, intended for his new grandson, Tomlin. It was a gift, presented by the Great Lady herself incognito. Each flower emanating from the stem resembles a tiny bell that when rung, emits, along with its irresistible sent, a music that, as Ned remarks somewhat tautologically, "reminds me of, well, of something I've forgotten," a remark that brings to mind the Queen's earlier observation, "Better a little doll, maybe, than no memory of *Faery* at all" (49).

When Smith informs his son that there will be no extended journeys in future, Ned commiserates his loss but also anticipates with pleasure the prospect of learning and working at his father's side. Sometime thereafter, having listened in breathless silence to the smith's narrative of his final visit to *Faery*, his awestruck son comments, "Do you remember the day you came back with the Flower? And I said that you looked like a giant by your shadow. The shadow was the truth" (50). Like other gothic heroes, Smith Smithson has achieved transcendence, to a greater or lesser extent, of both his own personal limitations and those of the society to which he belongs. By faithfully, courageously, and sometimes recklessly following his guiding star, i.e., his spiritual and aesthetic gifts, deep into the *terra incognita* of the Perilous Realm, and by his unselfish decision to voluntarily relinquish his passport to that enchanted realm, he has acquired an authenticity that has earned him the respect and affection of his family, his community (with the exception of Old Nokes) and the exalted of *Faery*. In the course of his solitary journey, he has also acquired the stoicism to contemplate with equanimity the finitude and loss and that life inevitably entails. To para-phrase the ancient Greek dramatist Aeschylus, suffering, through the terrible grace of God, has brought wisdom, and the giant shadow that the protagonist casts in the evening of his earthly existence is the shadow of his own approaching death.

The final pages of Smith of Wootton Major are devoted to a burlesque gothic epilogue that focuses on the relationship between Alf and Old Nokes, the retired Master Cook. As the reader has long suspected, Alf is no ordinary apprentice. When the previous Master Cook, Rider (like Bilbo Baggins in *The Lord of the Rings*) suddenly and inexplicably resigns his post to embark upon a mysterious journey, he leaves the pretentious and narrow minded Nokes to take his place with the able assistance of a "ridiculously young" apprentice. Taking credit for his achievements, Nokes exploits Alf's talents, scoffing maliciously at his frequent allusions to *Faery* and *fay-stars*. Fat and fraudulent, like the detestable but risible Vernon Dursley in J. K. Rowling's epic fairy story, this increasingly corpulent Philistine is a type of all those in this world for whom originality of thought and imagination are either a delusion or an affectation.

Having long been troubled by the unexplained "disappearance" of the *fay-star* at the first *Twenty-four Feast* at which he presided, a trinket that has now mysteriously reappeared in the spice drawer of the kitchen in the *Great Hall*, he finally concludes that Alf must of secreted it away at the time instead of placing it in the *Great Cake,* as instructed. Confronting Alf one last time, in what he subsequently interprets as a bad dream, Nokes commu-nicates his mistaken version of events to his successor with all the certainty and self-satisfaction that only those devoid of imagination can muster. Attempting to correct him, Alf replies: "Your knowledge is so great that I have only twice ventured to tell you anything. I told you that the star came from *Faery*; and I have told you that it went to the smith. Now at parting I will tell you one thing more. Don't laugh again! You are a vain old fraud, fat, idle and sly. I did most of your work. Without thanks you learned all that you could from me-except respect for *Faery*, and a little courtesy" (54).

Contemptuously dismissing this earnest injunction, Nokes says that he sees no courtesy in Alf's insolent form of address to an "elder and better" and that only if his former acolyte is able to produce a fairy to make him thin again by waving a wand, might he think better of Alf's fantastic beliefs. At that moment, the apprentice reveals his true identity as King of *Faery*, stating majestically that his unworthy adversary is at least not his elder. With sudden *noblesse oblige*, Alf reflects that the terrified figure who cowers before him is more deserving of pity than wrath. Relenting, Alf places him in a deep sleep. Nokes, upon awakening, is shaken by the alarming nature of his "dream," which (like Ebenezer Scrooge) he attributes to bad eating habits. Vowing to shun in future all bilious, potentially nightmare-inducing fare, he soon finds himself so reduced in girth that the village children take to calling him "old Rag-and-Bones," rationalizing this outcome as an inevitable result of his new diet, he satisfies himself that, "If you stop eating you grow thinner. That's natural. Stands to reason. There ain't no magic in it," thereby affirming his reductionist view of reality (56).

After presiding over the next *Feast of Good Children*, making sure to pass the *fay-star* to young Nokes of Townsend, in accordance with the smith's wishes, the Master Cook announces his imminent departure from the village. Unaware of "what a shocking thing has happened in his family," Nokes pronounces a final malediction on his erstwhile assistant: "He's gone at last! And I'm glad for one. I never liked him. He was artful. Too nimble you might say." (58) This amusing conclusion, provides a welcome, major-key resolution to what is, despite it burlesque elements, a hauntingly minor-key tale. While stirring us to *Sehnsucht*, Tolkien's *Smith of Wootton Major* ultimately affirms the intrinsic value of the gothic hero's quest (and by extension that of the artist and religieuse) for existential validation and insight.

At a time in history when young and old alike are encouraged to equate personal worth with market value, identity with product identification, and the democratic "pursuit of happiness" with a visit to the local shopping mall, the understated counter-cultural significance of Tolkien's modern contribution to the nineteenth-century cult of childhood is clear. Authenticity, which like happiness, calls for "the exercise of all ones powers along lines of excellence" (a familiar ancient Greek definition), remains a largely solitary pursuit dependent upon imagination and critical introspection. It presents appalling perils as well as profound pleasures and its rewards are more likely to elicit laughter gratitude or admiration from one's contemporaries. The first romantic generation and the neo-romantic generation to which the Inklings made their appeal have this in common: Both experienced the hope and heartbreak of unprecedented political and social upheaval (an idealistic era of confrontation and revolutionary expectations followed by a long, often brutal, retreat into political, religious, and cultural denial). What *Sehnsucht* and the "ineffable blue flower" were to Schumann and Novalis, *Faery* and the Shire were to J. R. R. Tolkien, C. S. Lewis, and the other Inklings, i.e., allusive possibilities—perhaps remembered and certainly hoped for—that modernity has either rejected or grotesquely deformed. Ultimately the distant mirror that the cult of childhood holds up to the modern world is a Mirror of Erised.

8 Magic Is Might: A Political Gothic Parable

Shortly after the seventh and final volume of J. K. Rowling's Harry Potter saga (*Harry Potter and the Deathly Hallows*) was published, its author made headline news by announcing to her fans that 1) she had always conceived of Dumbledore as gay and 2) that a healthy distrust for authority was one of the messages embedded in her tale. The first of these revelations may indeed have come as a surprise to some, but in retrospect, it is difficult to see how anyone could have missed the blatant iconoclasm implicit in such conceptions as the Order of the Phoenix (a secret society of wizards formed to combat He-Who-Must-Not-Be-Named and, for a time, the Ministry of Magic as well) and the D.A. (Dumbledore's Army, an independently formed student wing of the Order). These subversive organizations form the backbone of the fifth book in Rowling's Harry Potter series entitled *The Order of the Phoenix*. At a more prosaic level, the Dursleys, Harry's philistine aunt and uncle, who represent parental authority as well as the routine denial of the wizarding world practiced by Muggle society, are consistently held up to ridicule.

In a variety of ways, the political establishment of the wizarding world and its minions in the press closely mirror the unprincipled venality, and hypocrisy of the Muggle political establishment. It is not only Muggle authority that is pilloried by Rowling, however. Fudge and Scrimgeour, the two Prime Ministers of Magic with whom Harry has dealings, are worthy of comparison with the least savory of their British and American counterparts in real life. The former is a posturing miscreant who spends most of his wizarding tenure choosing to disbelieve and discredit both Dumbledore and Harry rather than face up to the politically inconvenient truth that the Death Eaters and their leader, the Dark Lord, have returned. Fudge's chief ally in this ill-conceived policy of denial is the editorial staff of *The Prophet*, the wizarding world's newspaper of record and its scandal-mongering star reporter, Rita Skeeter. The later wizarding Prime Minister (though his character is somewhat redeemed by a final act of self-sacrifice on Harry's behalf) is portrayed in the *Half-Blood Prince* as dishonest, manipulative, and committed to expediency over principle—as attested by his willingness to imprison the thankless Stan Shunpike, who he knows to be innocent, and by his continued support for Dolores Umbridge, under whose ministry-approved regime of "educational reform" Harry and a host of other Hogwarts students had been subjected to disciplinary measures amounting to torture.

In the *Half-Blood Prince*, Rowling details the origins of Lord Voldemort through the mentoring of Dumbledore, who, via the *Pensieve* (a magical devise that enables one to enter another's past experience), escorts Harry on a guided tour of key episodes from Tom Riddle's past experience. It is only in the *Deathly Hallows*, however, that her readers are finally initiated into the origins of the modern-day dispute between Death Eaters and the Order of the Phoenix, i.e., between the coercive and unjust anti-Muggle doctrines of Grindelwald and Lord Voldemort and those of his chief rival and adversary, Albus Dumbledore. The thousand year old rupture between Salazar Slytherine and the other three founders of the Hogwarts School is chronicled in the *Chamber of Secrets*, in which we learn that this schism was a result of Slytherine's obsession with racial purity.

"Pure bloods," i.e., those born of wizarding parents, are, according to Slytherine superior to lesser breeds and therefore deserving of power over them. These inferior strains consist of "Muggles," defined by Harry's friend, the half-giant Hagrid as "non-magical folk," "mudbloods," i.e., those whose ancestry is allegedly tainted by a Muggle strain, and "squibs," or those born to wizard parents who are nevertheless devoid of magical abilities. All three are equally proscribed, according to Slytherine's racial ideology. Gindelwald and Lord Voldemort are simply latter-day exponents of this racist creed, which is clearly modeled on the political theories and practices of a tribe of central European Muggles who called themselves "Nazis" in the first half of the twentieth century.

The motto adopted by Grindelwald's disciples is "Magic Is Might." Peace through victory, rather than justice, is their goal—a goal they rationalize in the name of "the Greater Good" for all concerned. This utilitarian rationale, as revealed in Rita Skeeter's hastily researched biography of the Hogwarts headmaster *The Life and Lies of Albus Dumbledore*, was originally suggested to the evil wizard Grindelwald by a naive and idealistic young Dumbledore himself. "You cannot imagine how his ideas caught me, Harry, inflamed me" explains Dumdledore posthumously in Kings Cross station, "Muggles forced into subservience. We wizards triumphant. Grindlewald and I, the glorious young leaders of the revolution. Oh, I had a few scruples. I assuaged my conscience with empty words. It would all be for the greater good..." (*Deathly Hallows* 716). The circumstances surrounding this revelation and its true implications with regard to Dumbledore's subsequent views are, however, wildly misconstrued in the journalist's slanderous best-seller (a volume that might have been more aptly entitled *The Half-Truths and Unwarranted Assumptions of Rita Skeeter*).

Glib plausibility is the hallmark of the Skeeter school of journalism, and her scurrilous attack on Dumbledore's integrity is, for a time, sufficiently credible to shake Harry's faith in his martyred former friend and mentor, particularly in light of certain comments made by Ron Weasley's malicious Auntie Muriel at the wedding of Bill Weasley to Fleur Delacour immediately prior to the collapse of the *Ministry*. Despite the anguish these comments causes him, Harry, like all gothic heroes, is determined to discover the truth, however inconvenient or controversial it might prove to be. "Harry," protests Hermione, "do you really think you'll get the truth from a malicious old woman like Muriel, or from Rita Skeeter? How can you believe them? You knew Dumbledore!" Harry's response is typical: He looks away, trying not to betray his resentment but thinks to himself, "There it was again: Choose what to believe. He wanted the truth. Why was everybody so determined that he should not get it" (*Deathly Hallows* 85).

Rowling's attitude with regard to journalistic standards and truth-telling generally, is nuanced. Her ethic throughout is perhaps best described as "situational." Dumbledore—partly from weakness (or, if you prefer, compassion), and partly from a wise realization that the hardest lessons in life are only learned from firsthand experience—withholds from his favorite student much of the truth about Harry's past as well as his destiny (just as he deliberately withholds much of the truth about his own sacrificial journey and the personal tragedies that have shaped his decisions and sensibilities as Headmaster of Hogwarts). In a world that is often not as it appears to be, however, Rita Skeeter's brand of journalism (with regard to Dumbledore's youthful relationship with Grindelwald and *Dark Magic*, the tragedy of Dumbledor's sister Ariana, his grave-side brawl with his brother, Aberforth, his motives in promoting Harry, and his unswerving, seemingly irrational, support of Professor Severus Snape) demonstrates that mendacious half truths can be as misleading as outright lies. In the *wizarding* world as in the *Muggle* world, secrecy and prevarication have a valid role to play as does an unyielding and probative commitment to the truth, depending on the situation at hand. Here, as elsewhere, gothic narratives recognize the value of ambiguity.

Most of us, of course, regardless of our religious, philosophical, or ideological orientation are practitioners of situation ethics when it comes to shielding a loved one ("You don't look a day older than when we last met...twenty years ago") or withholding the identity of someone whose life might be at risk were it to be revealed. Where the issue is joined is when chivalry becomes enablement and secrecy becomes the common currency of power. When lies help an alcoholic to deny his or her alcoholism or disinformation campaigns are used as weapons with which to protect illegitimate authority, the tipping point on life's ever-shifting ethical scale has been exceeded. As ever, according to the gothic imagination, the ideal is a dynamic equilibrium, i.e., a synergy between life's oppositional energies (*Ying* and *Yang*, law and grace, Right and Left, idealism and expedience). As today's ever- multiplying religious and political fanaticisms amply attest, a dogmatic approach to nuanced and complex situations is likely to result in the familiar spectacle of the super-righteous/super-patriotic being hoisted on their own petard. Only in the religious tracts of Victorian England, are "good" children and their parents perfectly truthful and forthcoming. Rowling pays homage to the need for the flexible standard that life's ambiguities require by allowing her children the freedom to choose between erring on the side of discretion when they deem full disclosure to be indiscrete, just as she accords them the dignity of facing up to the consequences when their choices prove to be unwise (thereby affirming the requirements of a morally conditioned universe). In *Deathly Hallows*, Harry insists on speaking Voldemort's name aloud, despite Ron's plea that he not do so, because—as Dumbledore points out—"Fear of the name only increases fear of the thing itself" (*Deathly Hallows* 273). The principal involved is sound, but the consequences are serious when, as a result of ignoring this wizarding world taboo, i.e., breaking the rules, he and his two compatriots are captured by the fearsome werewolf, Fenrir Greyback.

The Politics of Magic

Though the philosophical/religious aspects of Rowling's mythic world have received considerable attention, the political implications of her stories have been largely ignored. This all the more remarkable given the centrality of the power struggles depicted in the Harry Potter saga. Indeed, if asked to prioritize the principal genres of gothic narrative (supernatural, psychological, and political) as they relate to Rowling's work, I would—despite the story's obvious supernatural trappings—unhesitatingly choose political gothic as the primary genre, especially in *The Order of the Phoenix*. Why, because, as Rowling herself suggests, her plot has more to do with ends than means, it's more about the uses to which power, including non-magical power, is put than it is about the techniques and instrumentalities through which it is implemented. Magic in the wizarding world parallels technology in the Muggle world. It is, therefore, merely a tool whereby difficult ethical choices that plague both worlds are realized. For Rowling, the crucial question is not how magic works, but what are its appropriate, i.e., just, and inappropriate, i.e., unjust, uses. Admittedly, the Dark Magic favored by Death Eaters can have no worthy end; but that is because it is a means employed to subjugate and coerce.

Though the magical, supernatural elements of the wizarding world are undoubtedly responsible for much of the fascination it exerts on its Muggle readership, in a way, they are irrelevant to the substance of the story. On its face, this may seem an absurd statement, but its meaning is clarified by a passage from the first chapter of the *Half-Blood Prince* in which Fudge, the former Prime Minister of Magic, and Scrimgeour, his replacement, visit the Muggle Prime Minister to appraise him of the fact that *He-Who-Must-Not-Be-Named* is staging a coup. "But for heaven's sake," protests the befuddled human politician, "you're *wizards*! You can do *magic*! Surely you can sort out—well—*anything*!" To which Fudge replies patiently, "The trouble is, the other side can do magic too, Prime Minister" (*Half-Blood Prince* 18). Accordingly, the balance of power, in so far means (whether magical or mundane) are concerned, is symmetrical. In effect, the ostensible advantage enjoyed by the wizarding community over the Muggle community is neutralized. The political gothic theme of perverse, or asymmetrical, power still plays a vital role, however, with regard Wizard/Muggle relations. In Rowling's dualistic universe, the influences, for good or ill, on *Muggledom* emanate from an alternate reality to which few humans are privy, i.e. from a human standpoint; they are completely unpredictable and therefore utterly uncontrollable.

Another example of the finely calibrated ambiguity of Rowling's tale of abusive power and intrigue has to do with the recurrent gothic motif of the *Doppelgänger*, or double—a term derived from a spectral entity popular in German folklore and fantasy. Throughout the *Harry Potter* series, one finds hints that Harry and his arch-nemesis, Tom Riddle (a.k.a. Lord Voldemort) are inextricably linked. Like Luke Skywalker and his father, Darth Vader or Bat Man and his evil counterpart the Joker, Harry Potter and the Dark Lord share more than magical wands fashioned from a common core: Both were orphaned at an early age raised in an impersonal and uncongenial environment by Muggles. Both were wizarding prodigies who exhibited powers early in their lives that neither could understand nor control. Both came to regard Hogwarts as their true home, i.e., the first and only place where they felt accepted. Both speak *Parselmouth,* the snake language long associated with Salazar Slytherine. Finally, both are linked telepathically through Harry's scar. It is because of these numerous connections that Harry is, at one point, suspected of being the heir of Slytherine, responsible for reopening the *Chamber of Secrets* (and thereby responsible for unleashing its mythological monster the basilisk). From his arrival at Hogwarts, the question of Harry's penchant for the Dark Arts becomes an issue. It is only as a result of Harry's protest that the Sorting Hat refrains from assigning him a place in Slytherine. When the one-time Death Eater and potions professor, Severus Snape is interrogated by the fanatical Voldemort loyalist Bellatrix Lestange concerning his loyalty to the Dark Lord, she demands to know why he did not dispose of Harry during Voldemort's latent period (following his failed effort to procure the Sorcerer's Stone (recounted in the first installment of Rowling's saga). Snape replies that for a time he, along with other Death Eaters, conjectured that Harry might be "a standard around which we could all rally once more" (*Deathly Hallows* 31).

The essence of this *Doppelgänger* motif (as well as that of the Horcrux) in gothic story-telling is the danger inherent in the divided self which finds classical expression in Robert Louis Stevenson's novella, *The Strange Case of Dr. Jekyll and Mr. Hyde.* Though familiar to many (thanks to its many cinematic adaptations over the years) Stevenson's fundamental message is often missed. In the original story, Mr. Hyde, the good doctor's evil twin, is not an enemy but rather an indispensable ally of Dr. Jekyll. Prior to Jekyll's well-intentioned, though ill-considered, decision to separate himself from his complimentary alter ego, Hyde functions as what the Swiss psychologist C. G. Jung refers to as the balancing archetype that he terms the Shadow. According to Jungian psychology, true rationality is marked—as in gothic literature—by the finely balanced tension of oppositional forces within individuals and social structures, not by the willful eradication of one side over the other. According to proverbial wisdom, a house divided against itself cannot stand. Neither can an individual or a civilization function effectively if its constituent elements are truly at war with one another. It is this insight into the spiritual dangers of psychic fragmentation that accounts for the frequency with which Gothic narratives introduce the theme of mutilation and disfigurement. Such mutilations are outward manifestations of an inward, or spiritual, condition. In the case of Voldemort, this theme is illustrated by Tom Riddles's horrific act of self-mutilation whereby he dismembers his soul six times over, concealing it in the six Horcruxes that Harry must find and destroy (along with the seventh part of Voldemort's soul which still resides within himself). The moment he commits to this darkest of all Dark Magic, Voldemort's fate is sealed. Harry must finish the job, but in freely choosing to follow this dark path, *He-Who-Must-Not-Be-Named* has committed a species of psychic suicide that guarantees the outcome of his climactic duel with Harry following the Battle of Hogwarts. "Neither can live while the other survives," states the enigmatic prophecy that Voldemort fails to retrieve from the Ministry of Magic, not because "good" and "evil" are mutually exclusive, but because Voldemort (like Jekyll) has liberated himself from restraints that define his human synergy. In Harry and Dumbledore, we see what the Dark Lord might have become but for the demonic choices he has made. In targeting Harry, Voldemort is, in without realizing it, creating the very conditions that will lead to his own inevitable downfall, as Dumbledore emphatically tells Harry (*The Half-Blood Prince* 510). Riddle's monstrous transformation from human into reptile is the inevitable precursor to his own destruction and the destruction of all that he most cherishes and wishes to preserve (though by the time he is finally vanquished, Voldemort cherishes little beyond his own survival and lust for power).

Rowling acknowledges this precept by depicting the utterly corrupt Tom Riddle as one who has severed all links to humanity—his own and that of others—in order to pursue an obsessive quest for immortality: "There is nothing worse than death' Voldemort snarls at Dumbledore during their confrontation at the Ministry." "You are quite wrong," replies Dumbledore (*Order of the Phoenix* 814). At the conclusion of the *Deathly Hallows*, when Voldemort has been reduced to a grotesque, whimpering infant writhing on the floor of the Charring Cross train station, Dumbledore's statement is horribly confirmed. Voldemort's earlier transformation from a handsome youth into a grotesque human/reptile hybrid is obviously emblematic of his spiritual decline (as is Darth Vader's disfigurement in the *Star Wars* saga). What distinguishes and illegitimates the Dark Arts from their counterpart recalls us to the political gothic in that it has to do with two radically different conceptions of the use and abuse of power. The methods employed by Voldemort and his followers are invariably coercive. The three unforgivable curses (Cruciatas, Confundus, and Avada Kadavra) hinge on magic as a tool of domination, an application of power that violates its victim's fundamental humanity by torturing them into submission, stripping them of free will, or depriving them of life itself.

By contrast, the magic on which Harry ultimately relies, much to his chagrin, has nothing to do with coercion: When Harry questions Dumbledore as to the meaning of the prophecy uttered by Professor Trelawny, he is deeply disappointed. "So, when the prophecy says that I'll have 'a power the Dark Lord knows not," asks Harry, "it just means love?" Yes—just love," replies the wizard sardonically (*Half-Blood Prince* 509). Dumbledore, who has his own reasons for appreciating Harry's unfailing capacity to embrace the light, reminds him that it was his mother's love that saved him from Lord Voldemort—just as he had earlier soothed Harry's *angst* over his obviously similarities to the Dark Lord by reminding him that it is not our abilities but our choices that define our humanity. The connection, of course, is that whereas Voldemort's choices in life are invariable informed by egotistical will to power, Harry's are guided by an instinctive concern for the welfare of others. For the same reason that he cannot bow to the power of death, Voldemort can no more value the power of love than he can value the magic of house elves like Creature: "Nothing I have seen in the world," remarks Riddle when he returns to Hogwarts seeking employment as a teacher, "has supported your famous pronouncements that love is more powerful than my kind of Magic, Dumbledore. "Perhaps you have been looking in the wrong places," rejoins the Hogwarts headmaster" (*Half-Blood Prince* 444).

A Smooth and Silent Coup

Of all the politically incorrect truths that plague recent Muggle history, none is more inflammatory than the postulate that events of national and international import have resulted of political calculation rather than happenstance, i.e., that the traumatic trajectory of modern American and world history from November of 1963 to September of 2001 may have been shaped as much by bullets and bombs as by ballots. The notion that these occurrences are related as part of a hidden history, an Orwellian exercise in social engineering carried out by covert arms of our own government in association with interested parties in the private sector, is currently regarded as a fringe view on a level with belief in UFOs and Sasquatch (to invalidate one unproven assumption with another). Media news commentators across the entire ideological spectrum vie with one another in discrediting "conspiracy theorists" as cranks and crackpots. In doing so, they invariably compare thinkers who are qualitatively incomparable. To equate, for example, scholars such as David Ray Griffin (a distinguished theologian critical of the official version of 9/11) with a demagogue such as David Irving (the notorious Holocaust denier) is like equating Jascha Heifetz with Jack Benny because they both played violin. To the editorial staffs of both the Right-wing *National Review* and its left wing counterpart *The Nation*—despite a steadily mounting torrent of documented criminal conspiracies for over half a century (some trivial, some deeply troubling)—all conspiracy theories are equally invalid according to the political consensus arrived at by this media phalanx. Only citizens who are credulous, unpatriotic, or irrational (probably all of the above) lend any credence to them. Moreover, anyone who dares to challenge such a prejudicial and uninformed stance is simply added to the growing list of undesirables whose opinions are regarded as too eccentric to merit serious scrutiny. This circular reasoning on the part of influential skeptics is to impose a news blackout virtually equivalent in its effect to that of official censorship.

Apparently, Jo Rowling's name needs to be added to the ever-expanding media black list, as her fictional world, at least, is rife with conspiracies. Following the Tri-Wizard Tournament from which Harry emerges with certain knowledge that the death of his schoolmate Cedric Diggory was no unfortunate but politically meaningless accident and that Lord Voldemort has indeed returned, the Ministry of Magic, in conjunction with its journalistic mouth piece, *The Daily Prophet*, mount an orchestrated cover-up designed to placate public opinion. Harry is nearly expelled from Hogwarts for using under-age magic to defend himself and his Muggle nephew, Dudley from an attack by the dreaded Dementors of Azhkaban in the Muggle suburb of Little Whinging (an attack which, of course goes unreported in the *Daily Prophet*). When summoned to a summary hearing before the Wizengemot (the wizarding community's Supreme Court), Dumbledore appears in Harry's defense, thereby thwarting a combined Ministry/Death Eater plot to discredit the Chosen One. Thanks to Dumbledore's able defense, however, Harry is acquitted; and from that point on, both he and Dumbledore are *persona non grata* to the political and journalistic establishments of the wizarding world.

Cornelius Fudge, convinced that Dumbledore covets his position as Prime Minister of Magic, allows himself to be persuaded by Lucius Malfoy, Dolores Umbridge and others sympathetic to the cause of Lord Voldemort that the conspiracy theories of the Hogwart's headmaster and his star pupil pose a threat to the Ministry, and by extension, the wizarding world itself. In reality, of course, Fudge's stubborn resistance to mounting evidence of Voldemort's resurrection is a classic example of the projection that inevitable results from a policy of denial. Ironically, it is the Ministry's misguided policy of denial that threatens wizarding security just as it is the covert adherents of the Death-Eater creed who are the true subversives, not Harry, Dumbledore, the Order, or its tatterdemalion student branch known as Dumbledore's Army. If this narrative pattern sounds strangely familiar, it should.

Both of Rowling's two most subversive characters, Albus and Harry, find themselves in a position identical to that occupied by other well-known outcasts and heroes of the political gothic imagination such as Agent Fox Mulder of the *X-Files* television series, architect David Vincent of *The Invaders*, or New Orleans District Attorney Jim Garrison in Oliver Stone's conspiratorial docudrama, *JFK*. Deprived of official status, ridiculed or shunned by the guardians of politically correct history (i.e., consensus history) branded as paranoiacs in the popular press, and discredited in the eyes of the general public, such individuals have no responsible option but to pursue their lonely quest for the truth that is "out there" until they are either defeated or vindicated. Small wonder that such individuals are often scarred (as Harry is) by the burden they must carry, frequently finding themselves estranged from even their closest allies. When he returns to Hogwarts following the tragic outcome of the Tri-Wizard Tournament (recounted in *Harry Potter and the Goblet of Fire*) Harry, for example, finds himself estranged from classmates, his two inseparable companions (Ron and Hermione) and his one powerful ally, Dumbledore. While one might be inclined to dismiss such comparisons on the grounds that fictional conspiracies are by definition fictional, such fictions necessarily arise and gain plausibility from real-world circumstances. Whether or not Rowling herself subscribes to any particular real-world conspiracy theory, the fact that she has created an elaborately conspiratorial narrative suggests that her literary sensibilities—and by extension those of her enthusiastic readership—are attuned to such possibilities.

Into the painful breach created by his temporary alienation from his support group steps Luna Lovegood, perhaps the most intriguing and certainly the most frustratingly under-developed characters in Rowling's extensive cast. As her name suggests, she is both a personification of the gothic ambiguity of madness (Luna) and the one character whose unfailing love is equal to that of Harry himself (Lovegood). Uncompromisingly honest, disconcertingly candid, unswervingly loyal, unabashedly eccentric, and endowed by suffering with a precocious wisdom, Luna is able to understand, to an extent, lessen, Harry's acute sense of isolation during his turbulent fifth year at Hogwarts. She is, perhaps a literary echo of the hippies and flower children of the early 1960s, with whom, I suspect, Rowling's younger self identified. Luna's single-parent father, the eccentric sorcerer, Xenophilius Lovegood, publishes an independent tabloid journal called the *Quibbler*. News items and opinions beneath the notice of respectable outlets such as the *Daily Prophet* are provided a venue in its pages.

Though many (perhaps most) of the views advocated by Xenophilius are invalid, his conspiracy theory regarding the Death-Eaters is well founded, and it is in an issues of this fringe journal that Rita Skeeter's coerced vindication of Harry's (who has been vilified as just another crank conspiracy theorist) is published, thanks to some deft maneuvering on Hermione's part. While on the run and in hiding from the Death-Eaters, Harry—protected from detection by various wizarding charms—overhears another group of refugees from Voldemort discussing the relative merits of the *Daily Prophet* and the *Quibbler* to the following effect: "*The Prophet*," scoffed Ted Tonks (father of Nyphadora Tonks). "You deserve to be lied to if you're still reading that muck, Dirk. You want the facts, try the *Quibbler*..."The Quibbler? That lunatic rag of Xeno Lovegoods," responds the skeptical Dirk. Ted replies, "It's not so lunatic these days...Xeno's printing all the stuff the *Prophet's* ignoring" (*Deathly Hallows* 299).

Perhaps Rowling's subversive message here is that in an age when the differences that once separated responsible reporting from tabloid journalism (superseded, in turn, by the even less reliable internet sites) have diminished to the vanishing point, the reputation of the source from which one's information is obtained isn't always a reliable gauge of its veracity. Where conspiracy theories are concerned, she seems to imply, enquiring minds are constrained to seek for truth in whatever venues it is to be found, occasionally including even a series of fantasy novels for children. The wizarding world of Harry Potter is a world in which the political establishment is increasingly overshadowed and controlled by sinister forces from within and without. The *Prophet*, its newspaper of record, has been reduced to little more than a propaganda tool for a compromised Ministry of Magic, and those who oppose these disturbing developments are demeaned and vilified in its pages. To cite once again the conspiratorially minded Oliver Stone, "Black is white, and white is black."

Lord Voldemort's cabal of *Death Eaters* is by no means the only conspiracy that figures in Rowling's epic. Once Voldemort comes to power and the Ministry falls, the natural order of things is virtually inverted: Voldemort's recently reassembled coterie of Death Eaters and fellow travelers, whose very existence was once contemptuously dismissed as" the paranoid style" in wizarding politics, quietly assumes its post-coup role as an ongoing, legally sanctioned criminal conspiracy while those loyal to the old Ministry, scattered and forced into hiding, find themselves hounded for treason. Meanwhile, as Voldemort consolidates his power, the general public continues to be kept in the dark, uncertain of whom to trust or believe until it is too late to mount an effective resistance—which, of course, was Voldemort's intention all along.

In noting certain parallels between Rowling's fictional world and real world conspiracy theories, it is interesting to observe that the *Prophet's* editorial stance of denial stems, in part, from a laudable desire to prevent history from repeating itself. Voldemort's perspective on wizarding history rests on his belief that the current world order—enforced by the International Statute of Wizarding Secrecy, a statute that sent the wizarding community into hiding from Muggle intolerance and persecution—is a conspiracy against the innate superiority of so-called "pure bloods." Voldemort's right-wing Nazi-like conspiracy, in other words, is inadvertently abetted by the left-wing conspiracy hatched by Prime Minister Fudge and his comparatively liberal minions in order to head off the kind of wild speculations and public panic associated in their minds with the first, unsuccessful Death-Eater coup.

The political factions within Rowling's fictional world seem eerily reminiscent of events in post-W.W. II American history. They reluctance of the wizarding political establishment to entertain Dumbledore's conspiracy theory mirrors the reluctance of today's liberal media to entertain even the most thoughtful and well-documented probes into the veracity of official explanations concerning a wide range of issues from the political assassinations of the 1960s to the terrorist attacks of 9/11. Ultimately, that reluctance (denial would be a more apt term) stems, on the Left at least, from a laudable motive; namely, a desire to discourage the kind of red-baiting conspiratorial fervor that led to the McCarthy Era and ultimately to a Cold War that nearly provoked a catastrophic nuclear exchange. For such individuals, the notion that the very extremism they most fear has taken root at the core of American power (under the cover provided by a misguided anti-conspiracy bias on the part of liberals) is simply too terrible to contemplate. It follows that anti-conspiracy faction on the political Right (like Rowling's Death-Eaters) have their own, very different, reasons for wanting to suppress speculations about the legitimacy of American democracy since 1963.

When Remus Lupin shows up at the Black residence (where Harry, Ron, and Hermione have been incommunicado since the aborted wedding festivities for Bill and Fleur) he brings news of recent political developments. He informs them that though Harry has come under official suspicion for his alleged role in the assassination of Dumbledore, rumors are rife that the Death-Eaters were responsible and that Lord Voldemort is behind the repressive policies implemented by the Ministry since Dumbledore's death. "However," explains Lupin, "that is the point: They whisper. They daren't confide in each other, not knowing whom to trust; they are scared to speak out, in case their suspicions are true and their families are targeted. Yes," concludes Lupin, "Voldemort is playing a very clever game. Declaring himself might have provoked open rebellion: Remaining masked has created confusion, uncertainty, and fear." As a result, reflects Remus, "The coup has been smooth and virtually silent" (207–208).

Though a resident of England, Rowling came of age during an era dominated by America's Cold War with the former Soviet Union and the numerous subsidiary conflicts, black ops, and right-wing paranoia it spawned. That she should eventually have created a literary fantasy in which these dark, largely unacknowledged, realities are mirrored should come as no surprise—though the enthusiasm her books have generated on the part of those who would otherwise condemn conspiracy theories is remarkable (especially considering that they are marketed for children). Perhaps it is precisely because of their primary market that their controversial political implications have escaped notice. Any attempt to point the rather obvious parallels between Rowling's imagined patsy (Harry Potter) and other officially promoted patsies in the real world such as Lee Harvey Oswald, Sirhan Sirhan, James Earl Ray, and that surrealistic band of lap-dance-loving, aerial-acrobatic Muslim zealots led by the ever-allusive Osama bin Laden will no doubt illicit howls of protest from those whose who regard a "failure of imagination" (the wildly improbable official explanation for the systemic breakdown of America's national security apparatus) as a tenable explanation for what occurred on 9/11. Nevertheless, disturbing similarities between the "smooth and silent coup" that overtakes the wizarding world in Rowling's cult-of-childhood novels and parallel developments in Muggledom since the end of Second World War are difficult to ignore.

Faith and Politics in Rowling's Universe

If the Chosen One's terrible sense of alienation and abandonment, following his confrontation with Voldemort in the Hall of Prophesy was, in Christian terms, his Gethsemane—his Dark Night of the Soul—then his solemn wilderness journey into the Forbidden Forest for the last time is his Via Dolorosa, i.e., his dolorous journey toward death. Each memory or unfulfilled yearning serves as a marker, as station (as in the Stations of the Cross) bringing Harry one step closer to the pain, loneliness, and humiliation of his final confrontation with Voldemort (his Golgotha). This portrayal of Harry as a *figura Christie* and of his seemingly inevitable martyrdom on behalf of his friends and loved ones is all the more convincing for being rendered without sentimentality or, for that matter, any explicit reference to Christian mythology. Its tragic authenticity is no more weakened by Harry's ultimate triumph, i.e., Tolkien's *Eucatastrophe*, than is the power and veracity of the crucifixion by the resurrection that reverses its outcome. Indeed—as in Cooper, Bradbury, Barber, and L'Engle—the finality and mystery of death are only deepened by an understanding that, under certain circumstances, to save one's life is to lose it. The ultimate denial of death, suggests the religious imagination, is the ultimate failure of the imagination to acknowledge the possibility of life after death (with its implicit possibility of moral accountability). It is not, as religious skeptics often suggest, the refusal to accept life as a meaningless farrago punctuated by extinction (as if yielding to such a desolate prospect was somehow heroic). On the contrary, what such a nihilistic philosophy interprets as a cowardly flight from reality into the arms of religious superstition or escapist literature the gothic imagination portrays as an audacious leap of faith into a higher, truer reality, i.e., a source of consolation that, when properly understood, affirms and defines the human condition.

It is therefore all the more remarkable that Rowling's sacramental vision has been especially targeted for its alleged advocacy of occultism. As the web-mistress of the *Leaky Cauldron*, one of the more popular internet fan sites, points out, "Jo Rowling has said she's never had someone come up to her and thank her for introducing them to witchcraft" (Anelli 181). In writing of Georgia housewife Laura Mallory's Evangelical Christian crusade to have the *Harry Potter* books banned in schools and libraries across the country, she points out that such attempts at censorship by fundamentalist sects have not been confined to Christian extremists. Islamic and Jewish fundamentalists have also censured Rowling's series (186). The pride, denial and self-righteous projection implicit in these efforts to obstruct an innocent past time are not lost on Ms. Anelli, nor is the fact that many of Harry's right-wing detractors literally don't know what it is they are talking about—Laura Mallory included—in that they admit to never having read the books or seen the films to which they so strenuously object.

Laughable as such one-dimensional criticism might be, the obstreperous ignorance it represents should not be taken lightly. The modern-day alliance of religious literalism with a conservative political and social agenda is a manifestly undemocratic mix (as are the "Islamo-fascism" of *Al Qaeda* as well as the "cryto-fascist" means advocated by some who oppose it). Comparisons between such present–day ideologies and that of European fascism in the 1930s and 1940s are discouraged by mainstream news outlets such CNN and CSNBC (though no such taboo is enforced at the Fox news network). This is ironic considering that Rupert Murdock's disingenuous brand of far-Right journalism comes perilously close to emulating Joseph Goebbels—Hitler's propaganda minister. The infamous Third Reich, we are told by that who discourage such comparisons, was a complex historical singularity that can never be repeated. "To describe Hitler and National Socialism as one of the forms of Fascism...is wrong," writes historian John Lukacs, "as is the imprecise and mistaken leftist practice of applying the adjective 'Fascist' to all movements and regimes of the radical right" (Lukacs 118).

In a footnote to this unambiguous statement, he approvingly cites another well-known historian of the Nazi era to the effect that "Nothing is more misleading than to call Hitler a Fascist." With due deference to the importance of nuanced thinking, one might reasonable respond by asking, "If even Hitler and Nazism do not deserve that damning appellation, who or what in the world does?" The mantra on the Left is *It Can't Happen Here* (to cite the title of Sinclair Lewis's 1935 novel about the coming of President Buzz Windrip's Hitler-like regime to America). Indeed, Windrip himself exemplifies of the folksy, Sarah-Palin-style populism and anti-intellectualism that currently dominates the Republican Party (as well as its "Tea Party" political base). Consequently, See-No-Evil on the Left is offended by terms such as "Islamo-Fascist" when applied to militant Muslims while Hear-No-Evil (his counterpart on the Right) is equally dismissive of terms like "theocratic-fascism" when applied to so-called "faith-based" initiatives. Both adjectives, I would argue, are imperfectly justified (but justified nevertheless).

Moreover, our failure to recognize the growing threat posed by a resurgent, though veiled fascism in Muggle affairs is responsible for much of the confusion that bedevils modern political discourse, both in England and the United States. John Christopher deals explicitly with that threat in his gothic, sci-fi trilogy (as does Lucas in the *Star Wars* films). So does J. K. Rowling through the provocative parallels she draws between Death Eaters and Nazis. If, as Rowling suggests, fear of the name only increases fear of the thing itself, knee-jerk leftist objections to drawing parallels between pre-war ideologies in central Europe and similar ideologies in other regions of the post-war world—United States included—is a questionable policy (notwithstanding the fact that He-Who-Must-Not-Be-Named magically tracks down members of the Order who violate a commonly observed stricture against voicing his name).

As suggested previously, from the Slytherin perspective the "International Statute of Wizarding Secrecy" is the outcome of an official conspiracy to deprive wizards and witches of their right to rule ("Magic Is Might"). Given that assumption, Voldemort's followers no doubt regard their ethically-reprehensible means as expedient in light of their counter-conspiratorial ends. Similarly, many of today's right-wing super-patriots no doubt genuinely believe that they are championing the Spirit of 1776 when, in reality, they are destroying it. Meanwhile, the fact that those on the Left who oppose such extremism are infinitely preferable—ethically, politically, and spiritually—to those who practice it does not excuse a stubborn refusal on their part to recognize the devastating role played by domestic conspiracies from the Right in our national and international life long after they have been documented. Indeed, to anyone not mired in denial, the "hidden history" of the previous half century is no longer hidden. Only the uninformed (or the willfully blind) can fail to detect its outline.

Perhaps it's time the Left overcame its paranoia about being paranoid. While the Right confidently shouts "The old Cold War is dead; long live the new War on Terror!" the Left blandly accepts the premise that either war was necessary. Was Rowling mindful of such modern controversies while writing her Harry Potter books? Perhaps not, but then again, she did emphatically warn her readers not to trust authority. Whatever her current views on Muggle politics, it seems plausible that the popularity of her books—with

readers sophisticated enough to appreciate their political gothic implications—rests in part on the parallels they yield between a primary world
drifting toward some form of global Fascism (a drift to the Right not the
Left) and the secondary world of gothic fantasy for the young created by
their author.

Werewolves and Time Travelers

Though all of Rowling's books are drenched in the conventions of supernatural gothic literature in that they all deal with paranormal phenomena (telepathy, prophecy, portents, bi-location, talking pictures, alternate realities, and
non-human intelligences such as ghosts, monsters, and mythic beasts) there
is a dramatic shift in mood between books two and three. The initial three
chapters of *The Prisoner of Azkaban,* those that recount Harry's misadventures at Number Four Privet Drive, retain the burlesque gothic flavor of the
earlier books. Indeed, the "blowing-up" of Aunt Marge employs the same
hyperbolic humor as Hagrid's visit to the absurdly implausible location
chosen by uncle Vernon to sequester Harry from wizarding influence on the
occasion of his eleventh birthday—an abandoned lighthouse on "a large rock
way out at sea" (*Sorcerer's Stone* 54). Beginning with the fourth chapter of
Azkaban, however, the tonality of Rowling's work modulates to a minor key,
where it remains for the duration of her saga. While her delightful sense of
humor is evident throughout the entire series, her canvas definitely shifts to a
more somber palette. In keeping, no doubt, with the 'coming of age" motif
that figures prominently in cult-of-childhood narratives, the remaining
portions of Rowling's saga focus increasingly on the negative end of the
human emotional and psychological spectrum.

   With the arrival in her story of the alleged criminal Serius Black and the
otherworldly Dementors who pursue him (following his escape from Azkaban—the wizarding world's maximum security prison), Rowling's literary
landscape is overshadowed—as if by an immense cloud bank blotting out the
sun. The first two books in her series deal essentially with Harry's transition
from an insignificant Muggle to a lionized celebrity universally known
within wizarding circles as the Chosen One. Once this transition is ratified
(as it is when Harry succeeds in killing the basilisk in *The Chamber of
Secrets*), Rowling's focus shifts to Harry's impending rendezvous with
destiny, a dark journey that will entail a mounting catalogue of hardships,
dangers, and personal losses. As a consequence, Rowling's gothic narrative

deepens as she explores back stories that delve into the psychological complexities and hidden facets of principal characters such as Serius Black, Severus Snape, James and Lilly Potter, Remus Lupin, Albus Dumbledore, and the house-elf, Kreature.

One of the more intriguing and apparently incongruous themes introduced by Rowling in *The Prisoner of Azkaban* is time travel—a theme typically associated more with adult science fiction than children's fantasy. Nevertheless, many stories belonging to both genres have to do with the paradoxes of re-membering a reality that has been temporally dis-membered, i.e., changing a timeline that has been disfigured and mutilated by evil design, accident, or simple human folly. Whether on the personal plane (as in Antonia Barber), a mythic plane (as in Ray Bradbury and Susan Cooper, or on the cosmic plane (as in Madeleine L'Engle) the desire to atone for past misdeeds and their consequences by returning to their point of origin and rectifying them exerts a powerful hold over the gothic imagination. While Rowling repeatedly warns against the dangers of dwelling on an irretrievable past (exemplified by the dangers inherent in the Mirror of Erised or the Sorcerer's Stone), in *The Prisoner of Azkaban*, she indulges a universal fascination with the notion of averting tragedy by turning back the clock.

The Hogwarts hippogriff (Buckbeak) is sentenced to execution by the Ministry to for having retaliated against an intentional provocation on the part of the ever-obnoxious Draco Malfoy (who thereby manages to sabotage Hagrid's very first Care of Magical Creatures lesson). Professor Lupin (Harry's mentor in Defense Against the Dark Arts) is on the point of being exposed as a werewolf, and his boyhood friend Serius Black, who has been unjustly accused of murdering Harry's parents, is faced with the prospect of being subjected to the "Dementor's kiss" (a particularly nasty form of punishment involving loss of soul as well as loss of life). Dumbledore, at this point in the story, encourages Harry's precocious friend, Hermione to use her "time-turner." Worn as a necklace, this miniature time machine is activated by a turning mechanism—hence its name. Accordingly, she returns with Harry, with whom she shares this device, to a moment from which all of these undesirable outcomes can be averted by their future selves (through changing the sequence of events leading up to them). In order to accomplish this, the two intrepid time-travelers temporarily become their own *Doppelgängers*—at one point jeopardizing their primary objective, which is to save Buckbeak, by very nearly encountering their previous selves.

Paradoxically, their experience of reliving the past informs (and even alters) their future actions, e.g., Harry's confidence in casting the Patronus Charm in order prevent both Serius stems from his realization that he has previously seen himself casting the charm successfully. In the annals of parapsychology, this phenomenon is referred to as FIP (Future Influencing the Past). Theoretically, FIP is premised on the theory— advocated by certain modern physicists—that we inhabit not a universe but a multiverse in which every point in time intersects with an infinite number of possible outcomes. According to this hypothesis, not only is the future indeterminate, but so too is the past.

The problem with time-travel narratives is that they inevitably raise a host of philosophical and theological conundrums. If the future already exists, i.e. if it is determined, what becomes of human free will? If free will is an illusion, what becomes of moral responsibility, i.e. if our actions and moral choices are pre-determined as part of an unbreakable chain of cause and effect extending infinitely in both directions, how can we be blamed for them? As a correlative of this line of reasoning, one might restate the issue in theological terms: If human actions are governed by a divine providence that is irresistible, i.e. if everything happens according to God's will, how does God escape ultimate responsibility for Auschwitz, cancer, and the host of other existential atrocities that have plagued humankind? In the simplest possible terms, the issue boils down to a starkly simple proposition: If God is omnipotent then he is not good. If he is not omnipotent, then he is not God. Such questions are as old as theological reflection itself. Obviously, it was not Rowling's intention to write a philosophical or theological tract anymore than it was her intention to produce a political manifesto. Nevertheless, as suggested elsewhere in this volume, the connection between the religious imagination and the gothic imagination is a close one. Moreover, an over-view of the time paradoxes explored in gothic literature for young readers suggests a consensus among the ones discussed in this volume (with regard to enigma of time and its ethical implications).

Broadly speaking, all of them, including J. K. Rowling, reject a binary model of reality whereby free will and determinism are the only available options. On the contrary, all seem to postulate the existence of a cosmos in which human actions are both undetermined and yet, in some unspecified way, shaped by a transcendent moral authority. At the same time, the realms they imagine are equally and truly open to influence by both human and *daimonic*, i.e. otherworldly forces—not to be confused with "demonic" forces (see Patrick Harper's *Daimonic Reality: Understanding Other World Encounters*). These cult-of-childhood authors propound models of reality that are, in other words, dualistic, i.e. premised on the existence of alternate realities that co-exist with everyday human experience but remain hidden from ordinary perception, such as the wizarding world in Rowling or the "Perilous Realm" in Tolkein's *Smith of Wootton Major*. These secondary worlds offer a wide spectrum of temporal settings that have one thing in common. They all explore possibilities that challenge our common sense view of time as a straight arrow—an irreversibly forward trajectory comprised of an unalterable past, an elusive present, and an unknowable future.

In *The Prisoner of Azkaban* and subsequent volumes, Rowling both validates and pokes fun at those who claim to have transcended time's mysteries in the character of Sybil Trelawny, Hogwart's Professor of Divination. Throughout most of the Harry Potter saga, she is a figure of fun—a theatrical imposter who annually impresses her more gullible students by inaccurately predicting that one of them will die within the year. She is also a dipsomaniac who surreptitiously hides her discarded bottles of cooking sherry in the Room of Requirement. Often, she attempts to conceal her lack genuinely prophetic power behind an impressive-sounding barrage of mystical verbiage such as, "Broaden your minds, my dears, and allow your inner eyes to see past the mundane" (*Azkaban* 105). Accordingly, Professor McGonagall issues a timely warning to her transfiguration class that divination is one of the least precise and unreliable branches of magical learning. The ever-rational Hermione, who rejects its validity even before McGonagall's warning, is uncharacteristically contemptuous of Professor Trelawny.

Even Dumbledore, a model of tact and tolerance, is impatient at times with the resident seer's incessant complaints about the centaur Firenze (or "Dobbin," as she prefers to call him). His staffing problems, quips the kindly magician, have proven to be more difficult than he could have foreseen—never having himself studied Professor Trelawny's subject. Despite such gentle mockery, both he and McGonagal rush to Trelawny's defense against the sadistic Dolores Umbridge. Moreover, Dumbledore acknowledges that despite her airs and pretensions, Professor Trelawny has, on at least two occasions, rendered prophecies that deserve to be taken seriously. This suggests a degree of ambivalence on his part (as well as that of her creator) with regard to the subject of precognition. Trelawny's many misses do not invalidate her sporadic hits, anymore than the lunatic beliefs of Xenophilius

Lovegood concerning Gernumblies, Wracspurts, and Crumple-Horned Snorkacks necessarily invalidate his views on the Death-Eater conspiracy.

Once again, Rowling's gothic imagination refuses to sanction the conveniently glib either/or thinking into which the narrowly rational mind so easily slips. Such ambivalence is based an orientation to reality that recognizes the complexities and incongruities inherent in the human condition. The irrationally skeptical debunking mentality, on the other hand, seeks to simplify reality by forcing it into discrete categories, e, g., possible or impossible, right or wrong, superstition or reality. When Emerson famously denounced consistency as the "hobgoblin" of little minds, he instinctively seized upon a gothic metaphor. It is, however, important to recognize that the trans-rationality of heroes such as Harry is not the same thing as irrationality. Such heroes are open to the possibility of non-rational modes of perception (including ESP, divination, and even divine revelation as well as more mundane sources such as intuition, dreams, and simple hunches) but they also employ critical thinking skills. In other words, logic—according to the gothic imagination—is a good servant but a poor master. Harry listens to both the logical Hermione Granger and the impulsive Ron Weasley; but in the end, he invariably takes his own council.

Tales of Beedle the Bard

Rowling's literary sequel to the *Deathly Hallows* is a slender volume of wizarding *Kunstmärchen* (translated into modern English from ancient runes by Hermione Granger). Naturally enough, it illustrates some of the political points and ethical dilemmas explored in the Harry Potter novels (in which these apocryphal tales are referenced). A copy of the Bard's tales figures prominently in Rowling's final volume as a bequest to Hermione from the deceased Dumbledore, along with a Quidditch snitch and magical sword for Harry and a "deluminator" (or "Put-Outer" as Rowling sometimes calls it) for Ron. Rightly surmising that Dumbledore's motives in making such unusual bequests were clandestine, the former Auror and Fudge's successor as Minister of Magic, Rufus Scrimgeour, interrogates the three beneficiaries—though without tricking them into an admission. Harry, Ron, and Hermione are themselves puzzled until, at a later point in the story, they pay a visit to Xenophilius Lovegood in the hope that he will be able to explain the strange runic symbol on the cover of Hermione's copy of *Tales* (which they interpret as a possible clue to Dumbledore's intentions that might have been missed by Scrimgeour). They consult Luna's father because he had worn this identical symbol on his outer garments at the wedding party for Bill Weasley (Ron's facially mutilated elder brother) and his beautiful Veela bride (Floeur Delacour). On this occasion, one of the invited guests, (Victor Krum, an internationally known *Quidditch* star with an amorous interested in Hermione) is outraged to discover a symbol associated in his mind with the Dark Wizard Gindelwald brazenly displayed by Luna's father.

The editor of the *Quibbler* explains to his three unexpected guests that Grindelwald's use of this symbol was a misappropriation of what was originally a sign associated with the so-called Deathly Hallows (objects of transcendent magical power—allegedly mythical). Xenophilius, however, believes in the historical reality of Deathly Hallows, which further attests to his penchant for conspiracy theories according to most of the wizarding community). Elaborating on this theory, he mentions that that their veiled historical origins are recounted in one of Beedle's stories, *The Tale of the Three Brothers*. When his Muggle-raised guests, Harry and Hermione, plead ignorance of this story (familiar to every wizarding child) Xenophilius proposes that they read it aloud. This proves to be a stalling tactic designed to delay Harry's departure. Xenophilius, in apparent contradiction of his previously stated support for Harry) has summoned the Death-Eaters. As we eventually discover, his beloved daughter, Luna (schoolmate of the three renegades) has been captured and imprisoned by Voldemort's cohorts on account of her father's outspoken pro-Muggle views. Desperate to secure her release, her distraught father hopes to negotiate an exchange of hostages.

As the nervous and distracted Xenophilius reads aloud, Harry learns that in the course of their travels, the three fabled brothers one day encounter Death himself on a narrow bridge. The hooded specter cleverly offers each of them a gift in exchange for his freedom. Accepting an invincible wand— variously known as the Elder Wand, the Wand of Destiny, or the Death Stick—the eldest brother steps easily in Death's wily trap. Subsequently boasting of its prowess to fellow lodgers while in a drunken stupor, he is murdered and relieved of his wand. The middle brother asks for a magical stone capable of restoring the dead to life. The gift bestowed upon him by the Grim Reaper proves to be none other than the Sorcerer's Stone, featured in Rowling's first Harry Potter novel. Driven mad by an unrealizable longing, its new owner commits suicide after conjuring a tantalizing simulacrum of his lost love. The youngest brother, wiser than his two siblings, asks for a Cloak of Invisibility. This allows him to elude Death for many years. At the end of a long and satisfying life, he willingly accompanies his one-time nemesis (now perceived as an old friend) to his unknown bourn.

The point of this tale, apart from the political gothic moral stressed in Rowling's introduction (that wizarding magic, like Muggle technology, is a double-edged sword) is baldly stated in Dumbledore's commentary: "Human efforts to evade or overcome death are always doomed to disappointment" (*Tales* 94). The relevance of this moral to Voldemort's sinister bid for immortality is obvious, despite the headmaster's ironic dismissal of those who would interpret it too literally. The sorcerer's stone, a.k.a. the philosopher's stone (Rowling's preferred title for her initial novel in the series), like the Mirror of Erised, offers only a pale and false substitute for the "deepest, most desperate desire of our hearts." As Dumbledore warns his distinguished student shortly after Harry's arrival at Hogwarts, "It does not do to dwell on dreams and forget to live, Harry" (*Sorcerer's Stone* 265). The prospect of death, suggests Rowling, need not terrify us into relinquishing our humanity nor should it be allowed to spoil our pleasure in living. Indeed, when properly understood, death can be viewed as a goad to achievement, a unifying bond with our fellow creatures, and even as a welcome release from a world in which "the deepest, most desperate desire of our hearts" is ultimately unattainable—in short, as a friend and companion. In this respect, her message, like that of Ray Bradbury is that the Reaper, though ineluctable and unavoidable, need not be considered grim.

As for the Wand of Destiny, which provokes Dumbledore's most elaborate commentary as well as his harshest ethical strictures, it clearly represents the ultimate weapon so coveted by those who believe that "Magic Is Might" (and their Muggle counterparts who seem to believe that might is magic). Rowling is not of their number, perhaps because she belongs to the first Muggle generation to have matured within the shadow of a doomsday weapon. On the contrary, the weight of her social commentary is cast in the scale of peace over war and compassion over hatred and revenge—though she clearly implies that there are circumstances under which armed resistance is a necessity. In light of the moral dilemmas posed by the Nazis of modern Muggle history (on whom she has obviously modeled her Death-Eaters) it is difficult to see how she could have concluded otherwise. Nevertheless—as the finale of John Christopher's sci-fi trilogy suggests—the uncompromising commitment to non-violent resistance advocated by authentic Christianity (as well as other world religions) must surely command respect in any truly just society. It was the young John F. Kennedy, a recent war veteran reporting on the founding of the United Nations, who observed that the world would only achieve lasting peace when it accorded pacifists the same prestige it currently bestowed upon its warriors (Douglas 324). In an era of weapons of mass destruction capable of wiping virtually out all human life (along with most plant and animal life) the claims of absolute pacifism are strengthened. When the probable outcome of "realism" in international affairs is so plainly suicidal, the idealism of men such as Jesus and Gandhi begins to look like common sense. Proponents of coercive power (according to the religious as well as the gothic imagination) inevitably defeat their own agenda. The would-be eaters in Rowling's adult fairy tale become the eaten—an outcome, suggests the gothic imagination, reserved for all who pursue peace through victory rather than peace through justice.

Harry Potter, like Kennedy, is clearly a reluctant warrior. He seeks neither wealth nor glory and in every circumstance in which his powers are tested, all of his considerable ingenuity is directed at avoiding, rather than inviting, martyrdom. If the artistic cult of childhood is a distinctive by-product of a culture shaped by Christian parables of the Kingdom, as I believe it is, then the adventures of the Chosen One belongs to an essentially Christian literary genre, notwithstanding the protests of its Evangelical detractors. Indeed, since many of these same detractors seem to enthusiastically embrace the spread of theocracy from the barrel of a gun, one might argue that Rowling's anti-authoritarian commitment to an ethic of nonviolence is the true basis of their objection and not, as they claim, her alleged occultism. The theme of innocence and gentleness menaced by evil (qualities that are often personified in gothic literature by children or women) lies at the core of the gothic imagination, as it lies at the core of Christian ethics. Indeed, in his isolation, unconventional outlook, rebellion against the religious (Jewish) and political (Roman) establishment of his day, his unwonted martyrdom, his access to alternate realities, and his world-weariness as a " Man of Many Sorrows," Christ (like Harry) is a transcendent gothic hero.

As for Beedle's other tales, fans of Rowling's primary narrative will perhaps find them less entertaining than their accompanying commentary. In his remarks about "The Wizard and the Hopping Pot," Dumbledore reveals fascinating facets of both wizarding and Muggle history: We learn, for instance, that this forward-looking story of brotherly love for *Muggles* (in its original, pro-*Muggle* version) fell out of favor during the early fifteenth century, an era of *Muggle* witch hunts, and was later revised into an anti-*Muggle* tale in which "non-magical folk" are portrayed as a "torch-bearing, pitchfork-toting" mob. These *Muggle*-instigated persecutions, says Dumbledore, eventually induced witches and wizards to go into hiding, a development that led ultimately to the complete schism established legally by the International Stature of Wizarding Secrecy in 1689. Subsequent to this statute, Brutus Malfoy (editor of an anti-Muggle periodical and no doubt ancestor to Lucius, Bellatrix, Narcissa, and Draco) promotes the notion that befriending Muggles is the mark of an inferior wizard. In short, we learn that the Malfoy's predilection for the Death-Eater philosophy has a long and distinguished pedigree, traceable to one whose very name (Brutus) suggests violence, conspiracy, and treachery (*Tales* 11–19).

In this same commentary, we also learn that Beedle's uncompromising tales underwent a Victorian process of Bowdlerization under the guise of a children's anthology by one Beatrix Bloxam (perhaps a sardonic corruption of Beatrix Potter, famed author of the *Tales of Peter Rabbit*). This soon-to-be discredited anthology (entitled *Toadstool Tales*) offered a supposedly wholesome alternative to Beedle's allegedly "unhealthy preoccupation" with horrid subjects such as "death, disease, bloodshed, wicked magic and bodily effusions and eruptions of the most disgusting kind" (17). It produced unfortunate side effects in its target audience, however—"uncontrollable retching" for example, according to Dumbledore. From such a humorously hyperbolic remark, one can easily infer J. K. Rowling's attitude toward those who object on principle to the introduction of crudity into literature for children (though there may be some readers, myself included, who view her fascination with mucus, vomiting, and toilet humor as somewhat immature, without necessarily endorsing either the prudery of Beatrix Bloxam or the "family values" of Rowling's more conservative critics).

Rowling's fascination with the gruesome and the grotesque (as well as her adolescent fascination with vulgarity) are abundantly evident in the tale of *The Warlock's Hairy Heart*, in which we encounter the gothic themes of sexual obsession and sadism, i .e., the sexual sublime. The essence of this theme has to do with the humanizing effects of love and its perverse mirror image—a lust for power that transforms the self-sacrificing power of love into a need to control (*Eros* into *Thanatos*). Though Beedle naturally avoids even the faintest approach to anything salacious (as does Rowling in her primary narrative), he clearly suggests a quality of psycho-sexual sadism whereby the protagonist, unable to love (Harry's outstanding virtue), resorts instead to domination. In seeking such a perversely asymmetrical relationship, the warlock undergoes a monstrous transformation that leads ultimately to the Jungian *enantiodromia* reserved for all who would choose the violent ways of coercion over the gentler arts of suasion and reasoned argument. As a result, he ends by literally stopping his own heart and that of the woman he seeks to marry.

The fairy tale premise of this story hinges on the warlock's decision, at an early age, to employ the *Dark Arts* in order to guard against the foolishness of human attachments. To accomplish this aim, he removes his heart in a symbolic act of self-mutilation, placing it within an enchanted crystal casket for safekeeping. Increasingly given to denial, he projects his own emotional inadequacies unto others whose penchant for yielding to the more tender human emotions he naturally views with contempt. Observing parents at play with their children, for instance, he conjectures that their hearts must be empty husks. Dedicating his life to selfish pursuits, the warlock is quite content until one day—goaded, not by love but by wounded pride at overhearing a servant express pity concerning his solitary lifestyle— he decides to affirm his male potency by feigning love for a beautiful and accomplished maiden.

The maiden, intuiting her admirer's lack of emotion and imagination, states that she would be delighted by his attentions if only he had a heart, never suspecting, of course, that her commonplace figure of speech holds a terrible significant for her would-be suitor. Intent on proving that he is, indeed, possessed of a heart; he takes her to the dark castle dungeon where the crystal casket lies hidden. Removing its pulsating contents, he exhibits a diseased and withered organ covered in coarse hair. Using magic to re-insert this atrophied thing into his empty chest cavity, he discovers that through years of neglect "its appetites had grown powerful and perverse" (51). Heedless of the consequences for her, he extracts the maiden's heart from her living body, selfishly seeking to exchange it for his own. A short time later, the lifeless, mutilated bodies of both the warlock and his innocent victim are discovered.

At the climax of this flagrantly gothic tale—reminiscent both in its subject matter and its nightmarish atmosphere to the tales of E. A. Poe—the demented warlock is described as holding the maiden's "smooth, shining, scarlet heart" in his hands while he strokes and licks it (52). One can only imagine what Mrs. Bloxam must have made of this "age-inappropriate" image. Nevertheless, it captures with horrible vividness the dementia of one who (like Lord Voldemort) has willfully stripped himself of the ability to relate to others at an emotional or imaginative level. The perverted warlock—in choosing to devalue and ignore a part of life without which he cannot function properly—dismembers that which he is subsequently unable to remember. In Dumbledore's commentary, he notes the resemblance between the warlock's ill-considered acts of Dark Magic and Voldemort's creation of the six Horcruxes. Both cases involve the division of that which is not meant to be divided (heart from head/soul from body/past from present), i.e. the fatal loss of a wholeness (holiness) whereby the individual components of a healthy organism can perform their proper function only in conjunction with all the other components that comprise the system.

The handsome-but-misguided warlock in Beedle's tale and the handsome-but-misguided Tom Riddle in Rowling's primary narrative are both victims of the divided self, of their own fatally alienated Shadow side (which they willfully discard without realizing the danger in which they have placed themselves). A psychic fault line exists within each of these gifted but deeply flawed characters, one that illustrate the gothic interdependence of head and heart, rational and trans-rational. To seek to suppress or privilege one term over another in a balanced equation is to forfeit its synergistic balance, suggests the gothic imagination. As in Robert Louis Stevenson's *Dr. Jekyll and Mr. Hyde*, the monstrous product of such a schizophrenic imbalance is not unhampered rationality but a condition best described as sub-rational, i.e., bestial. In one of his more gothic mysteries (*The Adventure of the Creeping Man*) Sir Arthur Conan Doyle's protagonist (Sherlock Holmes) warns that when we leave the narrow path of nature, seeking to rise above it, we are liable to fall beneath it. Once again, irrationality, as understood by the gothic mindset, does not imply the subordination of head to heart but the fatal consequences that can result from a deficiency or *excess* [emphasis mine] of either. Harry Potter, like all true gothic heroes, represents a balanced synthesis, a merging of the best qualities of his two constant companions and alter-egos (the rational and reflective Hermione Granger and the impulsive and emotive Ronald Weasley).

The Fountain of Fair Fortune is the second of Beedle's five tales (as presented in his book). It relates the adventures of three witches and one Muggle Knight. Each year, according to Beedle, a single aspirant is permitted to bathe in a fountain whose waters have the ability to impart good luck (i. e. fair fortune). The first witch, Asha is ill and therefore seeks health. The second, Altheda is poor and therefore desires prosperity. The third, Amata (jilted in love) seeks relief from a broken heart. The name of the Muggle Knight (Sir Luckless) tells us all we need to know about his motivation in seeking out the fountain's enchanted waters. All four aspirants are permitted within the confines of the walled garden that encloses the fountain. Together they embark upon their quest, knowing that ultimately only one of them can prevail. After overcoming a series of obstacles designed to test the worthiness of their cause and character—an obstacle course in which the unique suffering of each provides the key to their further progress—they finally arrive within sight of the fountain.

At this point, Asha collapses in agony. Altheda proceeds to gather the herbs necessary to create a healing potion. Out of gratitude, Asha (who upon drinking her sister's concoction is immediately cured) relinquishes her claim on the fountain in favor of her compassionate sibling; but Altheda, realizing that her previously undervalued gifts as a "potioneer" (Rowling's term) are sufficient to insure her future prosperity, defers to the lovelorn Amata—a noble gesture emulated by Sir Luckless. In passing one of the preliminary tests during which she was required to shed tears into a broad stream that separated the supplicants from their objective, Amata discovers that the stream has already washed away her grief. In doing so, her eyes are suddenly opened to the unworthiness of her former lover. In acknowledgement of the knight's unselfish gallantry, Amata insists the he be the one to bathe in the fountain. Emerging from its reinvigorating waters with a renewed sense of purpose and confidence, Sir Luckless immediately proposes to Amata, who instantly accepts his offer of marriage. The four aspirants, having solved their problems through cooperation and self-sacrifice, depart the garden together never suspecting that the only magic necessary to improve each of their fortunes came not from the fountain, but from within themselves.

This fable (reminiscent of an episode from t the *Half-Blood Prince* in which Harry pretends to use *Felix Felicis* to bolster Ron's *Quidditch* skills. Ron, fooled into thinking that Harry (now captain of the Gryffyndor team) has spiked his breakfast drink with the good luck potion, performs admirably on the Quidditch field, never realizing that the only magic imparted by Harry's placebo came from his own enhanced sense of self-confidence (295). Both tales have to do with the nature and limitations of magical power stressed throughout Rowling's saga: In each of the Bard's five tales, the misuse of magic or an over-reliance upon its powers leads to either misfortune or else—as in the tale we have just considered—misunderstanding. Dumbledore's editorial comments are largely devoted to a discussion of what the marriage of Amata and Sir Luckless implies with respect to the issue of pure blood/Muggle relations. In a possible parody of the kinds of censorship advocated by detractors who have sought to remove Rowling's works from the shelves of local schools and libraries, the reader learns that Lucius Malfoy had once led an effort to have books that depict interbreeding between wizards and Muggles removed from the library shelves at Hogwarts. The school's enlightened headmaster, of course, refutes Malfoy's argument, informing the supercilious Death-Eater that owing to decades of interracial breeding "pure-bloods" no longer exist, adding that his petition is therefore nonsensical as well as immoral. Hagrid, of course expresses the same point of view in his defense of Hermione against the racial slurs hurled at her by Lucius's son Draco in the *Chamber of Secrets* (116).

In Beedle's remaining tale, *Babbity Rabbity and Her Cackling Stump*, the Bard recounts the misadventures of a vainglorious *Muggle* king who seeks magical powers at a time when witches and wizards are subject to persecution by *Muggles*. Needless to say, when the king advertises for a mentor, the only applicant he attracts proves to be a charlatan. After subjecting the king to a futile regime of false magical training, the king finally demands results, threatening to behead his mentor if the particular result he has in mind should fail. Realizing that he is about to be exposed (if not executed) the opportunistic con artist enlists the aid of a washerwomen who is, in reality, a witch driven into hiding by Muggle intolerance. When the king proceeds to stage a public exhibition of his newly acquired magical prowess in the courtyard of his castle, it is this witch (stationed behind a near-by bush) who actually performs the stunts requested by his fawning subjects.

All goes well until a spectator requests the resurrection of a recently deceased animal. Sounding one of Rowling's leitmotifs, Beedle's youthful readers are reminded that there is no magic that can restore the dead to life (just as there is no potion that can induce genuine love). Realizing that he is destined to fail, the charlatan blames the concealed witch who flees into the forest pursued by an angry mob of Muggle vigilantes. Transforming herself into a rabbit, the witch/washerwoman scurries for cover into the trunk of a tree. Seeing the pack of hounds gathered at the base of the crone's leafy refuge, and assuming that witch and tree are one and the same entity, a henchmen of the king (on orders from the sham Muggle wizard) fells the tree with his axe. Seizing upon the charlatan's mistake, the cackling voice of the witch is heard to emerge from within its stump, pronouncing a terrible malediction (possibly the *Cruciatus Curse*, according to Dumbledore) on any Muggle who would henceforth harm any witch or wizard.

This same disembodied voice demands that a statue in memory of the poor washerwoman be erected on the spot to ratify the king's solemn pledge of tolerance (and to serve as a reminder of his foolishness and hypocrisy in having sought magical powers inappropriate to his kind). Muggle persecution and pretension are thereby foiled by the cunning of a witch. Moreover, it is through this tale, as Dumbledore recounts, that many wizarding children first learn that death cannot be reversed by magic. With characteristic humor, Rowling disposes of this potentially corrupting notion (the very notion that has corrupted Tom Riddle) with unambiguous finality. Citing the eminent wizarding authority Bertrand de Pensées-Profondes (Bertrand the Profound Thinker) she offers the following eloquently phrased *coup de grâce*: "Give it up. It's never going to happen" (80).

Taken together, *The Tales of Beedle the Bard* provides fans of the *Harry Potter* series with a welcome encore as well as an added narrative dimension—a tertiary world within the larger narrative framework of her primary and secondary worlds (the wizarding world and the world occupied by Muggles). The house-of- mirrors effect created by such an ornate and elaborately realized fantasy is, in itself, one of its more gothic features. Moreover, these tales stand on their own inherent literary merit. From the salty peasant humor of the *Hopping Pot* and *Babbity Rabbity and Her Crackling Stump* (memorable for its Edward Lear-like title alone) to the chilling horror of *The Warlock's Hairy Heart* and from the delicate poignancy of *The Fountain of Fair Fortune* to the cautionary wisdom of *The Tale of the Three Brothers*, these stories (which might easily have been exploitive pot-boilers) are instead entertaining and artfully crafted fantasy in their own right. *The Fountain of Fair Fortune,* in particular, invites comparison with Tolkien's shorter works, such as *Smith of Wootton Major* (complete with a parody of the donnish scholarship that has been lavished on such literature by Tolkein himself, among others—present company included). Collectively, the Beedle stories are impressively varied, each one a finely etched vignette. Consistent with the style and themes of the novels—into which they are neatly interwoven—these interpolated tales within a tale might even be said to offer a more satisfying sense of closure to her primary narrative than Rowling's somewhat perfunctory epilogue in the *Deathly Hallows*.

9 Psychological Gothic: Reflections on Rowling's Back Stories

Kreature's Tale

The psychological gothic, as pointed out in the preceding chapter on Rowling's political gothic imagination, is a genre that deals primarily with the divided self. It explores interior conflicts resulting from psychic dismemberment that can shade easily from angst and neurosis into obsession and even madness. In the supernatural gothic genre, such transformations are frequently portrayed in terms of a physical transformation from man into beast (or monster) as in Mary Shelley's the *Frankenstein: The Modern Prometheus* and R. L. Stevenson's *Dr. Jekyll and Mr. Hyde.* Just as frequently, however, gothic writers and film makers toy with ambiguous situations that can be interpreted as either psychological or supernatural in nature.

The shadow-side of the divided self often eludes detection until it is too late for us or others to mount an effective defense against it. Our dark compulsions can appear in the guise of an unsuspected beast-within or, more terrifying still, in the guise of a reassuring friend, lover, or neighbor. "Complicated creatures we are," writes Madeleine L'Engle, "aware of only the smallest fragment of ourselves" (*Walking on Water* 131). In a similar vein Lurie Sheck observes, "So much of life is invisible, inscrutable: layers of thoughts, feelings, outward events entwined with secrecies, ambiguities, ambivalences, obscurities, darknesses strongly present even to the one who's lived it—maybe especially to the one who's lived it" (Sheck x).

The existence of hidden dimensions lurking deep within the psyches of those we least suspect is portrayed in gothic arts through a variety of recurrent symbols and motifs. The *Doppelgänger*, or mirror image (often a dark alto-ego), is one of these. The many connections between Harry and the Dark Lord referred to in the previous chapter suggest that Riddle is Harry's *Doppelgänger*. Mirrors themselves, reflect back to us an uncanny reverse image of ourselves that, under the right (or wrong) circumstances, can be disconcertingly unfamiliar. Masks are another frequent devise for concealing an identity too terrible to acknowledge or one that we simply choose not to reveal. The German romantic painter, Caspar David Friedrich conveyed his awareness of psychological complexity (and its alienating effects) by always depicting his human figures as either having their faces turned away from the viewer (*Traveler Overlooking a Sea of Fog*) or else as being so remote from the viewer's vantage point that their faces are unrecognizable (*Monk by the Sea*). Charlotte Brontë and Robert Schumann, both of whom contributed significantly to gothic mythology in their respective art mediums as well as to the cult of childhood, made the masquerade ball a central literary or musical motif.

These artists suggest that our true identities are ultimately a mystery closer than our dearest companion, yet more remote than a distant planet. During times when the protagonists of gothic literature and film (whether for children or adults) experience psychotic breaks or supernatural transformations they themselves are often unaware of their actions and motivations. In keeping with the recurrent gothic theme of "dismember/remember," their loss of humanity is almost invariably accompanied by a loss of memory. Unable to recollect their dark deeds in any detail, internally conflicted monsters like Lon Chaney's *Wolf Man* (or Rowling's werewolf Remus Lupin) agonize over their condition and its consequences, real or potential. Sometimes, even if they are able to recall their actions while under the spell of some personality-altering potion or sinister enchantment, they are unwilling to confide in others.

Most of us (in moments of exceptional candor) would have to plead guilty to the charge of having betrayed our better instincts, at some point in our lives. Whether we did so under the influence of drugs, fear, greed, ambition, or lust (to mention only a few of the more common human motivators), it is likely that guilt and shame will have served as strong inducements to concealment afterwards, i.e., inducements to hide our folly from others (or worse, from ourselves). It is precisely this circumstance that enlists our sympathy for the "monsters" of gothic literature and film. Sometimes—often in fact—the protagonists' struggles are waged behind the scenes, well away from the prying eyes of the reader or viewer. When finally revealed, they can drastically alter our perception of the character involved as well as those with whom they interact. The Walker's tragic undoing in Susan Cooper's *The Dark Is Rising* (see Chapter 1 above) is a clear example. Kreature's tale from the Harry Potter saga, to which we will now turn our attention, is another.

When we first encounter the Black family house elf, skulking about Grimmauld Place in *The Order of the Phoenix*, turning up his pug nose at Hermione Granger (and all such Mudblood filth), he is a singularly unlovable character—old, unwashed, disheveled, sullen, and rude. Fiercely loyal to his former mistress (Serius Black's deceased mother who still hurls pro-Death-Eater/anti-Muggle sentiments at passers-by from a portrait hanging on the wall of a staircase landing), her *Death-Eater* relation, Bellatrix Lestrange (an irrepressible sadist responsible for having tortured Neville Longbottom's parents to the point of madness), and Sirius's younger brother Regulus Arcturus Black (another deceased Black family member who figures prominently in Kreature's own tragic back story). This unfavorable first impression is confirmed when we learn, later on, that it was he who betrayed Serius to Voldemort thereby setting the stage for the pre-mature death of Harry's godfather at the Ministry of Magic.

Consequently, when Harry commands this newly acquired servant (a bequest from Sirius Black) to follow Draco Malfoy day and night or when he harshly enjoins the foul-mouthed house elf to desist from using terms like Mudblood, no one, other than Hermione, truly objects. House elves, a lowly caste within the wizarding community—particularly in the eyes of the "purebloods"—are magically obligated to comply with their master's orders (or else punish themselves mercilessly for failing to do so). Hermione takes a stand against this wizarding tradition through founding S. P. E. W. (Society for the Promotion of Elfish Welfare). As she is herself a victim of the pureblood ideology, her objection to Harry's heavy-handed treatment of Kreature is obviously based not on approval of the racial prejudice inflicted upon this servant class, but rather on her conviction that the routine neglect and abuse suffered by house elves at the hands of their wizarding masters is politically dangerous as well as ethically wrong. At this point in the narrative, it has already backfired against Sirius and will ironically do so again against He-Who-must-Not-Be-Named.

The crisis in Harry's relationship with his house elf comes while the three truant Hogwart's students (Harry, Ron, and Hermione) are in hiding at Number Twelve, Gimmauld Place, the Black family's ancestral home. The Ministry has fallen to the Death-Eaters, and the three friends are at the threshold of their quest to retrieve the remaining Horcruxes, i.e. the remaining parts of Voldemort's dismembered soul that are magically preserved and protected within a series of well-concealed objects that Harry must find and destroy. In *The Half-Blood Prince*, he had visited an enormous cave with

Dumbledore to retrieve one of them (a small, golden locket that had once belonged to Salezar Slytherine, one of four master wizards responsible for the founding of Hogwarts School of Witchcraft and Wizardry). This particular Horcrux was hidden on a small island in the middle of a subterranean lake, like the underground lake depicted in Jules Verne's adventure classic *A Journey to the Center of the Earth*. The locket is, of course protected by many enchantments, not the least of which is a legion of Inferi (zombie-like corpses animated solely by the will of Lord Voldemort). The least contact with the lake by anything or anyone, other than the tiny boat that Voldemort has prepared for his own journey to the island will summon these creatures to the lake's surface.

Once Harry and Dumbledore have hazarded this dark crossing, the challenge that awaits them on the island is equally daunting. The locket is placed within a goblet filled to the brim with a potion that must be consumed in order to remove the locket. The effect of this potion is the exact inverse of that produced by the Mirror of Erised. It forces its victims to relive their most traumatic memory. Moreover, the potion induces a tormenting thirst, intensified by the surrounding water. Any attempt to slake that thirst will, of course, summon Voldemort's legion of Inferi. Professor Dumbledore, who drinks the potion, is compelled to relive the tragic death of his sister Arianne (about which, more later) while Harry, who has promised to resist Dumbledore's protestations should his resolve falter, forces him to drain the goblet. The locket, once examined, proves to be a substitute. The genuine Horcrux, whose whereabouts is, of course unknown, was stolen by someone bearing the initials R.A.B, as Harry learns from an enigmatic note placed within the locket by its present owner—a note in which the thief expresses his intention of destroying the Horcrux in the hope that when its maker finally meets his match, he will do so as a mortal subject to death and defeat. In as much as Dumbledore's searing experience on the island serves as a prelude to his own demise at the hands of Harry's hated nemesis, Professor Snape. The futility of their shared mission only adds to Harry's subsequent grief and bitterness. It also anticipates a revealing confession from Kreature.

While hiding out at Grimmauld Place, Harry discovers that "R.A.B." coincides with the name of Sirius's brother, Kreature's beloved former master, Regulus Arcturus Black. He also suddenly remembers that, while helping Mrs. Weasley in the Herculean task of sorting through years of accumulated rubbish at Gimmauld Place, they had tossed aside a locket strikingly like to the one found on the island. Thinking this locket might be the real Horcrux, Harry interrogates Kreature as to its present whereabouts. It is at this point that the distressed house elf reveals both the connection between R.A.B and the Lord Voldemort and his own tragic involvement in their dispute. For Harry, Ron, and Rowling's readers, this narrative casts Kreature (and by extension his species) in a startlingly new light.

Harry learns that the locket, slated for disposal by Mrs. Weasley and subsequently reclaimed by Kreature, has been removed from Gimmauld Place by the sneak-thief wizard, Mundungus Fletcher. When asked how Kreature came into possession of the locket in the first place, the elf collapses in an agony of remorse and self-recrimination, accusing himself of the worst offense a of which a house elf can be guilty, i.e. a failure to carry out his masters orders. When asked to explain, Kreature spins the pitiable tale of having accompanied Regulus Black to a dark subterranean lake, a location only too familiar to Harry. He tells of how Voldemort had earlier used him as a guinea pig on which to try the effects of the enchanted potion, laughing at his agony, how he "disapparated" (teleported) from the island on his master's instructions, how Regulus, thoroughly disillusioned with Voldemort and his Death-Eaters, returned to the island himself, drank the enchanted brew, substituted the locket Harry retrieved for the actual Horcrux, and was dragged below the lakes surface by Inferi—though not before ordering Kreature to refrain from telling his mistress, mother to Regulus and Serius, of these occurrences and to destroy the locket by any means necessary. Anguished by his inability to inform the grief-stricken Mrs. Black of her missing son's fate and unable to pry open the Horcrux, Kreature repeatedly and cruelly punishes himself for his failure to obey orders.

When Harry, thunderstruck by this narrative, asks how—given Regulus's change of heart—Kreature could have betrayed Serius to Voldemort, an act that resulted ultimately in the death of Harry's godfather, a distressed Hermione intervenes saying, "Oh, don't you see now how sick it is, the way they've got to obey" (*Deathly Hallows* 198). Defending the house elf, she points out that Kreature has been loyal to those who have treated him with consideration, and that Kreature's kind simply parrot the Death-Eater philosophy of those they serve. The premature death of Sirius, she maintains, was an indirect consequence of the injustice traditionally visited upon house elves by their wizard masters and a direct outcome of Serius's invariably harsh treatment. "I do not think," Dumbledore had once remarked to Harry, "that Sirius ever saw Kreacher as a being with feelings as acute as a human's" (199). Moreover, Voldemort's arrogant indifference to elfish ways and welfare—specifically his lack of foresight in failing to realize that elf magic would enable Kreature to disapparate from the island and later assist Harry to find Slytherine's locket—leads ultimately to the defeat of the Death-Eater conspiracy

In light of these revelations, Harry and Ron dramatically alter their tone and demeanor, politely soliciting Kreature's help in locating Mundungus and the lost locket. The house elf responds favorably, as Hermione knew he would, collaring the thief (though not the locket, which has come into the possession of the sadistic Mrs. Umbrage) and turning their brief tenure together at Gimmauld Place into a culinary delight. Rowling's point is not so much an illustration of the "Golden Rule," as it is an example of the core insight of the psychological Gothic imagination: even the most unpromising among us, harbor a history and potential that might well undo the elaborately contrived prejudices and expectations of our detractors. Kreature's seemingly ingrained racial bigotry, i.e., his evasiveness, resentment, and treachery, proves to be more the products of nurture than nature. In light of his extreme suffering, our attitude toward him and his species is significantly revised. A former enemy of the *Order* is converted into an ally and a perversely asymmetrical and destructive relationship is transformed into a synergy of interests from which both parties benefit. The back stories of Snape and Dumbledore prove to be even more instructive.

Snape's Story

One of the most heated Rowling-related controversies, prior to the publication of her final book in the series, had to do with the character and motives of Professor Severus Snape. "Snape is loyal" reads a decal that was distributed at bookstores on the night *Deathly Hallows* was released. This partisan view was not shared by many Potter fans, however, as attested by the following: "The hottest debates," writes David Langford, in a book dealing with internet fan mail published prior to the *Deathly Hallows*, "are centered on Dumbledore's trust and Snape's betrayal...if trust and betrayal are the actual truth of the situation" (Langford 128). Snape's ostensible motive throughout the saga is to thwart Harry. A former Voldemort lieutenant, Severus (whose very name suggests his divided, i.e., severed, loyalties) aspires to the position of Dark Arts Teacher at Hogwarts, a position that Dumbledore refuses to bestow. From the outset, this seemingly sinister figure conceives a dislike for the Boy Who Lived (or "the Potter boy" as he prefers to call him) bordering on pathological hatred that manifests in repeated insults aimed at Harry's deceased father James as well as at Harry himself).

When, in the *Half-Blood Prince*, Snape kills Dumbledore, all doubt as to his allegiance is apparently settled...but is it? Not until the *Deathly Hallows* do Harry and Rowling's readers learn the surprising truth about the *Half-blood Prince*—a truth involving a chivalric tale of unrequited love, remorse, and heroism equal to any found in the pages of Arthurian legend. Just prior to the climactic *Battle of Hogwarts*, Voldemort subjects his lieutenant and supposed ally to a horrifying ordeal: Thinking it necessary to the realization of his plans, he allows his venomous pet snake, Naginni (named perhaps after the devilish nineteenth-century violin virtuoso Nicoló Paganini) to bite Snape. Harry, having witnessed this "regrettable" betrayal surreptitiously, rushes from his hiding place to the side of his dying nemesis. In extremis, Snape demands that Harry lock eyes with him as he presents the "the Potter boy" with a phial of distilled memories gleaned from his oozing wounds.

Upon returning to Hogwarts and emptying the phial into Dumbledore's Pensieve, i.e., a time-travel device that allows one to observe one's own past and that of others, Harry learns of Snape's unsuspected love for his departed Muggle-born mother, Lilly Evans. Having met as children prior to their matriculation at Hogwarts, Snape and Lilly are inseparable friends until the dashing prankster James Potter (who delights in tormenting his young Slytherine peer) claims Lilly's heart. Both Severus and James are pure-bloods, though only one is attracted by Dark Arts and hence to the anti-Muggle bigotry on which the Death-Eater ideology is founded. Initially repulsed by his arrogance as well as his cruelty to her friend, Lilly is eventu-ally attracted to the boy who will one day become Harry's father. Unable to tolerate her blossoming love for the magically and athletically gifted young wizard, Snape provokes a final breach between himself and Lilly. Lashing out at her in humiliation following one of James's many pranks at his expense, Snape angrily announces that he has no need of her mudd-blood assistance. Despite his subsequent apologies, the rift proves to be irreparable on her side.

Later, when Voldemort learns of the prophecy and decides to murder the infant Harry in order to preempt its fulfillment, Snape pleads with him to spare Lilly's life, but to no avail. Upon learning of her death (and that of her husband), Snape repents of his Death-Eater sympathies and agrees to serve Lilly's memory by acting as a triple-agent for Dumbledore and the *Order of the Phoenix*. From that moment on he becomes Harry's secret protector at Hogwarts, Dumbledore's trusted confederate, and the *Order's* most valuable ally. As Lord Voldemort's apparent spy, the grieving Snape places his life in constant peril on condition that Dumbledore never reveal his true allegiance or its motivation. "My word," asks Dumbledore, "that I shall never reveal the best of you...if you insist" (679).

In retrospect, all of Snape's ostensible hostilities and betrayals are explicable in terms of his dangerous assignment on behalf of Dumbledore and the woman he loved to his dying breath. His otherwise irrational dislike for Harry is rooted in jealousy and painful memory. His murder of Dumbledore is a pre-arranged act of self-sacrifice aimed at foiling the Death-Eater conspiracy. His frustration over Harry's inability to learn "occlumency" (the wizarding art of closing one's mind to telepathic influence) stems from his own super-human efforts in keeping his secret from the powerful Lord Voldemort and from his awareness of the dangers to Harry posed by his openness to the Dark Lord's influence. His protection of Draco Malfoy (Harry's nemesis among his peers at Hogwarts) and his sympathy for Draco's mother Narcissa are not marks of his devotion to Voldemort's cause (as Rowling's reader are led to suppose), but acts of genuine compassion that serve to advance the cause of Dumbledore by reinforcing Snape's credibility in the eyes of Narcissa's sadistic sister, Bellatrix Lestrange. Finally, his insistence on meeting Harry's gaze as his life ebbs away is due to the striking resemblance, with regard to this particular facial feature, between Harry and his mother—a resemblance frequently alluded to by James's former friends and classmates Professor Lupin and Sirius Black. In looking into Harry's eyes, Snape is, in fact, gazing one last time at the eyes of the woman he still loves, a friend for whose sake he has ultimately surrendered his life.

It is on account of Snape's secret devotion to Lilly, hidden by Snape's skill at occlumency, that Harry will one day name his youngest son after the school master he once detested. On the point of departing for his first year as a student at Hogwarts, anxious over the possibility that the Sorting Hat will place him in Slytherine House rather than Gryffindor, Harry reminds his anxious offspring, Albus Severus, that he was named after two former Hogwarts headmasters. "One of them," says the adult Harry, "was a *Slytherine* and he was probably the bravest man I ever knew" (758). Who, other than the author, could have suspected that beneath the bat-like academic garb of the villainous Potions Professor beat the heart of a Gothic hero transformed and redeemed by his remorse for an unrequited love? In a series of books replete with poignant episodes, despite the humor so effectively used by Rowling to deflect and lighten their impact, none is more poignant than the exchange (long after Lilly's death) in which Snape reveals to Dumbledore that his own altered Patronus is that of a silver doe.

A wizard's or witch's Patronus (a magical projection in the shape of an animal) is their most intimate and characteristic mark of identification, one that can only change under the influence of some profound emotional trauma. The silver doe was Lilly's Patronus during her brief span on earth and the fact that Snape has involuntarily adopted it attests to the durability and strength of his devotion. It is this projection, sent by Snape, which points Harry to the Sword of Gryffindor at the bottom of a frozen pond, much as Rowling's story points her readers to an understanding of the unexpected treasures of the human spirit that are sometimes submerged beneath the hardened and opaque surfaces we present to others. The world is as it is because people are often neither what they should be nor what they appear to be. This is certainly true of Albus Dumbledore, whose personal integrity, regard for Harry, and commitment to justice are all called into question in the course of Rowling's narrative.

Dumbledore's Story

If the Harry Potter series can be said to have a hero (other than Harry himself) that hero's name is Albus Percival Wulfric Brian Dumbledore. Throughout the first six volumes, the headmaster of Hogwarts conforms to the Jungian archetype of the Wise Old Man, fulfilling in Rowling's saga the role assigned to Merlin in Arthurian legend (and its prodigious offspring, such as Cooper's *Dark Is Rising* series) and Gandalf in Tolkien's *The Lord of the Rings*—though Rowling disavowal Tolkien as a source (Granger, 281). As Harry's principle sponsor and unofficial mentor, Dumbledore is responsible for his placement with the Dursleys following the death of his parents. He guides Harry's educational process once Harry arrives at Hogwarts, and later on in his development, even becomes his personal tutor assisting Harry, with the aid of a Pensieve, to explore the biography of Lord Voldemort prior to the Death Eater rebellion. Though Dumbledore's master plan with regard to Harry's pedagogical process is perhaps best characterized as an example of "tough love," at no point in the earlier stages of Rowling's serialized epic does Harry ever question either his motives or his integrity.

All this changes dramatically following Dumbledore's death at the hands of Professor Snape in *The Half-Blood Prince*. Harry's first inkling that his knowledge of Dumbledore's past is woefully inadequate comes at the wedding of Bill Weasley and Fleur Delacour, thanks to the malicious gossip of Ron's octogenarian Great-Aunt, Muriel. Disguised, by means of Polyjuice Potion as a Weasley cousin (cousin Barney), Harry listens with mounting alarm as the vituperative old woman dissects Dumbledore's character and reputation with undisguised glee. In an exchange between the sharp-tongued gossip monger and Elphias Doge, author of a glowing pro-Dumbledore epitaph in the pages of *The Daily Prophet*, Muriel raises disturbing questions concerning the famous wizard's commitment to Muggle rights, his youthful involvement with the infamous dark wizard Grindlewald, his strained relationship with other members of his immediate family, his sister Ariana's mysterious ailment and premature death (Muriel conjectures that she was a non-magical person born to a wizarding family, otherwise known as a "squib"), his mother's role in hiding her daughter's shameful condition from the wizarding community by virtually holding her prisoner in her own home (and perhaps, speculates Muriel, disposing of her when the opportunity arose), Dumbledore's willing acquiesce in the nefarious treatment of Ariana, and his alleged resentment at the responsibilities that devolved to him upon the untimely deaths of both his sister and mother. Three circumstances, in particular, lend credence to these distasteful and shocking allegations. One has to do with a tantalizing comment concerning Dumbledore that Harry finds in a partially destroyed letter written by his mother to Sirius Black. Another concerns a hastily written tell-all biography of Dumbledore penned by Harry's old journalistic nemisis, Rita Skeeter. A third implicit confirmation comes from the simple fact that the Hogwarts headmaster withheld from Harry the astounding fact that the Potters and Dumbledores were virtually neighbors—both having been raised in Godric's Hallow, where Harry's parents were killed.

The discovery of the fragmentary letter occurs the morning after the three second generation Marauders—Ron, Hermione, and Harry (the first generation having consisted of James Potter, Remus Lupin, Serius Black, and Peter Peddigrew)—seek refuge from Death Eaters in the London residence of the Black family, former headquarters for the Order and now part of the legacy bequeathed to Harry by Sirius. This becomes necessary when word arrives at the hastily curtailed wedding reception for Bill and Fleur that the Ministry of Magic has fallen to Lord Voldemort. Feeling lonely and distraught by what he has overheard concerning his mentor and one time role-model, Harry wanders into an upstairs chamber that had once served as the bedroom of Sirius's brother, Arcturus Regulus. Like other rooms in the house, this one is disheveled, having been ransacked by Death Eaters in search of useful information. It is while sifting the discarded remnants of their efforts that Harry happens upon a torn photo of his infant self and his father, James together with the fragment of the letter from Lilly Potter to her friend Sirius. After scouring the room unsuccessfully in hopes of finding the missing portions of these treasures, Harry sets about scrutinizing the fragments in his possession. One unfinished sentence from his dead mother's letter having to do with Bathilda Bagshot (author of *A History of Magic*, one of the Hogwart's texts familiar to Hermione and largely ignored by Ron and Harry) is of particular interest and concern, in that it seems to fit an unsettling pattern: "Bathilda drops in most days, she's a fascinating old thing with the most amazing stories about Dumbledore...I don't know how much to believe, actually, because it seems incredible that Dumbledore..." It is at this crucial point that the recovered fragment abruptly breaks off. Could Bagshot's "incredible" allegations against Dumbledore, Harry wonders, confirm the scandalous rumors retailed by Muriel (*Deathly Hallows*, 180, 181)?

As mentioned above, it was during the course of a conversation between the acerbic Auntie Muriel and Dumbledore's peer and champion, Elphias Doge that Harry first began to question his own convictions concerning the renowned Hogwarts headmaster and former head of the Wizengemot (the ruling assembly of the Ministry of Magic). The specific context within which his doubts were awakened had to do with the impending publication of Rita Skeeter's much anticipated biography, *The Life and Lies of Albus Dumble-dore*. In a promotional blurb (an interview with Skeeter published in *The Daily Prophet*), the loose-tongued biographer had hinted at the list of old scandals and unresolved controversies surrounding Dumbledore that led to the altercation between Doge and Muriel. Later, Hermione filched a complimentary copy of Skeeter's book found in Bathilda's cottage on the nearly fatal occasion of a visit to Harry's birthplace in search of the Sword of Gryffindor (a magical relic capable of destroying Horcruxes). Despite her awareness of Harry's growing disillusionment with Dumbledore and her many protestations against the reliability of Skeeter's sources and opinions, Hermione shares the book with Harry, principally in the hope of making amends for having inadvertently broken his phoenix-feather wand while struggling with Voldemort's gigantic snake Naginni during their ill-fated trip to Godric's Hallow. In reading passages from Rita's anti-Dumbledore screed (a noun that suggests the possible origin of her surname), Harry discovers that his own worst doubts are apparently documented.

According to Skeeter's account, Dumbledore had befriended the infamous Gellert Grindlewald and joined him for a brief time in plotting the defeat and subjugation of Muggles "for "The Greater Good," thereby overturning statute of secrecy on which the wizarding community's safety had rested since the middle ages. In effect, Dumbledore had, at a comparable age, advanced the very cause that Harry and his friends were currently risking their lives to defeat. Though hazy as to the details, Skeeter maintains that upon the death of Ariana (Albus's allegedly squib sister), her precocious brother broke off his relationship with Grindlewald and did a volte-face with regard to that dark wizard's political agenda. She goes on to relate a graveside brawl between Albus and his brother Aberforth at Ariana'a funeral, speculating that the latter may have had just cause to blame his precocious brother for their sister's untimely death, even suggesting that she may have become "the first person to die for "the greater good," a signature Death-Eater phrase that—according to a letter from the youthful Dumbledore to his then friend and compatriot Grindlewald—was suggested by Dumbledore (359). Despite Hermione's unswerving defense of Dumbledore and her equally fierce denunciations of Skeeter, Harry confesses that his faith in Dumbledore's love and rectitude are shaken. The plausibility of Skeeter's account, in light of what has been hinted at by others and Dumbledore's own silence, have convinced him that it was not love that motivated Dumbledore's involvement in his life. "He shared a damn sight more of what he was really thinking with Gellert Grindlewald," Harry declares resentfully, "than he ever shared with me" (362).

The danger posed by journalists such as Skeeter is that their omissions, distortions, and half-truths are covered by a thin but compelling veneer of plausibility. It is not unreasonable to conclude that Rowling sees her as representative of the profession she practices—in the Muggle as well as the wizarding world. It is only through comparing Skeeter's damning version of reality (which serves the Ministry's disinformation campaign admirably) with Dumbledore's own account at the conclusion of the book that we gain insight into the means by which a disingenuous fourth estate, i.e., one that panders to a popular appetite for sensationalism, can become an unwitting pawn in the hands of a corrupt political establishment. Skeeter belongs to no organized conspiracy. She has (unlike her more honorable but less pliable colleague Xenophilius Lovegood) been subjected neither to intimidation nor to overt censorship. Moreover, Rowling supplies absolutely no reason to surmise that she is in the pocket of either Voldemort or the corrupt upper echelons of the Ministry. Nevertheless, her cleverly worded character assassination does more to undermine Harry's resolve, and thereby threaten the Order and its liberal agenda, than either. Her career contributes to and is powered by the iconoclasm of an egalitarian culture that confuses cynicism with realism and equates a glib facility with words with incisive social commentary. Skeeter's malice resonates to a culture that celebrates mediocrity and distrusts the very possibility of a disinterested idealism. She infers that his life-long activities on behalf of Muggles were motivated by guilt over his youthful flirtation with Death-Eater values (which they no doubt were, in part), and that his high-minded opposition to Voldemort was therefore a hypocritical pose (which it most certainly was not). She even suggests that Dumbledore was a sexual predator. Witness her off-color insinuation that Dumbledore's interest in Harry as was "unnatural" (28). In short, her school of journalism—reproduced by Rowling with pitch-perfect accuracy—exploits the political and psychological Gothic realization that the world is not as it appears to be by ignoring the other half of the equation that it is not as it should be. Lacking an inner compass that points her toward the truth, the indiscriminate skepticism of investigative journalists such as Rita Skeeter sustains the status quo by undermining public confidence in those who would seek an alternative to it. By sniping at our heroes, under cover of journalistic objectivity, suggests Rowling, we protect our villains.

When Harry, suspended between life and death, meets Dumbledore in King's Cross station, he (and the rest of us) learn the tragic truth behind Skeeter's plausible, though wildly inaccurate, conjectures. Ariana was not a squib imprisoned by an unfeeling mother more concerned with her family's reputation than with her daughter's welfare, nor was she disposed of by an ambitious brother intent on suppressing his seditious activities. In reality, she was the victim of a brutal rape by a group of Muggle boys who left her permanently scarred psycologically and in need of constant attention. Her condition was hidden from prying eyes, whether wizarding or Muggle, asserts Rowling, not to spare the family embarrassment but in order to spare Ariana any further anguish—and, no doubt, to indulge Kendra's understandable impulse to guard her daughter's privacy. She had, after all, effectively lost not only a beloved child but—as Albus's father was sentenced to life in

Azkahban Prison for having murdered Arianna's assailants—a husband as well.

As for Ariana's death, it was an indirect consequence of an argument between Aberforth and Grindelwald. Having challenged his brother's right to shift the care of Ariana entirely to his shoulders in order to pursue his vainglorious dream of Muggle domination, Grindlewald entered the fray on behalf of the doctrine that "Magic Is Might." A heated exchange ensued in which deadly magical charms were cast, one of which struck the unfortunate Ariana. This accident marked the turning point in Dumbledore's attitude toward the use and abuse of magic and the paternal role that wizards should adopt toward their Muggle brethren. In this sense (and in this sense only) Skeeter was right to interpret Dumbledore's later crusade for Muggle-born rights as a compensation for the harm he had done. Having been complicit in Grindlewald's plans (a complicity that was no doubt justified in his mind by the Muggle assault upon his sister), he later sought to atone for his youthful sins firstly by defeating Grindlewald in a wizarding duel and secondly by devoting the remainder of his life to promoting wizarding tolerance and justice toward Muggles . He could not, of course, undo the fate of his sister (as much as he longed to do so). She was dead, despite her mother's loving ministrations, and Albus was only too aware of his indirect responsibility for that outcome. Indeed, it is possible that it was he who cast the fatal charm. Later in the novel, when Dumbledore retrieves the Sorceror's Stone from an heirloom that Voldemort has converted into a Horcrux, he pays one last time for the recklessness of his youth by placing Salazar Slytherine's ring upon his own finger in the vain hope of restoring his mother, father, and sister to life long enough for him to express his profound remorse—thereby incurring a terrible curse that, had it been permitted to run its course, would ultimately have claimed his life (718).

This particular episode makes an important statement about the essential ambiguity of the gothic hero-villain's mythic journey. The same trauma that leads us to introspection—i.e., to an imaginative reconstruction of our past that enables us to integrate past failures and disappointments can also ensnare us into grasping at delusional solutions to our gothic dilemmas. Those familiar with the life of Charles Dickens, for example, will remember that, comparatively late in life, he reopened a correspondence with Maria Beadnell, whom he had loved thirty years earlier. She had declined his proposal of marriage at the insistence of her parents—who disapproved of the courtship between their daughter and a then untried author with dubious prospects. Irrationally imagining that the intervening years had melted away and that his festering sense of humiliation at this cruel and unjustified rejection was about to be miraculously assuaged (even though he was now a middle-aged married man of international repute) he arranged to meet with the recently widowed thirty-five-year-old. The outcome of this meeting is recorded in the pages of *Little Dorrit* in which she is somewhat callously lampooned as Flora Finching (Kaplan 327).

By 1855 when their reunion took place, the graceful fantasy-figure of Dickens's memory had transformed into a grotesque parody of her former self—a corpulent, garrulous, and absurdly flirtatious matron. Goethe's dictum that "Old age does not make childish; it merely finds us children still," is clearly a double-edged sword. Like Dickens at the height of his powers, Dumbledore is badly burned by a smoldering desire that the combined consolations of fame, experience, and wisdom had been able to quell— a desire that that was rekindled by a final opportunity to unite the Deathly Hallows (and in so doing relieve his inconsolable sense of loss): "I was such a fool, Harry," Dumbledore laments from beyond the grave, "After all those years I had learned nothing. I was unworthy to unite the Deathly Hallows, I had proved it time and again and here was final proof" (720). One cannot help but wonder if he considered using a "time-turner" to undo the tragic consequences of his youthful indiscretions (as he did to alter the fates of Serius Black and the Hypogriff Buckbeak). If so, he clearly rejected the idea—perhaps realizing that the very wisdom that benefitted Harry, Ron, and Hermione had been forged in the crucible of his own pain—a pain that it would therefore be unwise to prevent (or possibly he simply refused to play a game of cosmic dice to benefit only himself and his immediate family when the stakes for the wizarding and Muggle communities were so high). Whatever the true explanation, Dumbledore was (as Harry at one point informs the headmaster's censorious brother, Aberforth) never free from the torments of his own guilt-laden conscience (567). The price of transcendence, the gothic imagination seems to suggest, is perpetual remorse. The alternative, however, is even worse, as Voldemort's ultimate destiny clearly demonstrates.

Like all gothic heroes and their parents (or surrogate parents), Dumbledore is a flawed human being; and like all offspring (or substitute offspring), Harry must struggle to accept this truth with regard to his idealized role-model. It has been said that there are no such thing as perfect men in this world, merely perfect intentions. That insight, and the unsettling realizations that flow from it, constitute an adult secret that defines the imaginative boundaries of childhood. What truly differentiates adults from children is a mature capacity to tolerate ambiguity, i.e., an ability to see beyond the particular to the general, to separate the man or woman from the message, and to avoid making the perfect the enemy of the good. It is a secret that is deeply offensive to the innate literalism, idealism, and uncompromising intolerance of youth. I suspect that children find this secret at least as disturbing as adult sexuality and violence though it receives far less attention from "conservative" guardians of virtue.

Self-styled "liberals" are equally remiss in scoffing at those who object to prevalence of graphic sexuality and brutality (and their attendant vocabulary) in the modern entertainment industry. Neil Postman, who attributes the breakdown of adult authority, in part, to the indiscriminate exposure to adult sexuality enjoyed by today's youth, is a rare exception to the political partisanship of modern "Culture Wars" in that he also condemns the lack of historical and philosophical contextualization, in-depth coverage and follow-through, and aesthetic discrimination endemic to pop culture media (see Neil Postman, *The Disappearance of Childhood*). Meanwhile, what today's print and electronic news media offers is a surrealistic welter of incongruous images and inchoate facts: a lead story about famine in Africa juxtaposed to one about a three-legged dog, neither of which appeared yesterday nor will appear again tomorrow. The very sequence of images belies the asymmetry of their relative importance and carries the encoded message that we live in a random, value-neutral universe. By routinely negating the distinction between what is or is not intrinsically newsworthy, the media's inevitable fall-back position is one that favors the sensational over the substantive. The result is a self-serving institution that dilutes or altogether distorts the truth, placing corporate profit ahead of public service and abrogating its democratic mandate to enlighten and inform...in short, a journalistic community (on both ends of the political spectrum) comprised largely of Rita Skeeters.

The secret source of adult authority in previous times, suggests Postman, was privileged knowledge, not just about sexuality but knowledge covering a wide range of issues having to do with the darker side of the human spirit. Children of the moderately prosperous in Western civilization (circa 1800-1950), were, for the most part, shielded against direct exposure to life's horrors and mysteries until they had attained—or might reasonably be expected to have attained—a level of sophistication requisite to coping with them. Indirectly, of course, they were familiar with the more gothic aspects of life through exposure to such cultural artifacts as religious lore, folklore, and the fine arts (to say nothing of nightly news broadcasts)—but only through the filtering prism of adult sensibilities. Even then, their exposure was subject to the innate restraints imposed by their own limited experience and capacity to emphasize.

In advising her younger readers to question authority, Rowling is opposing a self-righteous standard of denial, the invariable hallmark of adults who fall victim to the arrested development brought on by pre-mature and uncontextualized exposure the darker, more disturbing dimension of life. Such individuals seem permanently encased within a transparent mental barrier that is at once protective and destructive, like dinosaurs encased in ice. Often, they confuse a mature ability to accept the moral complexities and ambiguities of adulthood with an inability to discriminate shades right and wrong, good and evil. Rather than cultivate a nuanced view of life that requires critical introspection, they embrace an easy cynicism that is, in reality, nothing more than an egotistical projection of their own fears and inadequacies.

As the gothic imagination illustrates repeatedly, evil is quite as likely to spring from good motives as from bad ones. Indeed, it is only those (such as Voldemort or Bellatrix LeStrange) who never question their motives or methods who are capable of radical evil. Men like Snape and Dumbledore, who submit to the painful discipline of remorse worked by time and memory, lack the boundless pride and self-confidence that can transform any of us into monsters. The repulsive, whimpering infant that Voldemort is destined to become is a poetic image of the true spiritual condition of those who are obsessed by a lust for power. The paradox at the heart of the cult of childhood is that our greatest strength lies in a willingness to nurture and respect the limitations imposed by a morally conditioned universe. The only real power we possess, as Dumbledore constantly reminds Harry, is the power of love (and our own remorse). Love—as saints, philosophers, and artists throughout history have reminded us all—is the antithesis of worldly power. According to Rowling, only that power informed and tempered by remorse could have saved Tom Riddle, and it was the one power that eluded the Dark Lord to the end of his life and beyond.

This is the great secret of the Deathly Hallows, those symbols of worldly omnipotence, i.e., the Wand of Destiny (the false security of coercive force), the Cloak of Invisibility (the false security conferred by stealth), and the Sorcerer's Stone (the false security associated with the illusory power to reverse time and death). Their allure is as irresistible to most of us as it is dangerous. Dumbledore's well-intentioned secrecy with regard to Harry's mission is entirely motivated by a desire protect him from that allure. As we learn from his back story, Dumbledore's soul was nearly destroyed by his youthful ambition to unite the Hallows (and his life was forfeit to a momentary renewal of that ambition as an old man). Countless others, including many who were innocent, have paid an incalculable price for the virus of power that seems to infect most of us to some degree and some of us to an inordinate degree. By surrounding Harry with the restraining influence of Hermione's rationality and Ron's impulsive nature, Dumbledore wisely sought to defend Harry against the rapid spread of this infection. By insisting that he grapple with the dilemma of choosing between Horcruxes and Hallows, he hoped to encourage the kind of critical introspection necessary to escape the "reversal into the opposite" (*enantiodromia*) that awaits anyone who—like Lord Voldemort—nurtures an appetite for power in conjunction with a capacity for denial.

When Dumbledore, averting his gaze, confesses to Harry his own youthful passion to possess the *Hallows*, he says, "You know what happened. You know. You cannot despise me more than I despise myself" (715). Harry, who relents in the face of Dumbledore's ruthless self-condemnation, protests that he does not hold his former teacher in contempt, though that for some months past he has come close to doing precisely that. Dumbledore angrily rejects Harry's protestations, insisting that he deserves contempt not consolation. It is Dumbledore's capacity for honest reflection, however painful—his willingness learn from guilt and terrible grief—that is the ineluctable price of, not only his shame, as he maintains, but also of his deliverance (717). That capacity is what fundamentally sets him apart from Tom Riddle (a.k.a. Lord Voldemort) who persists in projecting his own inadequacies upon both Harry and Dumbledore up to the very moment of his death. In light of what Harry learns about the transformation that Dumbledore's tarnished past has wrought within him, he knows unequivocally (without Dumbledore's admission) what the wizard would have seen within the Mirror of Erised, and that it would have had nothing whatever to do with a pair of warm woolen socks.

In the final duel between Harry and Riddle, the latter mocks Harry's assertion that he knows lots of important things of which his adversary is ignorant. "Is it love again, Dumbledore's favorite solution, love," jeers Riddle. He goes on to maintain that if what Harry has in mind is not the power of love, he must be laboring under the delusion that he possesses magical powers superior to one who has used magic of which even Dumbledore had never dreamed. When Harry replies that Dumbledore had dreamt of using such powers but was wise enough to refrain from doing so, Voldemort screams, "You mean he was weak…too weak to dare, too weak to take what might have been his, what will be mine?" "No," corrects Harry, "he was cleverer than you, a better wizard, a better man" (739). Earlier, when Harry upbraids Dumbledore for having repeatedly turned down the powerful post of Minister of Magic on the grounds that he would have done a better job than those who eventually accepted it, Dumbledore questions this conclusion, reflecting that when he was young, power had been both his weakness and his temptation. "It is a curious thing, Harry," reflects Dumbledore, "but perhaps those who are best suited to power are those who have never sought it. Those who, like you, have leadership thrust upon them, and take up the mantle because they must, and find to their own surprise that they wear it well" (718).

In accepting Harry as the Chosen One worthy of possessing the Deathly Hallows, Dumbledore in effect offers a metric against which it is possible to measure his own growth from a supremely gifted but callow young magus into the wise and humble teacher Harry has come to respect. Dumbledore's spiritual stature, as Harry now realizes, has been affirmed rather than diminished by his painful journey toward self-renunciation. Harry, on the other hand, is an archetypal child, untouched by either temptation or remorse. He instinctively avoids the pitfalls of pride and resentment that claim either the lives or the conscience of those around him (usually both). Like one of his literary precursors, Oliver Twist, he seems unaffected by the dangers and hardships of the potentially corrupting environments and situations in which he finds himself.

Nevertheless, anyone who had sustained the losses experienced by Harry Potter would surely have a formidable array of demons to exorcise in after years. His parents, his godfather, Dumbledore, Cedric Diggory, Lupin, Tonks, his pet owl Hedwig, Fred Weasley, Mad Eye Moody, and Dobby the house elf, all are taken from him in the course of his long ordeal—not to mention his own many near brushes with death, his temporary estrangement from Ron, Lupin, and Dumbledore, his eye-opening revelations concerning Snape, and the fact that he and Hermione are both subjected to physical torture. Are we truly to believe that these excruciating experiences have left no permanent scars? Even the notorious lightening-shaped scar vanishes after Voldemort's death. Apparently so, to judge from the epilogue of Rowling's final volume. Unlike the brooding Frodo (hero of Tolkien's *Lord of the Rings* trilogy who departs from the innocent life of the shire that he can no longer share), we find Harry, Ron, and Hermione, essentially unchanged nineteen years after the events recorded in the *Deathly Hallows* have transpired.

The youthful optimism of the Boy-Who-Lived is perfectly intact, his personal and professional ambitions are realized, and—apart from the fact that he is himself now the scion of a family of aspiring young wizards and witches—it is as if the traumatic events of his early childhood and youth had vanished along with his celebrated scar. Admittedly, the deepest desire of Harry's heart has been to escape from the burdens of life as the Chosen One into the kind of existence that he was denied in childhood—a life of domestic felicity, security, and normalcy. Nevertheless, Rowling's traditional happy ending, fails to convince. For one thing, Harry's understandable need to recoup the emotional deprivations of his own childhood bodes ill for the prospects of a successful marriage to Ginny Weasley. Psychology as well as common sense suggests that anyone who is looking for a spouse to double as a surrogate mother is probably asking for trouble. Perhaps Rowling's Dickensian ending is attributable in part to her own ambivalence with regard to her decision to pair Harry with Ginny rather than Hermione (just as most of Dickens's fraudulent happy endings end with lovers meeting rather than lovers enduring). Absent a clear vision of her protagonist as a mature gothic hero, she seems to have settled on a compromise to the problem of how to end her hero's coming-of-age tale without truly aging her hero. Consequently, when the Teflon Harry of the *Sorcerer's Stone* reappears in the epilogue to the *Deathly Hollows*, we are left wondering just how he and his companions have come to terms with their traumatic past lives during the intervening years (or have they simply lapsed into a pleasant state of amnesia?). Beyond the obvious facts, that Harry has obviously resolved his earlier issues with Dumbledore and Snape, Rowling leaves us with scant insight regarding the mature adult into whom the Boy Who Lived has evolved. Though it is difficult to see how could have done so, without producing a sequel of equal length and complexity, the ending she supplies is nevertheless superfluous in my view—in that it fails to provide a satisfying sense of closure to her narrative.

The appeal of the archetypal child as a romantic symbol of innocence is that it stands apart from the world and its sordid temptations and preoccupations. Harry endures the slings and arrows of the Dursley household in his earliest youth, just as he emerges from every other trial seemingly unscathed and incorruptible. Nevertheless, this conception of Harry is belied by Rowling's compelling portrayal of the psychological pain inflicted by the many hardships he has endured. Unlike Oliver Twist, Harry is neither perfect nor incorruptible, as attested by his over-reaction to Lupin's offer of assistance, his irrational willingness to believe the worst of Dumbledore, his implacable prejudice against Snape, his initial indifference to the plight of house elves, and a host of lesser offenses (such as his willingness to cut corners, lie, and cheat on occasion). Admittedly, most of these shortfalls are easily forgiven in light of his circumstances. Some are merely the flip side of his strengths while none outweigh his admirable qualities. Nevertheless, taken together they do suggest that Harry is more a work in progress than a finished and perfectly formed character, i.e., more an adolescent gothic hero than an archetypal child. Consequently, we expect the adult Harry to be more than a mere extension of his earlier self.

Perhaps, Rowling was simply tired of her subject, ready to lay down her authorial burden as quickly and gracefully as possible. Perhaps, she was uncertain as to how to relinquish it. Conversely, she may have been so invested in her characters that parting from them was a bitter sorrow. Given the valedictory sadness of her readers at bidding Harry and his world farewell, Rowling's own experience of letting go must have been akin to that of grief. Possibly, her artistic instincts were overwhelmed by her affection for the characters she had created. Like Dickens who supplied Pip with a second, happier, more unrealistic ending in *Great Expectations*, maybe Rowling sought to both appease her less exacting readers and escape from the implications of her increasingly somber narrative. Arguably, the ending proper of the *Deathly Hallows* was, in reality, its proper ending:

Harry, like Ignotus Peverell (his distant ancestor) resists the allure of both the Sorcerer's Stone (which he leaves behind in the forest) and the Elder Wand (which he restores to Dumbledore's tomb), retaining only the Cloak of Invisibility—a family inheritance. Moreover, the cyclic nature of her concluding chapter (*The Flaw in the Plan*) is reinforced by the fact that Harry uses the Elder Wand, for the first and only time, to repair his own broken holly and phoenix wand. This symbolic act of restoration—which brings Rowling's narrative full circle—parallels the synergy of past and present, wizarding world and Muggle world that Harry has achieved in his final, triumphant duel with Lord Voldemort. Whatever the explanation for her somewhat superfluous epilogue, the real story of what Harry Potter became nineteen years subsequent to his harrowing ordeal has yet to be told.

One can only hope that if and when it is, Rowling herself will do the telling. Otherwise, the sequel to Harry's gothic quest for synergy and personal integration is best left to flower silently in the imaginations of her grateful readers.

Conclusion:
Twilight of the Archetypal Child

The Gothic Imagination and the Cult of Childhood

At the dawn of the romantic century (circa 1800 A.D.), the medieval European social contract was under attack from many different quarters, e.g. exponents of democratic revolution, industrial revolution, and scientific progress. It was a time of great social and political turmoil, favorable to the fundamentally conservative backlash known retrospectively as the Romantic Movement. There is an historical irony involved here, in that it is usually the Classical ethos of the eighteenth century that is written about and thought of as "conservative" in relation to the more experimental attitudes of many romantics (though there was admittedly a hard right-wing element within the Romantic Movement from its earliest beginnings). Nevertheless, war and other social upheavals (or rather their emotional fallout) are always conducive to the gothic in arts. The late-eighteenth century neo-Gothic revival in literature, for example, coincided with the American and French revolutions as well as the industrial revolution. Practitioners of the gothic in the visual arts, such as the Spanish painter Goya, believed that the sleep of reason brought forth monsters, i.e., that narrow rationality and the scientific skeptics who exemplified it would give rise to a superstition more brutal and dehumanizing than the Judeo-Christian doctrines it condemned and sought to supersede. In its denial of the Sublime, such artists maintained, unbridled reason posed a threat to both the physical and spiritual well-being of Western civilization. Why…because beneath reason's philanthropic mask, its pose of disinterested objectivity, lurked a monster who, like Goya's Cronos threatened to devour his own children. Perhaps our modern fascination with all things gothic, undiminished since the 1960s, stems from a growing awareness that we too are threatened by this monster, a militaristic beast bent on "perpetual war for perpetual peace," to cite a phrase coined by historian Gore Vidal.

In any event, the romanticism that gave rise to a gothic preoccupation with the divided self (a. k. a. the "Shadow," a.k.a the "beast within") also gave rise to an enduring counter-symbol. That symbol proved to be the archetypal child—an image of a spontaneous joy often associated with nature, or communion with nature. Itself a romantic symbol of release from the confined spaces, spiritual despair, and ugliness of Blake's infernal factories, romantic nature offered a way out into the open expanse of what panentheists such as Caspar David Friedrich and Wordsworth sometimes referred to as "Nature's cathedral." Though often incorrectly identified as pantheists, these romantics believed that the moral ground of all being was discernable in nature for those innocent and discerning enough to see it— unlike the true pantheists who believed that God and nature were synonymous MacGregor 126–127). The distinction is crucial to an understanding of the cult of childhood in that the regard for nature that has figured so prominently in romantic educational theories (from those of Frobel and Rousseau onward) was not allied with savagery of a nature that is "red in tooth and claw." The natural child is a fantasy figure—a being unspoiled by the allegedly corrupting influence of civilization (as it untouched by the. It belongs (in the guise of the "noble savage") to a pantheistic idyll popularized by Rousseau at the end of the eighteenth century. This conception inevitably evolved into a celebration of idealized immaturity best illustrated by James Barrie (whose Peter Pan is obviously named after the reed-playing goat-god of Greek mythology—an archetype of untamed nature).

True pantheism provides no refuge from the gothic implications of life other than through a figurative retreat back into the womb. Rather than embracing "life's darkly mysterious, painful, frightening, and seemingly irrational experiences as a potential source of insight and transcendence," the pantheist must either seek to embrace life's harsher aspects as a terrifying model for human conduct or else to deny their existence by escaping into a fantasy world of pre-pubescent longings that can never be realized. To the worshippers of Pan, the archetypal child typifies a self-conscious refusal of life, an instinctive and essentially self-centered rebellion against the requirements of adulthood. The character of Sporos in Madeleine L'Engle's The *Wind in the Door* is a perfect example and type of the pantheistic cult of childhood (as well as a critique of its import). The archetypal child from Wordsworth and Brontë to L'Engle and J. K. Rowing, on the other hand, is "father to the man," i.e., a symbol of human qualities without which we are unlikely to successfully navigate the rough waters that separate early youth and adolescence from adulthood—qualities without which adulthood itself loses much of its zest and savor. This archetypal child-within, a trope that ideally exists in synergy with the gothic beast-within as a restraining influence, is also identified with other positive qualities thought by romantics to be threatened by modernity such as faith, trust, hope, humor, imagination, play, unconditional love, gentleness of spirit, intellectual openness, honesty, simplicity, innocence, creativity, and—above all—vulnerability. It goes without saying that there is bound to be a discrepancy (sometimes glaring) between even this romanticized vision of childhood and children in real life. It is a discrepancy of which romantics themselves, some of them at least, were well aware.

Charlotte Brontë, whose *Jane Eyre* is a literary landmark of the cult of childhood, though she never had children of her own (having died in child birth) worked for a time as a governess, as did her two gifted sisters. The bitterness of that experience is burned into the pages of both *Jane Eyre* and Anne Brontë's novel, *Agnes Gray*. Intended as an English adaptation of the German *Bildungsroman* (the novel of education) the point of Charlotte's cyclic *Kunstmärchen* (often likened to the Cinderella story) is to measure her protagonist's spiritual growth as an adult against a series of recurrent experiences dating from her childhood. The cyclic nature of Jane's educa-tional journey (*Bildungsreise*) is typical in romantic philosophy. Writing of this gothic pedagogical pattern in his study of romantic literature, literary critic M. H. Abrams says, "The protagonist [of the *Bildungsreise*] is the collective mind or consciousness of man, and the story is that of its painful pilgrimage through difficulties, suffering, and recurrent disasters in quest of a goal which, unwittingly, is the place it had left behind where it first set out and which, when reachieved, turns out to be even better than it had been at the beginning" (Abrams 191).

In Brontë's semi-autobiographical classic, the protagonist is (in many, though not all, respects) Charlotte herself. Jane's childish self and that of her one friend Helen Burns are therefore archetypal children endowed between them with most if not all of the traits associated with the romantic cult of childhood (though Jane's bitter resentment and rebellious nature belong more to the conception of the mature gothic hero than to the cult-of-childhood heroes of Wordsworth, Dickens, Eliot, and their literary progeny). Helen (as well as the wise and sympathetic Miss Temple) are modeled on Charlotte's two older sisters, both of whom died as teenagers while attending a negli-gently run charity school for clergymen's daughters similar to Lowood). Helen illustrate a hybrid archetype encountered frequently in nineteenth century cult-of-childhood literature—that of the "prophetic child." The prophetic child combines characteristics of the adult gothic hero with those of the idealized child-as-hero. Pearl (in Hawthorne's *The Scarlet Letter*) and

Mignon (in Goethe's *Wilhelm Meister's Apprenticeship*), and—to a certain extent—Brontë's orphaned protagonist in *Jane Eyre* are also examples of this hybrid type.

In sharp contrast with the mature heroes and idealized children of gothic literature (as well as the cloying Peter Pans of the genre), the Reed children (Eliza, Georgiana, and John) are depicted as greedy, selfish, shallow, and cruel. In the eyes of their precocious cousin, they are tyrannical monsters bent on persecution. Latter in life Jane's hyperbolic perception of them is tempered and deepened (though not eradicated) by a sympathy and wisdom acquired through bitter experience. Similarly, the great nineteenth-century German romantic composer, Robert Schumann (who launched the musical phase of the cult of childhood) makes a clear distinction between his *Scenes from Childhood* (*Kinderscenen*, Op. 15) and his latter music written for actual children to study and perform. The former he called "reminiscences of a grown up for grownups" (Taylor 156). The final selection in this cycle of thirteen character pieces is entitled *The Poet Speaks* (*Der Dichter spricht*). The poet in question turns out to be a sleeping child.

As in other cult-of-childhood masterpieces, memory is seen by Schumann as an indispensable agent of spiritual growth and development. In No. 6 (*Almost Too Earnest* or *Wichtige Begebenheit*), the self-importance of the child, which is immense and completely genuine, is conveyed from somewhere within an adult consciousness that is perfectly aware of itself. This at times uncanny hall-of-mirrors effect is analogous to the temporal and psychological complexities in the novels of Charlotte Brontë. For example, when Jane first meets the Reverend Brocklehurst (chief administrator at Lowood and a religious bigot comparable to today's most risible televangelists), the reader experiences simultaneously the dilemma of the inexperienced child and the detached bemusement of the mature narrator. Lucy Snowe, the heroine of *Villette*, Charlotte's last novel, engages in a dialogue with Paulina de Bassompierre whom she had known years earlier as a child. In a passage reminiscent of Madeleine L'Engle's assertion that to lose any part of one's chronological self is to be diminished, Paulina says of Lucy, "Her eyes were the eyes of one who can remember; one whose childhood does not fade like a dream, nor whose youth vanishes like a sunbeam... she would retain and add; often review from the commencement, and so grow in harmony and consistency as she grew in years." When Paulina suggests that the emotional edge of the days they spent together so many years ago must have softened, Lucy replies with uncompromising candor, "I have a good memory for those days," Paulina (puzzled as well as startled by vividness of Lucy's recollections) observes, "The child of seven years lives yet in the girl of seventeen" (Brontë 251–252). Together with Goethe's "Old age does not make childish...it merely finds us children yet," this passage might serve as the motto of the literary genre that is the focus of our discussion. To speak of nineteenth-century *Bildungsreisse* is to bring that discussion full-circle. "Tell them what you are going to say, say it, and then tell them what you've just said" is a familiar maxim among journalists. It is also a useful template for how to structure an argument. Having previewed this book's contents in its preface (and hopefully fleshed out that content in succeeding chapters) it is now time to review the recurrent themes of Kinder-Goth, i.e., to summarize those themes that define the gothic imagination in children's literature.

Christianity, the Cult of Childhood, and Supernatural Naturalism

The fundamental thesis of this book is that nineteenth and twentieth-century romantics rediscovered a scriptural motif (the child as spiritual role-model) that had been largely ignored previously in Western intellectual and cultural history; and they developed it into a distinctive sub-genre of gothic literature. Why, one may ask, was it ignored for so long by so many? It's difficult to say. One reason, certainly, is that children are, and have always been, a powerless constituency. The romantic sensibility that emerged at the end of the eighteenth century was perhaps responsive to this early Christian motif because of the many parallels it perceived between artists and children. The cultural agenda of the so-called Art Religion was to subvert bourgeois values, i.e., to replace a crassly consumer culture with an aesthetically enlightened one. Such a transformation would involve a "trans-valuation of all values" in that respect for wealth and power (in the worldly sense) would be subordinate to respect for wealth of imagination and creative power. In other words, art would be recognized as incarnational, i.e., an expression of humanity as a co-creator with the deity (and therefore the antithesis of the destructive impulses that find their fullest expression in predatory capitalism and the wars that nurture it) and artists would assume the role traditionally assigned to religious prophets, i.e., they would speak spiritual truth to worldly power. "When I am grappling with ideas which are radical enough to upset grown-ups," writes Madeleine L'Engle apropos of the subversive message of cult-of-childhood literature, "then I am likely to put these ideas into a story marketed for children, because children understands what their parents have rejected or forgotten" (*Walking on Water* 110). According to a Latin maxim, "Man acts toward man either as a god or as a wolf" (*homo homini aut dues aut lupus*). Romantics believed that in post-Enlightenment culture the wolf-within was definitely gaining ascendency over the god-within (a. k. a. the child-within).

The solution proposed by these romantics was a society that would be redeemed by art and inspired by childhood. Artists would no longer be mere ornaments of fashionable society but role-models for all of humanity. Curiosity, spontaneity, imagination, idealism, wonder, openness to radical possibilities, and an emotional susceptibility tantamount to vulnerability were the hallmarks of the artist as prophet—a psychological profile that corresponded almost exactly with that of children (another marginalized group within Western culture). Thus was born the concept of the prophetic child—a poetic archetype of all that was threatened by an industrialized society increasingly indifferent to its poorer and politically weaker members (such as its artists and children).

In this respect (as in others) European romanticism was not an attempt to secularize Judeo-Christian terminology, divesting it of its supernatural connotations, i.e., to create a "natural supernaturalism." It was rather an attempt to rehabilitate the spiritual world view by accommodating it to a climate of opinion dominated by the assumptions of scientific materialism and empiricism, i.e., to recreate a supernatural naturalism. Most nineteenth-century authors associated with the cult of childhood (e.g., Dickens, C. Brontë, Lewis Carroll, and George McDonald) were explicitly Christian in their orientation—though not all (George Eliot agnostic at least). Their immediate successors in the twentieth century were the Inklings (C. S. Lewis and J. R. R. Tolkien in particular). A more recent generation represented by L'Engle, Cooper, Barber, Christopher and Rowling are also clearly informed by traditions, such as Grail-lore and hermeticism, whose roots are histori-cally inextricable from those of Christianity (though, once again, Ray Bradbury does not fall within this scheme). My point is not that the cult-of-childhood is the exclusive province of Christian writers, (whatever a "Chris-tian writer" might be), but that it is obviously a literary product of sensibili-ties shaped (however belatedly) by a uniquely Christian trope—that of the child as prophet and role-model.

The Paradoxes of Power and the Religious Perspective

As we have seen throughout this discussion, it is especially the vulnerability of the archetypal child, i.e., his or her "weakness" when confronted by adult coercion, that we find a connection between the conscientious objection preached in the parables of Jesus and the literary/cinematic cult of childhood. Though he did not live long enough to become a parent himself, Jesus obviously did live long enough to have been a child. One therefore suspects that the children he set before the crowds of disciples, curiosity-seekers, and naysayers who followed him were not a special case or even a typical case. They were his own case, i.e., that is to say that they were extrapolations from his own childhood experience. "Whosoever shall not receive the kingdom of God as a little child," proclaimed Christ, "he shall not enter therein" (Mark: 10:15). Himself a prophetic child who astonished the scribes with his precocious understanding of scripture, Jesus matured into an exemplar of the child-like values he commended to his following.

Whoever these little ones may have been in real life, their representation as ideal images of God found in Mark is surely the literary origin of the archetypal child—an image that has haunted the imagination of artists for more than three centuries (and been forgotten by most Christians for more than twenty centuries). Christ as a Pied Piper leading a band of child-like adults into a kingdom that they, and only they, are fit to enter is not a popular conception, or if it is, it is a tradition that has definitely been honored more in the breach than in the observance. At any rate, one will not find this image etched into stained-glass windows, carved into the elaborate stone masonry of Catholic or Episcopalian cathedrals, nor preached from most of the nation's Protestant pulpits on Sunday morning. It is the Elders of the Church (not its children) whose voices carry loudest and the furthest. The infant Prince of Peace may temporarily gain the spotlight during Advent, but by the Lent it is the wrathful God of "peace through victory" (killer of his own child countless others, according to those who worship him) who is once again front-and-center. The authentic cult of childhood has fared no better in secular culture. Its values are not celebrated in our secular temples of law and learning (erected essentially as shines to the worship of Mars). Speaking of ancient Rome, no sane human being would dispute the fact that it is God (not Caesar) who has historically received the short end of the stick when it comes to rendering the world's resources or distributing the world's wealth. God's (intentional) will has not been done, nor has His kingdom come on earth as it is heaven. Nevertheless, the riches and values of that kingdom have been adumbrated in a certain body of literary art widely regarded as too insignificant (theologically, aesthetically, and politically) to warrant close critical attention.

The political and (to a lesser extent) theological implications of writers such as Tolkien, L'Engle, Cooper, Christopher, and Rowling have been basically ignored by even their more ardent readers. Evangelicals, who cooed contentedly over the conservative Christian sub-text of C. S. Lewis's *Chronicles of Narnia*, were less enthusiastic about Madeleine L'Engle's liberal Christian message (which speaks explicitly against violence and draws equally from apocryphal and extra-canonic sources as well as from scientific works). Such conservative Christians were positively hostile, many of them, toward J. K. Rowling's more secular portrayal of sacrificial love and redemptive suffering in the *Harry Potter* series. It is only in recent year, due to the commercial success of Rowling, that the Fluffys of public morality have been awakened to the dangers of witchcraft and magic in children's literature (except, of course, in the pages of C. S. Lewis).

Whether or not one subscribes to the humanist objections to the evil implicit in pantheistic policies, i.e. those that take the violence and cruelty of nature as warrant for political doctrines such as Manifest Destiny, the use of coercive and cruel methods to promote "the greater good," contradicts the character and teaching of Christ. The authentic Christian view is that such rationalizations are a demonic perversion of God's loving intentions toward his children. The cult of childhood in literature serves as a reminder that, "It's Jesus Who Put the Peace in the Phrase the 'Prince of Peace.'" The grotesque hybridization of Caesarism and Pauline Christianity that has been practiced since the days of Constantine has been tried and found easy (as well as politically expedient)—an observation that might be applied with equal aptness to other world religions, including the Muslim faith, whose core teachings have also been twisted by its literalists to suit a political agenda. Nevertheless, we are still left with a seeming paradox: if Rowling and other cult-of-childhood writers are pacifists, why do so many of their stories end in a pitched battle between the forces of good and evil, i.e., why do they end in war? The one unambiguous expression of pacifism in any of the books we have considered is to be found at the conclusion of John Christopher's trilogy (*Beyond the Burning Lands*) when a band of post-apocalyptic Christians place themselves in harm's way to catch the conscience of a prince.

If, as modern thinkers from Sigmund Freud to John Dominic Crossan are correct in their conclusion that civilization itself rests on a foundation of irresistible predatory impulses, then civilization is necessarily doomed to self-destruction. As our atavistic instincts continue their one-sided wrestling match with our growing awareness that ever-more-sophisticated technologies of death are bound to overwhelm us in the end, the bad news is that we have no clue as to how we might avert such a fate, or do we? Arguably, the greatest impetus for peace in Western civilization came two thousand years ago from a man who died horribly on a cross. Like a shaft of sunlight on a prison floor, the non-violent resistance of one who is purported to be the ultimate revelation of what modern theologian Paul Tillich called "the Ultimate Ground of Being," i.e., the source of life itself, (at a minimum) provides a clue that there is alternative to the collision course upon which humanity has embarked.

It suggests that something does exist beyond the perceptual limits of the dreary fortress of denial into which the demonic powers of this world have held us captive throughout recorded history. *That*, maintains the cult of childhood (and not some self-centered personal salvation requiring a "come-to-Jesus moment") is the true "Good News" of the Gospels. Christ, on this view, died because of our sins not for them. The heavenly father who sent his only begotten son to earth did so not out of a primitive blood-lust (blasphemously equated with love in Christian orthodoxy), but rather out of a desperate hope—born of divine compassion—that the Light of the World would prevail (or if not, that its ultimate indestructibility would be compellingly demonstrated). Unfortunately, as we all know, the world extinguished the light—apparently, at least. Fortunately, according to the same sources that chronicle its extinction, the light ultimately survived and the reality of the realm from which it had originated was affirmed in what J. R. R. Tolkien interpreted as the greatest *Eucatastrophy* in human history. Are we therefore justified in construing life finally not as a tragedy but as a comedy...a divine comedy? Is the genre to which the story of humankind truly belongs not theater-of-the-absurd (as so many have maintained in recent decades) but the adult fairy tale?

Those writers who comprise the literary cult of childhood imply that it is. Rather than renouncing the claim that religion is a fairy tale, they celebrate it. Nevertheless, like the rest of us, they too operate in the dark; grouping their way toward a light at whose source they can only guess. Is it to be wondered at that their imaginations, like ours, are contaminated by time-worn images and worldly metaphors (such as the trope of spiritual striving as cosmic warfare). Like the authors of the story of Abraham and Isaac or Psalm 51:17 (which informs us that a contrite heart—not a sadistic ritual of suffering and death—is the sacrifice most acceptable to the Lord) our modern prophets of peace on earth can only hint at a transcendent reality that refutes the legitimacy of violence—a reality that lies (as Madeleine L'Engle provocatively suggests) on the other side of the sun, somewhere beyond the spectrum of human sensory perception?

Death, Loss, and Aging

From the perspective of the cult of childhood's most representative and visionary artists, the harsh necessity of death (prefigured in the process of aging and the inevitable losses that accompanies it) is an inescapable concomitant of life. As the Freudian school has attempted to teach us, death defines the absolute limit of human knowledge. It is the ultimate boundary between the knowable and the unknowable—the undiscovered and undiscoverable borne—the veil that neither religion nor science has been able to penetrate (for all their pretensions to the contrary). What we cannot know we inevitably fear; what we fear we seek to deny, change, or destroy. In the case of death, however, our efforts have been unavailing (the horrific science-fiction scenario of virtual immortality achieved through robotics or cryogenic freezing may ultimately force us to choose between faith in life-after-death or the prospect of an existence that may prove to be a form of self-imposed incarceration). In short, what cannot be cured must be endured, as my grandfather advised. "The readiness is all," says Hamlet, and whether we agree with him or not, it is most certainly all that can be achieved this side of the grave. Though one hesitates to assign a utilitarian value to art, including that body of art classified in these pages as belonging to the cult of childhood, the aesthetic experience is undoubtedly one of humankind's greatest consolations in the face of death, if for no other reason than that it helps to mitigate the radical unknowability of what lies beyond the ultimate boundary that is death—if anything does. Serious art for all age groups openly confronts the anxieties inspired by our common mortality. Through grappling imaginatively with the Grim Reaper and his near relations, e.g., loss, divorce, and disillusionment, we can at least recognize that we are not alone in our struggle to wrest meaning from life's inescapable traumas.

From Bradbury's Joe Pipkin to J. K. Rowling's Harry Potter, the cult of childhood teaches us that we need not cower before the intimidating presence of death. We belong to an extended community (often constricted in our imagination to a small coterie of friends and immediate family) that shares our destiny and from whom we may draw strength, insight, and a sense of solidarity. We learn too that no matter how we may die (with dignity like Dumbledore or without it like Snape), we can chose to live with courage and self-restraint, that no matter how anxiety may occasionally cloud our judgment and warp our lives (as in the case of Susan Cooper's Walker) partial recovery and perhaps even redemption are real possibilities. Another related lesson to be inferred from the cult of childhood is that loss (which is sometimes for us, as it was for Dumbledore, the terrible price of our shame) can become a catalyst for improvement, though its pain may never entirely leave us. The key to such transcendence, suggests authors such as Antonia Barber, lies in accepting our rightful share responsibility for our disappointments and bereavements, as does the amazing Mr. Blunden. Like Job, we are at times innocent victims of an inscrutable fate; but most of us, if we are honest with ourselves, will be compelled to acknowledge that not infrequently our greatest traumas in life stem from our own deeply ingrained, repeatedly reinforced character flaws. That is why we so often recycle self-destructive behaviors and why time, memory, and critical reflection are so crucial if we are ever to escape their progressively constricting orbit. Few of us, perhaps are able to see the face of a friend hiding beneath the fearful mask of death, as do Tom Skelton and Joe Pipkin in Ray Bradbury's *Halloween Tree*, or as the youngest Peverell brother does in Beedle's *The Tale of the Three Brothers*. Even fewer of us, I suspect, are capable of graciously relinquishing our hold upon whatever idol we have chosen in which to invest our sense of identity and personal worth. Nevertheless, suggests the cult of childhood, the redemptive possibility of emulating the smith in Tolkien's poetic tale is always an option, provided we are able to achieve a genuine synergy between our past and our present. This, in turn, can only be accomplished by nurturing the archetypal child who prefigures our true identity and worth.

The ever-present past and the mysteries of time and consciousness constitute a recurrent theme in cult-of-childhood arts. The only remedy for having been dismembered (a gothic fate at least as old as the Egyptian myth of Isis and Osiris) is to be remembered. In a sense, this theme defines the fate of humanity, according to the gothic imagination, in that it presents the need

for atonement and redemption as symptomatic of our human estrangement
from the Ultimate Ground of Being, i.e., from self, nature, and God. In *The
Use and Abuse of Art*, cultural historian Jacques Barzun speaks of the deep
seeded separation anxieties engendered by the Enlightenment as the primary
impetus for European romanticism. Commenting on Schiller's famous essay
On Naïve and Sentimental Poetry, Barzun begins by pointing out the
inaccuracy of this English translation of the essay's originally German title.
He asserts that *On Primitive and Self-Conscious Poetry* would have been
more to the point; the point being that modern man suffers from a divided
and fractured sense of self in relation to the universe (like Rowling's Lord
Voldemort). "What does Schiller tell us," asks Barzun, "First, that modern
man is split—or as we should say in modern jargon, alienated. Being
divided, feeling not home in this world, he is unhappy, self-conscious."
When Schiller asks himself if there is any class of individuals who has
escaped this fate—any group within society that is still "primitive in the
sense of simple and *childlike* [emphasis added]," the conclusion at which he
arrives is that only artistic genius possesses this qualification. The historical
origin of what he terms "the art religion of the nineteenth century" resides in
this belief, according to Barzun. "In other words," he writes in summary of
Schiller's ground-breaking essay, "the way of salvation can only be shown
us by the genius, the artist, because he is not self-conscious like the rest of
us" (Barzun 28–29). The historical origin of what we have called the literary
cult of childhood resides there also.

The Prophetic Child and the Child as Gothic Hero

Gothic literature for or about the young presents us with two closely related
but distinct types of hero. The first, and historically earliest, of these representative types is the archetypal child to be found in Romantic poets such as
William Wordsworth, novelists such as Charles Dickens, painters such as
Carl Otto Runge, and musicians such as Robert Schumann. Wordsworth's
two most characteristic themes are linked. They are firstly, the child as a
"mighty prophet" who comes to earth "trailing clouds of glory," and secondly, adult consciousness as a "prison house" in which—as in Rowling's
Azkaban—we are stripped of memory ("our birth is but a sleep and a
forgetting"). Both themes are clearly sounded in his 1806 *Ode: Intimations of
Immortality from Recollections of Early Childhood*. Memory is for Wordsworth—as it is for all cult-of-childhood writers past and present—a redemp-

tive faculty that can both recompense us for our early loss of cosmic consciousness and preserve our primitive, childlike qualities (usually through exposure either to nature or art). To a greater or lesser extent, this symbolic figure of the prophetic child—Wordsworth's autobiographical hero—continues to appear throughout the second half of the twentieth century in the pages of stories and novels by writers from Ray Bradbury to J. K. Rowling.

The second type of protagonist favored by the gothic imagination in children's literature (as distinct from the "prophetic child") is the child as simply a diminutive version of the adult gothic hero, i.e., a child that exhibits most, if not all, of the characteristic strengths and weaknesses attributed to protagonists of adult gothic literature, e.g., pride, obsession, and access to alternate realities. Though by no means mutually exclusive, the second of these representative types is distinguished from the prophetic child in that he or she is exposed to a series of trials and traumas that must be dealt with either positively, i.e., with the kind of critical introspection that leads to personal integration, or else negatively, i.e., with denial and projection of the sort that leads ultimately to self-destruction. These mythic journeys are the classic options presented to all gothic heroes, whether young or old. Unlike the prophetic child, who is incorruptible, the child as gothic hero is presented as a work in progress destined for either *enantiodromia* or transcendence (a third type—the narcissistic child who refuses maturity) is exemplified by James Barrie's *Peter Pan*. Though hinted at in characters such as Sporos from L'Engle's *The Wind in the Door* and Lord Voldemort in Rowling's saga (whose ultimate destiny is to be permanently trapped within the body of a helpless, whimpering infant) this type does not belong to the authentic cult-of-childhood—a genre that celebrates the child-like not the childish.

The Synergy of Then and Now

Having mentioned Wordsworth's emphasis on recollection, i.e., his own life-long struggle to reconcile ecstatic memories of a childhood fraught with "recollections of immortality" (whether real or faux) with adulthood, brings to mind the cult-of-childhood emphasis on time and memory as transformative agencies. Whether through actually travelling back in time to alter past and future events (as the children do in *The Amazing Mr. Blunden*, as Will Stanton does in *The Dark Is Rising*, and as Harry and Hermione do in *The Prisoner of Azkaban*) or simply through recycling past experience mentally (in the manner of Professor Redlaw and Ebenezer Scrooge from the Christmas novellas of Charles Dickens) gothic heroes are required to "keep memory green." The desire to end our pain by severing our self psychically from past actions (or inactions) can only add to our pain, according to the gothic imagination; i.e., forgetfulness of our condition is a symptom, not a cure. That condition, as Schiller pointed out two centuries ago (and as Christ pointed out two millennia ago) is one of alienation and estrangement from the ultimate source of our well-being.

To "forget ourselves" is synonymous with dismembering ourselves psychically. It is to lapse into a state of mind identified by modern psychology as "denial." Conversely, to come to terms with ourselves by integrating and contextualizing past experience, however painful, is to reassemble the broken fragments of our lives, i.e. to "re-member" ourselves. "Maturity," writes L'Engle," consists in not losing the past while fully living in the present with a prudent awareness of the possibilities of the future" (*Walking on Water* 102). The temporal synergy she commends as essential to our spiritual well-being on a personal plane, is equally important to the preservation our identity and balance as a culture. The gothic imagination encourages us to plumb the depths of our social and political (as well as our psychological) malaise. The perennial challenges to each of us posed by personal loss, disease, and death are equaled by the perennial challenges posed by ideological and religious strife (and the large-scale loss, disease, and death to which they can lead). These related human dilemmas are foci of the books discussed in these pages. Bradbury's Halloween romp through the death-related rituals of diverse times and cultures, the dystopian world of John Christopher's political gothic trilogy, the biblically and scientifically inspired time-travel narratives of Madeleine L'Engle, Barber's ghostly tale of redemption through self-sacrifice spanning two centuries, J. K. Rowling's lengthy chronicle of Harry's quest to bind the broken fragments of the Muggle and Wizarding worlds occasioned by Voldemorts self-mutilation (as well as his personal quest to mend severed ties to his own wizarding past), Pensieves, time-turners and potions, the tesseract, journeys on the backs of mythical flying steeds to various "Whens," all of these imaginative motifs are pressed into the service of a single over-arching theme—the importance of achieving a dynamic equilibrium between then and now, the past and the present.

Fairytales and *Kunstmärchen*

As we have seen, the literature under consideration differentiates between categories of hero (the prophetic child, the narcissistic child, and the child as gothic protagonist). It also differentiates between categories of readership. From the earliest days of the Romantic Movement artists such as Schumann differentiated between those cult-of-childhood works that were intended for the enjoyment of the young, and those aimed at a more mature audience. Often these categories tended to shade into one another (more so, I suspect, for adults than for children). The distinction to which I refer has continued to the present day, with books such as those by J. K. Rowling appealing equally to immature and mature readers. Indeed, one could argue that the psychological nuances of the *Deathly Hallow* presuppose an adult perspective. Nevertheless, the distinction between fairy tales for children and adults (i.e., stories that are—in terms of their vocabulary, thematic range, and degree of psychological sophistication—better suited to one age group then another) has persisted. Though *Gulliver's Travels* can be read as a child's adventure story, it was clearly intended as a political allegory for adults. Conversely, though *Harry Potter and the Sorcerer's Stone* can and has provided pleasure to a great many adults, it is clearly aimed at a youthful audience. Where this method of classification becomes ambiguous is in the case of books that are both conceptually sophisticated and stylistically simple. This issue was perhaps first raised in the modern era by Madeleine L' Engle' Newberry Award winning, *A Wrinkle in Time*. Evidently, one of the unhealed wounds of her early career was that this now beloved fantasy was repeatedly rejected by prospective publishers on the grounds that it was too difficult for children—a religiously oriented science-fiction fairy tale (L'Engle *Walking on Water* 117)! Since then, the unspecified criteria that previously guided publishers have noticeably broadened. This ambiguity is only compounded by much larger controversies surrounding genre designations such as "romantic" and "gothic." Despite these unresolved issues of terminology and definition, the old German demarcation between domestic and artistic fairytales (*Hausmärchen* and *Kunstmärchen*) is plausible as well as helpful.

Is the Reported Death of Childhood Premature?

For some time now, so-called cultural conservatives, a category into which I would place myself in many respects, have bemoaned the supposed *Disap-*

pearance of Childhood (which happens to the title of a book by media critic
Neil Postman). Their argument seems boil down to the belief that childhood
is a time of innocence that was once protected by cultural mores and prohibi-
tions that no longer apply thanks to the immorality and irresponsibility of
liberals. Whether you blame this loss of innocence on the 1960s counter-
culture (like cultural historian Alan Bloom), on an entertainment industry at
odds with traditional family values (like film critic Michael Medved), on a
permissive and left-leaning educational system (like conservative author
Dinish D'Souza), or on the 'dumbing-down" of America by its addiction to
TV culture (like Postman), these critics agree that we now live in a world in
which young and old alike are swamped by daily exposure to steamy sex and
brutal violence. The young are adrift in a mass media universe that under-
mines literacy, critical judgment, and the psychological space once reserved
for the naïve and inexperienced—a space deemed necessary to the mental
and spiritual well-being of the young by those who bemoan its loss. Absent
that space, these critics contend, all that was once associated with cult of
childhood is imperiled by the "emergence of a symbolic world that cannot
support the social and intellectual hierarchies that make childhood possible"
(Postman 74). The defining characteristic of childhood, as a place apart from
adulthood, according to this critique, is adult secrecy with regard to certain
areas of knowledge (such as sexuality) and codes of conduct (such as the use
of profanity) that were formerly labeled "Adults Only," but which have now
become the public domain of pop culture, thanks to an undiscriminating
mass media.

Though one can readily sympathize with this critique (my own bleat
against pop culture vulgarity in Rowling has already been sounded), there are
several objections to it that can be raised in light of the survey undertaken in
these pages. In the first place, the membrane that separates conventional
ideas as to what adults know and what young people experience was never as
impenetrable as these critics pretend. With regard to sex, not only have the
young always sensed more than they were told, but it can be argued that in
some ways conventional mores and linguistic taboos shielded the predator at
least as much as they protected the young. It is impossible to defend against
that which can neither be understood nor communicated. The very young, as
Dickens observed with regard to the adult library plundered by the abandoned David Copperfield, have a built-in capacity to filter out that which is
not really relevant to their lives (including sexual innuendos)from which they
might otherwise suffer moral taint. As for those old enough to take an

interest in sex, no amount of Victorian vigilance will suffice, and in any event, would it not be better to deal with the erotic dimension of life responsibly by placing it within a moral context, as the best children's literature invariably does. Madeleine L'Engle states that she could not imagine herself ever being artistically tempted to confuse the sensuous with the pornographic—even in her adult novels.

The same principle applies to linguistic and visual codes. Indeed, it applies with even greater force in that the profanity and the graphic portrayal of violence linked with sex that characterize much of today's pop culture entertainment are arguably marks of a profound immaturity. Far from being the legitimate credentials of adulthood, they suggest its polar opposite. An inappropriate reliance on profanity is either a cultural affectation or an admission of intellectual inadequacy. An attraction to gratuitous violence and sex implies an almost childish addiction to sensationalism—an inability to take pleasure in the refined, the nuanced, and the thoughtful. Such "entertainment" is clearly rooted in a lack of imagination and empathy that is borderline psychotic. In short, the cultural conservatives are right to interpret pop culture's endorsement of sensation unmediated by an adult perspective as morbid.

Incidentally, this widely shared dread of introspection—which manifests itself as an inability to listen attentively to one's self or other—is symptomatic of denial, a denial finds expression in unquestioned behaviors so widely shared as to be effectively invisible. Go into almost any public resort (a restaurant, a night club, a mall, or sidewalk café) and you are likely to find yourself under assault from an unremitting barrage of auditory and visual stimuli, i.e., electronic sound systems blaring rock music and multiple television sets flashing a steady stream of inchoate images, often with an accompanying soundtrack to augment the chaos. The deafening noise levels that can result make either conversation or introspection virtually impossible. One has to wonder if this outcome is the point of the exercise. Is the appeal of this bizarre social behavior prompted by an innocent delight in festivity or by a psychological need to escape from ourselves and others, i.e., a need to fill a spiritual void created by an ever-more brutal and mindless culture addicted to ever-more trivial pastimes? Are the obscene salaries paid to our professional athletes, popular entertainers, and media celebrities a simple matter of economic "supply and demand," as defenders of the current status quo insist, or are they rather a tacit acknowledgement that a great many adults lack the interior resources necessary to entertain and inform themselves or one another. According to the political gothic imagination, it is even possible that this never-ending supply of trivial pastimes is a creation of those who seek to protect the politico-economic status quo from the kind of scrutiny that an informed, intellectually vital citizenry might otherwise demand. If so, suggests the cult of childhood, it may well be that in depriving not only our children but ourselves of the mental and emotional space traditionally set aside to cultivate inner resources and intellectual vitality, we are denying culture as a whole access to experiences that constitute the bedrock of any sane, truly democratic society.

The Sexual Sublime in Gothic Literature for the Young

Where one is justified in siding with liberals in the so-called "culture wars" is in recognizing the shallowness and inconsistency of the right wing critique of popular culture. The same brutality and vulgarity they abhor in films and "the music industry" (an apt term that implies pop-music's ersatz, disposable-product approach to art) they enthusiastically defend in life. Pro-life is not consistent with pro-war, and no amount of rhetorical sophistry can make it so. Self-righteous posturing is not consistent with a genuine commitment to spiritual values and no amount of Evangelical sophistry can make it so. The *ad hominem* attack is not an acceptable substitute for reasoned argument and no amount of right-wing, Fox-News-style invective can make it so. Moreover, media water-carriers on the right are frequently so misinformed about their adversaries that they mistake them for allies. At some point during the past year, for example, right-wing television host Glen Beck invited Stephanie Meyers (author of the wildly successful *Twilight* series) as a guest on his nightly television program. The tenor of his praise was that she had produced gothic literature for the young that is devoid of explicit sexuality. Ms. Meyers graciously (and rather roguishly, I imagine) accepted Mr. Beck's congratulations without objection, well aware that the erotic— though not the pornographic—figures prominently in her novels. In fact, one suspects that the natural curiosity and suppressed eroticism of her adolescent readership accounts in large measure for the popularity of her impassioned narratives having to do with eternal love between a mortal and an immortal (a theme common to nineteenth and twentieth-century romantic fiction). Unfortunately, the ignorance displayed by her conservative admirer was typical of the breadth and depth of right-wing thinking on the entire range of themes and motifs explored by the cult of childhood in gothic literature.

The sexual sublime is, of course, one of these motifs. Though it is dealt with, if at all, only tangentially in pre-adolescent children's literature, it's prominence in Meyers, and other purveyors of gothic literature for young adults, raises the issue of the disappearance of childhood in a somewhat different form. Neil Postman affirms G.K. Chesterton's observation that, "All healthy men, ancient and modern, Eastern and Western, know that there is a certain fury in sex that we cannot afford to inflame and that a certain mystery and awe must ever surround it if we are to remain sane" (Postman 85). His point, and that of other like-minded culture conservatives, is that unrestricted media exposure to the "fury" of sex by younger audiences has eroded the adult mystery and awe formerly protected by official or tacit forms of censorship—trespassing on the mental space reserved for childhood in the process. Admittedly, the entertainment media and its corporate sponsorship have exploited sexuality as an easy way to sell a product or tell a story. This, in turn (given the pervasiveness of the electronic media, especially the internet) has undoubtedly introduced a virus into our social programming that has been allowed to run rampant. As usual, however, the political Right has latched on to the wrong end of the stick. The real issue raised by the inclusionary nature of the modern media is not the easy access to sexual titillation that it affords, but the invasion of privacy and personal space that it mandates—including that space formerly reserved for childhood.

Writing of this issue, Caroline Kennedy notes that privacy covers many things from the solitude necessary to thought to our right to self-determination. She concludes that our right to privacy, a fundamental human right (like economic justice) not explicitly covered in our national charters of freedom, is ultimately what makes us civilized (Kennedy xiii). In its own way, the archetypal child symbolizes that right by affirming that part of us resistant to ideological propaganda, marketing manipulations, and pseudo-religious sophistry. What, if anything, has changed is not the potency of the archetypal child as a symbol of civilization, but the ability of society to provide a protected space separable from the stream of information and imagery that defines adult culture. In the modern world, children are encouraged to grow up fast while adults are encouraged to not grow up at all. Rough sex, constant noise, images of virtual and real violence, fast foods, fast cars, fast credit, and loose language target all of us indiscriminately—polluting our intellectual environment as surely as carbon emissions pollute our physical environment.

Nevertheless, as we have indicated throughout this discussion, the attempt to treat childhood in this exclusionary way was not the objective of those who originated the cult of childhood. According to these poets, painters, and musicians, childhood was not a privileged sanctuary for the young; it was a refuge for all healthy-minded men and women. Ultimately, what is good for our children, such artists suggested, is good for their parents and grandparents. Conversely, what is liable to harm the human spirit of children is liable to be damaging to adults as well. It was only in its later, decadent phase that cult of childhood artists began to speak and write of childhood not as a "seedtime of the soul" but as a "Never-never-land" of irresponsibility and delusional longings (thereby giving birth to what we referred to as the "narcissistic child" in literature). As this discussion has documented, both visions of childhood are still with us, though, as ever, only one of them offers any credible way through our adult dilemmas. The terrifying sense of futility felt by every self-reflective soul in today's world is a result of our centuries-long cultivation of the beast within. That is why the lilting voice of its concomitant, i.e. the child within, is still worth heeding. That prophetic voice is not merely a cultural artifact, i.e. the perishable product of Postman's "symbolic world." It is a private and sacred space impervious to the onslaughts of cultural forces working to facilitate a sterile Gulag of the mind (demonic forces according to David Ray Griffin). As the enthusiastic reception accorded the writings of Stephanie Meyer and J. K. Rowling affirms, the cult of childhood (however marginalized) is alive and well in the twenty-first century. That is because it belongs, those who endorse its values would argue, to an indestructible core of reality that is not subject to the allure of mass communication, pseudo-religious indoctrination, or political coercion. Like the Kingdom of God, to which it is historically linked, the cult of childhood lies within.

Bibliography

Adler, Mortimer. *The Angels and Us*. New York: Macmillian Publishing CO., Inc., 1982.

Abrams, M. H. *Natural Supernaturalism: Tradition and Revolution in Romantic Literature*. New York: W. W. Norton & Company Inc., 1971.

Aldertman, Ellen and Kennedy, Caroline. *The Right to Privacy*. New York: Alfred K. Knopf, 1995.

Anelli, Melissa. *Harry, A History*. New York: Pocket Books, 2008.

Barber, Antonia. *The Amazing Mr. Blunden*. Victoria, Australia: Puffin Books, 1972.

Barzun, Jacques. *The Use and Abuse of Art*. Princeton: The University of Princeton Press, 1974.

———. *The Beast from 20,000 Fathoms*. Dir. Eugene Lourie. Warner Bros., 1953.

Becker, Ernest. *The Denial of Death*. New York: The Free Press, 1973.

Bradbury, Ray. *The Halloween Tree*. New York: Yearling, 1972.

———. *A Graveyard of Lunatics*. New York: Perennial, 2001.

———. *Dandelion Wine*. New York: Bantam Books, 1982.

———. *Something Wicked This Way Comes*. New York: Bantam Books, 1983.

Brontë, Charlotte. *Jane Eyre*. Oxford: Oxford University Press, 1993.

———. *Villette*. New York: Dutton, 1977.

Chesterton, G. K. *Orthodoxy*. Wheaton, Illinois: Harold Shaw Publishers, 1994.

Christopher, John. *The Sword of the Spirits Trilogy*. New York: Collier Books, 1970-1972.

Cooper, Susan. *The Dark is Rising*. New York: Collier Books, 1973.

Coveney, Peter. *The Image of Childhood*. Baltimore, Maryland: Penguin Books, 1967.

Crossan, John Dominic. *God & Empire: Jesus Against Rome, Then and Now*. Harper Collins, 2007.

Dante Alighieri. *The Divine Comedy*. New York: Vintage Press, 1950.

Davies, Paul. *God & the New Physics*. New York: Simon & Schuster, 1983.

Dickens, Charles. *The Christmas Books, Vol. 1, A Christmas Carol*. New York: Penguin Books, 1982.

————. *The Christmas Books*, Vol. 2, *The Haunted Man*. New York: Penguin Books, 1982.

————. *The Oxford Illustrated Dickens*. Oxford: Oxford University Press, 1987.

————. *The Life of Our Lord*. New Jersey: Silver Burdett Press, 1987.

————. *Dombey & Son*. New York: A Signet Classic, 1964.

Douglas, James. *JFK and the Unspeakable: Why He Died & Why It Matters*. New York: Orbis Books, 2008.

Doyle, Sir Arthur Conan. *The Complete Sherlock Holmes*. New York: Doubleday, 1930.

Fiedler, Leslie A. *Love and Death in the American Novel*. Normal, Ill: Dalkey Archive Press, 1960 (reprint 1998).

Frankl, Victor E. *Man's Search for Meaning*. New York: Pocket Books, 1939.

Gaines, James R. *Evening in the Palace of Reason*. New York: Harper Collins, 2005.

Goethe, Johann Wolfgang von. *Faust: A Tragedy*. Trans. Walter Arndt. New York: W. W. Norton Company, 1976.

Granger, John. *Harry Potter's Bookshelf: The Great Books Behind the Hogwarts Adventures*. New York: Berkley Books, 2009.

Griffin, David Ray. *Christian Faith and the Truth Behind 9/11: A Call to Reflection and Action*. Louisville: Westminster John Knox Press, 2006.

————. *Cognitive Infiltration: An Obama Appointee's Plann to Undermine the 9/11 Conspiracy Theory*. Northampton, Mass.: Olive Branch Press, 2011.

————. *The New Pearl Harbor: Disturbing Questions about the Bush Administration and 9/11*. Northampton, Mass.: Olive Branch Press, 2004.

Guida, Fred. *A Christmas Carol and Its Adaptations*. London: Mc Farland & Company, Inc., 2000.

Harpur, Patrick. *Daimonic Reality: Understanding Otherworld Encounters*. London: Arkana, 1994.

Hawthorne, Nathaniel. *The Scarlet Letter*. New York: The Modern Library, 1937.

Hoecker, Marcia J. "Children in the Kingdom." *Sewanee Theological Review*, Vol. 48 No. 1, 2004.

Hoffmann, E. T. A. *The Best Tales of Hoffmann*. Ed. E. F. Bleiler. New York: Dover Publications, 1967.

Houghton, Walter E. *The Victorian Frame of Mind 1830-1870*. New Haven, Yale University Press, 1957.

It Came From Outer Space. Dir. Jack Arnold. Universal International, 1953.

JFK. Dir. Oliver Stone Warner Bros. Pictures, 1991.

Jung, C. G. *Modern Man in Search of a Soul*. New York: Harcourt Brace Janovich, 1933.Johnson, Edger. *Charles Dickens: His Tragedy and Triumph*. Boston: Little, Brown and Company, 1952.

Kaplan, Fred. *Dickens: A Biography*. New York: Avon Books, 1988.

Kung, Hans. *Great Christian Thinkers*. New York: Continuum, 1995.

Langford, David. *The End of Harry Potter?*. New York: Tor, 2006.

Lewis, C.S.) *The Chronicles of Narnia*. New York: Collier Books, 1953.

———. *Christian Reflections* ("The Psalms"). Grand Rapids, Michigan: William B. Eerdmans Publishing Company, 1967.

L'Engle, Madeleine. *Walking on Water: Reflection on Faith and Art*. Colorado Springs, CO: Waterbrook Press, 2007.

———. *A Wrinkle in Time*. New York: Dell Publishing Co., 1962.

———. *A Wind in the Door*. New York: dell Publishing Co., 1973.

———. *A Swiftly Tilting Planet*. New York: Dell Publishing Co., 1978.

———. *The Other Side of the Sun*. New York: Ballantine Books, 1971.

Lukacs, John. *The Hitler of History*. New York: Alfred A. Knopf, 1997.

———. *George Kennan: A Study of Character*. New Haven: Yale University Press, 2007.

MacGregor, Geddes. *Gnosis: A Renaissance in Christian Thought*. Wheaton, Ill.: Quest Books, 1979.

Miracle on 34th Street. Dir. George Seaton. Twentieth Century Fox, 1947.

Night of the Demon. Dir. Jacques Tourneur. Columbia Pictures, 1957.

Orwell, George. *A Collection of Essays by George Orwell* (*Charles Dickens*). New York: Doubleday & Company, 1954.

Pawles, Louis and Jacques Bergier. *Morning of the Magicians*. New York: Stein and Day, 1960.

Priestley, J. B. *Over the Long High Wall: Some Reflections & Speculations on Life, Death, & Time*. London: Heinemann, 1972.

Postman, Neil. *The Disappearance of Childhood*. New York: Vintage Books, 1982.

Rowling, J. K. *The Harry Potter Series*. New York; Scholastic Inc., 1997-2007.

———. *The Tales of Beedle the Bard*. New York: Scholastic Inc., 2008.

Sheck, Laurie. *A Monster's Notes*. New York: Alfred A. Knopf, 2009.

Stevenson, Robert Louis. *Dr Jekyll and Mr. Hyde.* New York: Signet Classic, 1978.

Sullivan, J. W. N. *Beethoven: His Spiritual Development.* Vintage Books, 1927.

Taylor, Ronald. *Robert Schumann: His Life and Work.* New York: Universe Press, 1982.

Thomas, Lewis. Late Night Thoughts on Listening to Mahler's Ninth Symphony. New York: Bantam Books, 1984.

Tolkien, J. R. R. *The Tolkien Reader.* New York: Ballantine Books, 1966.

———. *Smith of Wootton Major, Farmer Giles of Ham.* New York: Ballantine Books, 1967.

———. *The Lord of the Rings Trilogy.* New York: Ballantine Books, 1965.

Towner, Betsy. *AARP Bulletin,* Vol. 51 No. 7. September, 2010.

Tuchman, Barbara. *A Distant Mirror: The Calamitous 14th Century.* New York: Ballantine Books, 1978.

Universal Horror. Dir. Kevin Brownlow. Universal, 1998.

Wilde, Oscar. The Picture of Dorian Gray. Place, Pub. Date.

Wilson, Colin. *The Occult.* New York: Vintage Books, 1973.

———. *Beyond the Occult.* New York: Carroll & Graf Publishers, Inc., 1988.

Weatherhead, Leslie D. *The Will of God.* Nashville: Abingdon Press, 1972.

Wordsworth, William. *Selected Poetry.* New York: The Modern Library, 1950.

Index